Food Processor Cooking
QUICK AND EASY

Food Processor Cooking
QUICK AND EASY

by Greg Patent

TEN SPEED PRESS
Berkeley, California

To Suzanne S. Jones,
for her invaluable advice and help

ACKNOWLEDGEMENTS

I want to thank the following people for making this book possible.

Carl Sontheimer, for his encouragement, support, and good taste.

The staff of Cuisinarts test kitchen, who tested and retested these recipes.

My students all over the country whose comments shaped the development of many recipes.

My wife, Dorothy, my sons David and Jason, and the many friends who tasted and evaluated the recipes honestly and objectively.

My editors, Mimsie Beckwith and Ruth McElheny, for skillful surgery.

And my parents, Mabel and Joseph Patent, who encouraged me from the moment I showed an interest in cooking as an eleven-year-old.

🔟

TEN SPEED PRESS
P. O. Box 7123
Berkeley, California 94707

Published in association with Culinary Arts Television.

FIRST TEN SPEED PRESS PRINTING, 1992

Cover design by Fifth Street Design
Text design by Pamela J. Stewart
Photography by Jeffrey Weir
Edited by Ruth S. McElheny
Art directed by Christine Goulet
Author photograph by Marc A. Hefty
Food styling by Michael diBeneditto, Marjorie Foster,
    and Sarah Kerstin Gross Catering

This book originally appeared as
Patently Easy FOOD PROCESSOR COOKING,
copyright ©1985 by Cuisinarts Cooking Club, Inc.

Cuisinart ® is a registered trademark of
Cusinarts Corp., Stamford, CT 06902

Library of Congress Cataloging-in-Publication Data

Patent, Greg. 1939 -
        Food processor cooking : quick and easy / by Greg Patent.
            p.   cm.
        Includes index.
        ISBN 0-89815-479-0
        1. Food processor cookery.   I. Title.
TX840.F6P35   1992
841.5'89—dc20   92-4437
                                                    CIP

Printed in Singapore

7 8 9 10 — 01 00 99 98 97

CONTENTS

(Low-fat recipes are highlighted in the Index in blue.)

INTRODUCTION

I bought my first food processor in 1976, after years of longing for one. The clincher for me was a recipe for a praline cake that could not be made without it. That didn't impress my wife, a very practical person, that the machine was an essential kitchen tool. But she is very fond of dishes calling for quantities of chopped, minced, or sliced onions. When I pointed out that the food processor would enable her to create these dishes without tears, it did the trick.

With so many people working outside the home, the food processor is more necessary than ever. Although early owners used the machine primarily for preparing difficult dishes like pâtés and quenelles, today's cooks are much more likely to use it for speedy preparation of everyday foods like salads, stir-fry dishes, and chocolate chip cookies.

All makes of food processors come with a metal blade, and discs for slicing and shredding. Some also come with a plastic blade for kneading bread dough. I urge you to become comfortable with these basic tools before investing in accessory discs. If you've never used a food processor before, practice with a supply of different vegetables. You can always turn the results into a delicious soup. Once you've gotten the hang of using your machine regularly and with confidence, then you're in a position to decide which additional discs and attachments best suit your needs. At the end of this book (page 171), I've included a section on accessory discs with suggestions for their use. In addition, there is a section describing certain familiar and unfamiliar ingredients. All are available in supermarkets.

What excites me most about food processor cooking is the sheer *speed* with which I get *quality* results. You can do the same. For the past ten years, I have taught food processor cooking classes to thousands of people all over the country. I've learned that what people want most from their food processors is to prepare dishes that are quick, delicious, nutritious and attractive—food they can put together with a minimum of fuss and bother, and be proud to serve to family and friends. Quiches easily fit into this category, and there is a whole chapter of recipes for them. You can even make a quiche ahead and freeze it perfectly (see page 65).

Another important feature of cooking from scratch with the food processor is that you control what goes into your food. People with dietary restrictions can gain precise control of ingredients. For example, if you are watching salt intake, the recipes in this book give a suggested amount. So you decide how much to use. In addition, I have also given suggestions on how to reduce fat and cholesterol in recipes.

It was with these ideas in mind that many recipes in this book were created. Others were originally developed for my television show, *Big Sky Cooking*, which was on the air for many years in western Montana. Still others are from my new television series, *Patently Easy Food Processor Cooking*, which features 30-minute meals made entirely with the help of the food processor.

The way to get started with your food processor is first to read the section on Food Processor Techniques. This section describes ten basic techniques you're likely to use again and again, and it is based on questions I get repeatedly in my classes. What's the best way to process cheese? How do I get perfect slices of carrot rounds? Can I slice meat with the food processor? The answers to these and many more questions are at the beginning of the book.

All the recipes are written in such a way that you can follow the steps right through without having to wash the machine until you've completed the last direction. Remember, the machine has been designed to be your helper, and you are always the boss! Carl Sontheimer, the founder of Cuisinarts, once told me he didn't want food processor owners to feel as though they had to drag their machines by their power cords in order to use them. That's why I have tried to write the recipes in as user-friendly a way as possible.

I have made each of the recipes in this book dozens of times and have become very fond of them. To me they are like old friends—dependable and always welcome. To make sure that they are consistently reliable and easy to follow, the recipes were also thoroughly tested in the Cuisinart kitchen.

I wish you good luck and happy cooking, and I hope that you derive as much pleasure from using these recipes as I do in bringing them to you.

HOW TO CUT THE FAT AND CHOLESTEROL CONTENT OF RECIPES

Dozens of the recipes in this book are already low in fat and in calories (see titles in blue in the Index). And there are those whose fat, cholesterol, and calorie contents can be sharply reduced without sacrificing taste. In this section, I'll suggest ways you can reduce the fat in specific recipes as well as provide general instructions for fat reduction in similar recipes.

In most recipes, you can reduce fat simply by cutting back on the amounts called for. To reduce saturated fat, substitute margarine for butter and use polyunsaturated oils such as sunflower, canola and olive. The use of non-stick skillets and vegetable cooking sprays sometimes is enough to eliminate most of the fat in cooking. Trial and error will tell you what works best for you. In recipes calling for eggs, you can greatly decrease the amount of cholesterol by using egg substitutes such as EggBeaters®. These products are mostly egg white with natural food coloring to give the appearance of beaten real eggs, but there is no cholesterol in them. Or, if you'd rather, simply use fresh egg whites (3 tablespoons per egg).

Here is a chapter by chapter guide on how to go about reducing the fat.

APPETIZERS. The **Guacamole** recipe and **Pork Dim Sum Rolls** are already low in fat. In the **Hummus Bi Tahini** recipe, use half the amount of tahini and omit the olive oil topping. For the **Cheddar & Corn Crackers**, use reduced-fat sharp cheddar cheese and half the oil called for. In the **Swiss Cheese & Mushroom Cornbread**, use only 1 tablespoon butter in the topping, and use 1 tablespoon butter and ½ cup egg substitute in place of the butter and eggs in the cornbread batter. The **Party Focaccia** fat content can be reduced by using half the amount of Parmesan cheese, half the amount of ham, and half the amount of olive oil in the topping.

SOUPS. Most of these soup recipes are already low in fat and calories, but in many you can decrease the fat content further. For example, in the **Cold Cucumber and Walnut Soup**, use non-fat yogurt and only 1 tablespoon olive oil. In the **Chilled Avocado Soup**, use non-fat yogurt instead of low-fat yogurt, and low-fat or non-fat milk instead of the half and half. When sauteing vegetables for soup bases, decrease or eliminate the butter or oil called for. Use broth instead as the cooking medium.

PASTA. Even when egg is used, the pasta doughs are still low in fat. However, if you want to cut back on cholesterol, then use egg substitute instead of the whole eggs. For each "large" egg, use 3 tablespoons egg substitute and eliminate the oil in the dough. Adjust dough consistency with water. The recipes for **Water Pasta** and **Egg-White Pasta** contain no added fat.

Many of the sauce recipes for pasta are already low in fat, but you can lower the fat even further in some. For the **Tuna Sauce** recipe, use water-pack tuna instead of oil-pack. In **Montana Meat Sauce**, use extra-lean ground beef and only 1 tablespoon olive oil. For **Bolognese Sauce**, use extra-lean ground beef, half the Parmesan cheese, and only 1 tablespoon butter. The **Turkey Tetrazzini** fat content is reduced by using only half the amount of Parmesan cheese and substituting non-fat milk for the half-and-half.

To make the **Turkey Tetrazzini** sauce, slowly whisk the cold milk into the flour in a saucepan. Bring mixture to boil, stirring, and cook until thickened. Off heat, add only 1 tablespoon butter for flavor. Complete the recipe as directed. You can use this same technique for the **Pastitsio Sauce** recipe using non-fat milk and only 2 tablespoons butter. Use 1 cup egg substitute instead of the eggs.

In the recipe for **Cold Sesame Chicken with Noodles**, use half the tahini called for.

QUICHES. You may decrease the saturated fat and cholesterol content in the pastry by using regular stick margarine (not light margarine or margarine spreads which contain too much water) instead of butter, and use only three-fourths the amount of fat called for. In custard fillings, use low-fat or non-fat milk or evaporated skim milk instead of any of the following: whipping cream, sour cream, whole milk, or half-and-half. Also use egg substitute (3 tablespoons for each "large" egg) in place of whole eggs. You may also use lower-in-fat cheeses and less of them if you wish.

SALADS. The recipes for **Eggless Egg Salad** and **Tabbouleh** are already low in fat and cholesterol. But in the salad dressings for other recipes you can safely decrease the oil contents by one-third without loss of flavor.

MAIN DISHES. Many recipes are already low in fat, but you can trim away more. In the **Classic Pizza**, for example, omit the pepperoni and use part-skim mozzarella cheese (about 4 ounces instead of 6 ounces). In all the stir-fry recipes, which are already low in fat, you can cut even more fat out by using half the oil called for and cooking in a non-stick skillet. To be sure of extra-lean ground beef, buy cuts on sale and trim away all visible fat before chopping the meat with the metal blade. Even the **Lamb Pilaf** recipe can have less fat. Just be sure to use very lean lamb and only 2 tablespoons oil in the cooking.

POTATOES AND RICE. Again, most of these recipes are already quite low in fat, but there's always a way to cut back even more. In **Scalloped Potatoes**, for example, decrease the butter by half and use low-fat milk and egg substitute. For the **Potato Pancakes**, use half the oil and butter and cook in a non-stick skillet. For **Mexican-Style Potatoes and Cheese**, decrease the sharp cheddar by half and use a low-fat variety. Substitute low-fat milk for the heavy cream. Decrease the fat in the **Spanish Rice** recipe by omitting the bacon. And for the **Rice and Onion Casserole**, omit the Swiss cheese and use low-fat milk instead of heavy cream.

VEGETABLES. Many recipes are low in fat (**Julienne of Gingered Carrots and Zucchini**; **Sauteed Mushrooms with Basil**; **Zucchini and Red-Pepper Stir-Fry**; **Sweet and Sour Red Cabbage**). To decrease the fat in **Savory Butter-Crumb Tomatoes**, just use 1 tablespoon butter instead of the 3 tablespoons. In **Zucchini Stuffed with Onions**, omit the bacon and decrease the cheese to 1 ounce, using it only to sprinkle on top.

BREADS. All the yeast breads are low in fat with the exception of **Cinnamon Rolls**. The **Whole Grain Muffins**, a quick bread, is also low in fat. Here's how you can decrease the fat in some of the other quick breads. For the **Pumpkin Date-Nut Loaf**, use egg substitute instead of the eggs and only ¼ cup of oil. Decrease walnuts to 2 ounces. For the **Banana Bran Bread**, use egg substitute for the eggs and one-half stick margarine instead of the butter. Decrease the pecans to ½ cup. In **Yogurt and Jalapeño Corn Bread**, eliminate the cheese, use 3 tablespoons margarine instead of butter, non-fat yogurt instead of regular yogurt, and egg substitute (9 tablespoons) instead of the eggs.

DESSERTS. You may be surprised, but many of the dessert recipes in this book are low in fat. For example, **Almost Sugarless Apple Pie**; **Crunchy Raisin-Oatmeal Cookies**; **Rocky Mountain Marathon Bars**; and **Pineapple and Strawberry Sherbets** will not strain your fat and calorie budgets. Make the others for special occasion treats or when you feel like splurging. The **Apple-Ginger Crisp**, though, is a good candidate for fat and cholesterol reduction. Simply use 3 ounces margarine instead of the 6 ounces of butter. The crunchy mixture won't be as rich-tasting, but it will still be delicious! You can use this method to reduce fat and cholesterol levels in virtually all "crisp" recipes.

Food Processor Cooking

QUICK AND EASY

FOOD PROCESSOR TECHNIQUES

Frequent use of your food processor will teach you how to make it work to its utmost capability. Excellent instruction books come with most processors; this section is not meant to replace those. Yet in teaching all over the country, I constantly meet people who own machines and don't know how to use them to their fullest. That is the reason for this section. It does not cover every technique, but it should serve as a reference for certain procedures that you are likely to use again and again.

Strawberry Sherbet

SEQUENCING OF STEPS

When using your food processor to prepare a recipe from start to finish, your aim is to accomplish all the steps without washing the work bowl until the very end. In most cases, the best approach is to begin with the dry ingredients and end with the liquid. For example, if preparing a quiche, make the pastry, shred the cheese, process the filling ingredients, and finish with the custard mixture. Then clean up.

Very often, your first step will be to prepare the last ingredient of a recipe, like chopping parsley for a garnish, or grating cheese for a topping. When making salads, you will often begin with the dressing and process the vegetables into it.

All the recipes in this book are sequenced for quick, easy and efficient use of the food processor. When adapting other recipes, refer to chapters with similar recipes for additional guidelines. Eventually the sequencing of processing steps will become so natural that you'll do it without thinking.

PUSHER PRESSURE

The instructions in this book generally specify "light," "medium," or "firm" pressure. This section will help you translate those words into the appropriate actions. Suppose you want to slice mushrooms. First, buy mushrooms that feel firm, with caps closed on the underside and no gills showing. Trim them by cutting two opposite sides of the cap flat. Load one layer into the feed tube at a time, with a flat side against the disc. Lock the pusher into place and process with light pressure. That means you barely press the pusher with your fingertips. Apply only as much pressure as it takes to maintain contact between the pusher and the mushrooms. Think about *guiding* the food steadily and gently through the cutting edge of the disc, not *forcing* it through. Use the same procedure to shred cheese.

Generally speaking, use light pressure on soft foods and firmer pressure on harder foods.

Another point to keep in mind: the thickness of the slice affects the pressure you apply and the speed of processing. When you process mushrooms with the 4mm slicing disc, light pressure does the job nicely. If you use the 8mm slicing disc, apply only *very* light pressure; the job will take half the time. If you want to prepare even, paper-thin slices of mushrooms with the 1mm slicing disc, apply slightly more pressure for the best results. The idea is to apply a steady, guiding pressure on the food, so the disc will cut it evenly. Practice will teach you the correct "feel" for each food.

When an instruction calls for "medium" pressure, apply steady pressure with the palm of your hand. Foods like zucchini, cucumbers and onions require medium pressure.

Processing firm food like carrots and potatoes requires firm pressure on the pusher. The heel of your hand exerts the most pressure.

Whatever the pressure, be sure to apply it steadily. One of the most common reasons for uneven slices is uneven pressure on the pusher.

The best way to develop confidence is to buy a variety of soft, medium and firm foods and try slicing them with different discs. You will have fun, and all your processed vegetables can be turned into a marvelous soup. Any fruits used for practice make a terrific fruit salad.

FITTING FOOD IN FEED TUBE

Students often tell me they can't get perfectly round sections of carrots, zucchini or other food. There are two important things to remember:

1) Load the feed tube so the food is wedged in place and can't slip sideways. For example, cut carrots into lengths of about 3 inches (7cm) and

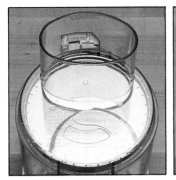

Positioning slicing disc   *Fitting carrots in feed tube*

stand them vertically so they have no space to tip over. The carrots should fit so snugly that they stay in the feed tube when you lift the work-bowl cover. Use firm pressure on the pusher, and you will get perfect round slices.

2) Make sure that all the food is resting on a flat part of the slicing disc, not on the cutting edge or on a raised ledge. Food placed on the cutting edge or ledge will be tipped at an angle, and slices will be uneven. Each time you load the feed tube, remember to rotate the disc so the flat part is under the feed-tube opening.

Keep these two points in mind and you should always get perfectly symmetrical slices.

PULSE CONTROL

Most food processors have a pulse control. This is a valuable attribute because it allows precise regulation of processing. Chopping onions is a good example. Use onions of medium size, peel them and cut them into quarters. Add only the amount recommended by the manufacturer. Pulse three times, with pulses lasting no longer than 1 second, and scrape the work bowl. Check the texture; the onions should

be coarsely chopped. If you want a finer chop, pulse once or twice more. The actual processing time is only a few seconds. By controlling the length and number of pulses, you can easily obtain the precise result desired, from coarse to very fine chop. More is said about the pulse control in other chapters.

PROCESSING CHEESE

Soft cheeses like Brie, Camembert, cream cheese and ricotta are easily puréed with the metal blade. These cheeses cannot be sliced or shredded with the food processor. Mozzarella, another soft cheese, shreds beautifully if it is well chilled. Take it straight from the refrigerator or put it in the freezer for about 10 minutes. Use very light pressure and you'll get perfect shreds.

Semi-soft cheeses like Fontina, Bel Paese or blue cheese can be puréed with the metal blade. If well chilled, they can be shredded. Use light pressure on the pusher. These cheeses cannot be sliced with the food processor.

Semi-hard cheeses can be chopped, shredded or sliced with the food processor. These include Cheddar, Monterey Jack, Swiss, Gruyère, Emmenthaler, Colby, Longhorn, Jarlsberg, Edam, Gouda and Provolone. The temperature is not critical for chopping, but these cheeses should be well chilled for shredding or slicing. Remember always to use only light pressure on the pusher.

Hard cheeses like Parmesan, Romano, Pecorino or Sapsago can be chopped or shredded, but not sliced. The temperature is not critical for chopping, but the cheese should be at room temperature when shredded. Use light pressure on the pusher.

One final word about shredding cheese. Usually, just as the last of the cheese is about to pass through the shredding disc, it "fights back" and seems to exert upward pressure on the pusher. Don't worry;

just keep steady pressure on the pusher and the cheese will go through. Remember, you're the boss!

CHOPPING PARSLEY

If you remember three things, you'll always get perfect results:

1) pat the parsley leaves completely dry,
2) use a dry work bowl,
3) use a dry metal blade.

Put the parsley in the work bowl (any amount from 2 tablespoons to a bunch or more, depending on the size of the bowl) and turn on the machine. In about 10 seconds, the parsley should be coarsely chopped. In 20 to 30 seconds, it should be finely chopped. A few seconds more, and it will be minced. I always chop just what I need since parsley loses flavor and fragrance if prepared hours in advance.

PREPARING CHICKEN BREASTS FOR SLICING

Place each boneless and skinless breast half on a sheet of plastic wrap with the original skin side down and the long side facing you. Fold over about an inch (2.5cm) of each end of the breast (left and right) and, starting with the side nearest you, roll the

 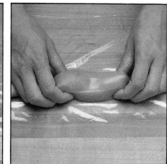

Folding ends over   *Rolling into cylinder*

breast into a compact cylinder. Wrap securely in plastic wrap. Repeat with as many breast halves as desired. Place the prepared chicken on a shallow tray or baking sheet and freeze until solid (or until it passes the knife test described below). Wrap securely in a plastic bag and store in freezer until needed. These will keep well for up to 2 months.

To slice the chicken, let the desired number of pieces stand at room temperature for about 20 minutes to thaw partially. The flesh should resist when squeezed — there should be no soft spots — but the tip of a sharp knife should pass completely through it without too much effort. If the chicken is as solid as an ice cube, wait a few more minutes and test again with the knife. Chicken that is too hard may damage the slicing disc, and chicken that is too soft will not slice properly.

Cut each piece of partially frozen chicken in half crosswise and fit the pieces snugly into the feed tube, cut side down. There should be no room for the chicken pieces to tip over. Be sure the chicken rests on the flat part of the slicing disc, not on a cutting edge or on the ledge. Process with firm pressure. Remove the chicken from the work bowl and let the slices thaw before using them in your recipe. Once you prepare chicken this way, you will never want to return to laborious and time-consuming hand slicing.

PREPARING RAW MEAT FOR SLICING

Flank steak, beef sirloin or pork tenderloin all slice well with the food processor, provided they're partially frozen and you use firm pressure on the pusher. Cut pieces of meat so they will slice across the grain and fit into the feed tube snugly. Arrange the meat in a single layer on a foil-lined baking sheet and freeze solid or until meat resists when squeezed but can be pierced through with the tip of a sharp knife. If the meat is frozen solid, let it stand for a few minutes at room temperature until it passes the knife test. After the meat is sliced, let it thaw before using it.

SECURING THE METAL BLADE FROM BELOW

This is the easiest way to pour liquid mixtures from the work bowl into another container. Remove the work bowl and hold the metal blade in place by inserting your middle finger into the hole in the bottom center of the bowl and grasping the side of the bowl with your thumb. The blade will stay put when you pour.

THE SPIN-OFF

When the work bowl contains heavy batters or whipped egg whites, there's a time-saving trick to get every bit out. Remove the work bowl, holding the metal blade in place. Scrape out as much as you can with the plastic scraper. Replace the work bowl with the metal blade and pulse for 1 second. Centrifugal force will spin every remnant off the blade. Remove the metal blade and scrape the bowl clean with a plastic scraper.

WHIPPING EGG WHITES

While I was working on this book, Cuisinarts introduced a whisk attachment to fit each of its four food processors. These whisks produce very stable, fine textured egg whites. Like those beaten by a French chef using a hand whisk in a copper bowl, eggs whites beaten by the Cuisinart® Whisk let you make feather-light meringues with only one-third the usual amount of sugar. The secret, I'm told, is in the fine wires used both in the French egg-beating whisks and the Cuisinart whisks. These also make light, fluffy mashed potatoes, whipped cream, and fruit whips.

When whipping egg whites, it is important to use a clean, grease-free work bowl and to work quickly. Beaten egg whites are ready if they hold their shape when lifted on a rubber spatula, and look creamy and light. Remove them from the work bowl and proceed with the rest of the recipe as quickly as possible.

When folding egg whites into other ingredients, be sure to use only a few brief pulses with the metal blade to incorporate them. Longer processing will beat out the air you've whipped in.

APPETIZERS

Appetizers traditionally set the scene for the dinner to follow. But you can offer several of them together as the entire menu for a cocktail party, or even an unconventional meal.

These recipes, most of which can be prepared in advance, draw on many cuisines.

The Gougère, from France, is made with a puff-shell dough that is prepared in the food processor. The Pork Dim-Sum Rolls are Chinese in origin, with an American accent — the wrapping is made from refrigerated biscuit dough!

The Party Focaccia, from Italy, is topped with a typically Mediterranean combination of ham, cheese and olives. Although it's made with a yeast dough, it can be prepared for the oven in about 5 minutes. Hummus bi Tahini, the delicious spread or dip based on garbanzo beans, is one of the most famous and popular dishes of the Middle East. And Greece is the inspiration for Spinach Triangles, phyllo leaves filled with a savory mixture of feta cheese, ricotta cheese, and spinach.

The United States is the source of Cheddar Cheese and Corn Crackers, Avocado and Yogurt Dip, and Swiss Cheese and Mushroom Cornbread.

Flaky Parmesan Twists

GUACAMOLE

There are many variations of this popular avocado dip. I have experimented with several, and this is the one that draws consistent raves in my cooking classes all over the country.

> 2 tablespoons fresh cilantro leaves *or* ¼ cup parsley leaves, washed and patted dry
>
> 1 large shallot (1 ounce, 30g), peeled
>
> 1 fresh jalapeño chile, halved lengthwise and seeded (see NOTE)
>
> 1 tablespoon lime juice
>
> 2 large ripe avocados (about 1 pound total, 455g), peeled, pitted and cut into 1-inch (2.5cm) pieces
>
> 1 large tomato (7 ounces, 200g), with stem end removed
>
> Salt and freshly ground black pepper, to taste
>
> Jicama slices *or* tortilla chips

Insert *metal blade* and put cilantro or parsley in work bowl. Turn on machine, drop shallot and jalapeño through feed tube, and process until finely chopped, about 10 seconds. Remove mixture and set it aside.

With *metal blade* in place, put lime juice and half of avocado pieces in work bowl. Pulse 2 or 3 times, then process until mixture is almost smooth, about 1 minute. Stop to scrape bowl as necessary. Add remaining avocado and pulse until mixture reaches desired consistency — slightly chunky or very smooth. (I like it slightly chunky.) Leave mixture in work bowl and remove metal blade.

Insert *French-fry disc*. Cut tomato to fit feed tube, if necessary. Place it vertically in feed tube and use light pressure to process. Remove French-fry disc, add cilantro mixture to work bowl, and stir gently to combine ingredients. Taste and adjust seasoning with salt and pepper.

Turn guacamole into serving bowl and accompany with sliced jicama or tortilla chips.

Makes about 2 cups (480ml).

NOTE: Protect your hands with gloves when working with fresh chiles, and afterward, wash your hands thoroughly with soap and water.

AVOCADO AND YOGURT DIP

Wonderful with cheddar and corn crackers, or with thick slices of fresh vegetables. It also makes an excellent and unusual sauce for pasta.

> 1 large egg *or* 1 large egg plus 1 egg yolk *or* 2 egg yolks (see NOTE)
>
> 2 teaspoons lemon juice
>
> 1 tablespoon oil
>
> 2 teaspoons Dijon mustard
>
> ⅛ teaspoon white pepper
>
> ½ cup (120ml) oil
>
> 1 large avocado (about 10 ounces, 285g), peeled, pitted, and cut into 1-inch (2.5cm) pieces
>
> 2 1-inch (2.5cm) cubes onion
>
> ½ cup (120ml) thick plain yogurt
>
> ½ teaspoon ground cumin
>
> Dash of Tabasco sauce
>
> Salt, if desired

Insert *metal blade*. Put egg, lemon juice, 1 tablespoon oil, mustard, and pepper into work bowl and process for 1 minute. With machine running, add ½ cup oil through feed tube in slow, steady stream.

Add avocado and onion and process until mixture is smooth, about 1 minute. Stop to scrape work bowl as necessary. Add yogurt, cumin, and Tabasco sauce and pulse about 3 times to combine. Taste for seasoning and add salt, if desired.

Makes about 1½ cups (360ml).

NOTE: Consistency of mixture depends on number of egg yolks used. Use egg yolks only for thick dip, 1 egg plus 1 yolk for medium-thick dip, and 1 whole egg for fairly thin dip.

Hummus bi Tahini

HUMMUS BI TAHINI

One of the most famous dishes of the Middle East — and deservedly so. Call it a dip, a spread, or a salad. Serve it with raw vegetables, with pita or French bread, or with crackers. It's wonderful, however you eat it. Garbanzo beans and sesame-seed paste, both high in protein, increase in protein value when combined.

2 tablespoons parsley, washed and dried
1 small garlic clove, peeled
1 15-ounce (425g) can garbanzo beans (chick peas), drained, rinsed in cold water, and drained again
½ cup (120ml) tahini (sesame-seed paste, see page 177)
2 to 4 tablespoons fresh lemon juice
¼ cup (60ml) water
½ teaspoon salt, if desired
Dash of Tabasco sauce
1 tablespoon olive oil
Paprika

Insert *metal blade* and put parsley into work bowl. Process until minced, about 30 seconds. Remove and set aside.

With *metal blade* in place, turn on machine and drop garlic through feed tube. Process until finely chopped, about 10 seconds. Scrape work bowl and add beans. Stir tahini until it is smooth, then measure and add it to work bowl along with 2 tablespoons of lemon juice, 2 tablespoons of water, salt, and Tabasco sauce. Process until mixture is very smooth and thick, about 1 minute. Stop to scrape work bowl as necessary. Add another 2 tablespoons of water and process until mixture is smooth. Taste and add more lemon juice, salt and Tabasco sauce, as desired. (There should be a distinct, but not tart, lemon flavor.) Adjust consistency with additional water, processing a few seconds to combine well. It should be thin if served as a dip, thick if served as a spread.

Transfer mixture to serving dish or bowl, film top with oil, and sprinkle lightly with paprika and parsley. Cover and let stand at room temperature for 2 or 3 hours before serving; paprika will dissolve in oil and give hummus a beautiful color.

Makes about 2 cups (480ml).

CHEDDAR AND CORN CRACKERS

These thin, crisp crackers are ideal with dips. Be sure to bake them until they are golden brown, or they won't crisp properly as they cool.

6 ounces (170g) sharp Cheddar cheese, well chilled
1 cup unbleached all-purpose flour (5 ounces, 140g)
2 tablespoons yellow cornmeal
1 teaspoon baking powder
½ teaspoon salt, if desired
1 teaspoon dry mustard
¼ teaspoon turmeric
¼ teaspoon white pepper
¼ cup (60ml) oil
⅓ cup (80ml) milk

Insert *medium shredding disc* and use light pressure to process cheese. Leave cheese in work bowl and insert *metal blade*. Add flour, cornmeal, baking powder, salt, mustard, turmeric and pepper. Pulse 2 or 3 times, then process continuously for 10 seconds.

Combine oil and milk with fork and add gradually through feed tube while pulsing quickly about 10 times. Process just until dough begins to mass together on blade. Do not overprocess. Carefully remove dough, shape it into ball, flatten it slightly, and wrap it in plastic wrap. Refrigerate for at least 1 hour.

Adjust oven rack to center position and preheat oven to 350°F. (175°C.).

Divide dough in half. Roll 1 batch out on lightly floured surface to thickness of ⅛ inch (3mm) or slightly thinner. Use cookie cutter or knife to cut dough into 2-inch (5cm) pieces and transfer them to ungreased baking sheet. Leave ½ inch (12mm) between crackers; they do not spread. Prick each cracker a few times with fork. Bake until crackers are lightly browned around edges and flecked with brown on top, 12 to 15 minutes. Crackers may puff up slightly as they bake. Transfer crackers to cooling racks and let stand until cool.

Repeat process with remaining dough. Reroll all scraps, incorporating as little flour as possible.

Crackers will keep well at room temperature for a few days if wrapped airtight. They may also be frozen. To refresh frozen crackers, place them close together on ungreased baking sheet and reheat them in center of preheated 350°F. (175°C.) oven for 5 to 10 minutes.

Makes about 4 to 5 dozen.

FLAKY PARMESAN TWISTS

These light and elegant pastries are made with a semi-puff pastry that is extremely simple to prepare. They provide a perfect accompaniment to drinks before dinner. Be sure to allow several per person; they disappear quickly!

6 ounces Parmesan cheese, at room temperature, cut into 1-inch (2.5cm) pieces
1⅓ cups unbleached all-purpose flour (6½ ounces, 185g)
¼ teaspoon salt, if desired

> **2 sticks unsalted butter (8 ounces, 225g), chilled and cut into 12 pieces**
>
> **½ cup (120ml) dairy sour cream**
>
> **1 large egg**
>
> **1 teaspoon milk**

Insert *metal blade*. Turn on machine, drop cheese through feed tube, and process until finely chopped, about 1 minute. Remove and set aside.

With *metal blade* in place, put flour, salt, and butter into work bowl. Pulse 3 times, then process continuously until mixture resembles medium-fine meal, 10 to 15 seconds. Add sour cream and pulse rapidly about 15 times, just until dough begins to mass on blade. Carefully remove dough and shape it into a ball. Flatten it slightly, wrap in plastic wrap, and refrigerate for at least several hours or overnight.

Adjust oven rack to center position and preheat oven to 400°F. (205°C.). Lightly grease 14 by 17-inch (35 by 43cm) heavy cookie sheet or line it with cooking parchment paper or heavy brown paper. (Do not use foil; pastries tend to stick to it.)

Work with half the dough at a time, keeping remainder refrigerated. If dough is very firm, pound it gently with rolling pin to flatten it slightly. Roll dough out on lightly floured surface into rectangle approximately 12 by 7 inches (30 by 17cm). Trim edges with sharp knife so that rectangle is exactly 12 inches (30cm) long and 6 or 7 inches (15 or 17cm) wide.

Beat egg and milk together with fork just to combine them. Brush one side of dough with egg mixture and sprinkle evenly with ⅓ cup of cheese (1½ ounces, 45g).

Place sheet of waxed paper over dough and gently press cheese into dough with rolling pin, using direct pressure rather than rolling motion. Remove waxed paper and flip dough over. Brush second side with egg mixture and sprinkle with

Cutting dough into strips   *Twisting strips*

another ⅓ cup of cheese (1½ ounces, 45g). Cover with waxed paper and press cheese into dough with rolling pin.

Lay ruler along long side of dough and use sharp knife to notch dough at ½-inch (12mm) intervals. Cut across dough to make 24 ½-inch (12mm) strips.

Twist each strip 3 or 4 times and place strips about 1 inch (2.5cm) apart on prepared cookie sheet. Press down gently near ends of strips to hold them in place. (Don't press ends; they may burn during baking if you do.)

Bake until twists are deep golden brown, about 15 minutes. Use wide metal spatula to transfer them immediately to wire racks. Cool completely. Repeat procedure with second batch of dough, remaining egg mixture, and remaining cheese.

These pastries are best when very fresh. If they are not to be served within a day, wrap them airtight and freeze them. To reheat frozen baked pastries, place them on ungreased baking sheet in center of preheated 400°F. (205°C.) oven for 4 or 5 minutes. Cool on racks.

Makes 4 dozen.

SWISS CHEESE AND MUSHROOM CORNBREAD

This light buttermilk cornbread is baked in a pizza pan and topped with Swiss cheese and sautéed mushrooms.

Topping

3	ounces (85g) Swiss cheese, chilled and cut into 1-inch (2.5cm) cubes
½	cup parsley leaves, washed, patted dry and loosely packed
1	medium onion (6 ounces, 170g), peeled and quartered
½	pound (225g) fresh mushrooms, cleaned and patted dry
3	tablespoons unsalted butter
1	teaspoon dried basil
½	teaspoon salt, if desired
⅛	teaspoon freshly ground black pepper
¼	cup (60ml) dry white wine *or* dry white vermouth
1	tablespoon lemon juice

Cornbread

⅔	cup unbleached all-purpose flour (3⅓ ounces, 95g)
⅔	cup yellow cornmeal (4 ounces, 115g)
2	teaspoons baking powder
½	teaspoon salt, if desired
1½	tablespoons sugar
3	tablespoons unsalted butter, chilled and cut in 3 pieces
2	large eggs
⅔	cup (160ml) buttermilk

Insert *metal blade*. Turn on machine, drop cheese through feed tube, and process until it is finely chopped, 20 to 30 seconds. Remove and set aside.

With *metal blade* in place, put parsley into work bowl and process until it is minced, about 20 seconds. Remove 1 tablespoon of parsley and set it aside, covered, for garnish. Add onion to parsley in work bowl and pulse 3 times. Then scrape work bowl and pulse 2 or 3 more times, until onion is finely chopped. Leave parsley and onion in bowl.

Insert *2mm slicing disc.* Put mushrooms in feed tube and use light pressure to process. Repeat until all mushrooms are sliced.

Melt butter in 12-inch (30cm) skillet over moderately high heat. When butter is hot, add mushrooms, parsley, and onions. Toss frequently with 2 broad wooden spatulas and cook until onion is wilted and mushrooms begin to release their juices, about 3 minutes. Add basil, salt, pepper, wine, and lemon juice. Increase heat to high and cook mixture briskly, tossing often, until all liquid is absorbed and mushrooms begin to brown lightly, about 5 minutes. Remove from heat and set aside, uncovered. Topping may be made 2 or 3 hours before bread is baked.

Wipe work bowl and metal blade with paper towels. Adjust oven rack to center position and preheat oven to 425°F. (220°C.). Butter 12- or 13-inch (30 or 33cm) pizza pan.

Insert *metal blade* and process flour, cornmeal, baking powder, salt, sugar, and butter for 15 seconds; mixture should resemble fine meal. Add eggs and buttermilk and pulse rapidly 5 times. Then scrape work bowl and pulse rapidly 2 or 3 more times, just until ingredients are thoroughly combined. Do not overprocess.

Spread batter in prepared pan and sprinkle it evenly with half the cheese. Distribute mushroom mixture evenly over cheese (fingers do the job best). Sprinkle top with remaining cheese and reserved parsley. Bake until cornbread is golden brown with darker spots at edges, and toothpick inserted into center comes out dry, 12 to 15 minutes. Remove from oven and let stand for 5 minutes. Cut into wedges and serve hot or warm. (This is best eaten with fork; it is too delicate for finger food.)

Makes 12 servings.

PARTY FOCACCIA

Most cuisines have a version of a flat bread. The Italians call it focaccia; they usually season it with olive oil and herbs. I call this a party focaccia because it is not only seasoned with the usual herbs and garlic; the topping is made especially festive with the addition of ham, cheese, and olives. Although the bread requires a yeast dough, it can be ready to serve in only 45 minutes.

1 package (1 tablespoon) active dry yeast

½ teaspoon sugar

½ cup (120ml) warm water (105 to 115°F., 40 to 46°C.)

2 tablespoons olive oil

½ teaspoon garlic powder

½ teaspoon dried oregano

½ teaspoon dried sage

1 teaspoon dried basil

½ cup (120ml) cold water

3 cups unbleached all-purpose flour (15 ounces, 425g)

2 tablespoons sugar

1 teaspoon salt, if desired

½ cup parsley leaves, washed, patted dry and loosely packed

1 small garlic clove, peeled

4 ounces (115g) Parmesan cheese, cut into 1-inch (2.5cm) pieces

4 ounces (115g) cooked ham, cut into 1-inch (2.5cm) pieces

6 pitted jumbo black olives, drained and patted dry

⅓ cup (80ml) olive oil

Butter 15½ by 10½ by 1-inch (39 by 26 by 2.5cm) jelly-roll pan. Adjust oven rack to center position and preheat oven to 450°F. (230°C.).

Sprinkle yeast and ½ teaspoon sugar over warm water in 1-cup (240ml) glass measure or small bowl. Stir and set aside until yeast is dissolved and mixture is very foamy, about 10 minutes.

Meanwhile, heat 2 tablespoons of olive oil in 1-quart (1L) saucepan over low heat. Add garlic powder, oregano, sage, and basil and simmer for 1 minute. Remove from heat, add cold water and stir in yeast mixture.

Insert *metal blade* and put flour, 2 tablespoons of sugar, and salt into work bowl. Turn on machine and pour liquid mixture through feed tube in a thin, steady stream, as fast as flour absorbs it. This may take 15 to 20 seconds. Once dough forms ball, process for 30 seconds longer. Carefully remove dough (it should be slightly sticky) and place in jelly-roll pan. Cover it loosely with oiled plastic wrap and let it stand for 15 minutes to relax gluten. Then pat dough evenly with lightly oiled hands to cover bottom of pan.

Wipe out work bowl and reinsert *metal blade*. Add parsley and process for 10 seconds. With machine running, add garlic through feed tube and process for 10 seconds longer. Add cheese, pulse 3 times, then process continuously for 30 seconds. Add ham and olives and pulse rapidly 10 times to chop them fine. Remove metal blade and add ⅓ cup (80ml) olive oil to work bowl. Mix well with plastic spatula.

Spread ham mixture evenly over dough. Use your thumb to make deep indentations in dough at 2-inch (5cm) intervals. Bake until top is well browned, 10 to 12 minutes. Cut into squares and serve hot, warm, or at room temperature.

Makes 24 servings.

FONTINA GOUGERE

This is a classic appetizer from Burgundy, varied by substituting an Italian cheese for the traditional Gruyère. It is made with puff-shell dough and has a texture similar to a popover — crisp on the outside, and tender as a custard within. It is baked in the shape of a wreath, and makes a marvelously festive appetizer for a cocktail party.

1 ounce (30g) **Parmesan cheese, in 1 piece**

4 ounces (115g) **Fontina cheese, in 1 piece, well chilled**

1 cup (240ml) **water**

1 stick **unsalted butter (4 ounces, 115g), cut into several pieces**

½ teaspoon **salt, if desired**

1 cup **unbleached all-purpose flour (5 ounces, 140g)**

4 large **eggs, cracked into cup**

⅛ teaspoon **white pepper**

1 teaspoon **dry mustard**

1 tablespoon **Dijon mustard *or* mayonnaise**

1 tablespoon **dry white wine *or* dry white vermouth**

1 teaspoon **sweet paprika**

Insert *metal blade*. Turn on machine, drop Parmesan cheese through feed tube and process until cheese is very finely chopped, about 45 seconds. Remove and set aside.

Insert *medium shredding disc* and use light pressure to process Fontina cheese. Remove and set aside.

Put water, butter, and salt in 3-quart (3L) saucepan. Set over moderately high heat and cook until butter is melted, stirring occasionally. Bring mixture to rolling boil, then remove from heat and immediately add flour. Blend thoroughly with wooden spoon and return to moderately high heat. Cook, stirring occasionally, until dough comes together in smooth mass and begins to film bottom of pan, about 1 minute.

With *metal blade* in place, transfer hot flour mixture to work bowl. Process until completely smooth, about 15 seconds, then add eggs all at once and process for 30 seconds, stopping once to scrape work bowl. Mixture should be very thick, shiny, and smooth; if necessary, process a few seconds longer. Add pepper, dry mustard, and Fontina, and process for 15 seconds, stopping once to scrape work bowl.

Adjust oven rack to center position and preheat oven to 400°F. (205°C.). Line 14 by 17-inch (35 by 43cm) baking sheet with foil, and butter foil. Butter outer side of 8-inch (20cm) round cake pan and place it, bottom side down, in center of foil.

Fit large pastry bag (18 inches, 45cm long) with plain or star tube measuring ½ inch (12mm) at its tip. Fill bag with dough and pipe in continuous loops, approximately 2 inches (5cm) wide, around outside of cake pan. Try to pipe loops very close to side of pan, but not touching it. (If you don't have pastry bag, place 14 to 16 heaping tablespoonfuls of dough around pan, touching each other, but not the side of pan.) May be prepared to this point a few hours before baking. Cover loosely with plastic wrap and refrigerate.

Bake until puffed and rich golden brown, about 30 minutes. (If put into oven directly from refrigerator, it will take a few more minutes to bake.) While it is baking, mix Dijon mustard and wine in small bowl. Combine Parmesan cheese and paprika in another small bowl.

Remove gougère from oven but do not turn oven off. Carefully remove cake pan from center. Quickly brush mustard mixture over top and sides of hot pastry and sprinkle evenly with Parmesan mixture. (At this point, pastry may settle and lose some volume; that is to be expected.) Return gougère to oven and bake just until cheese is melted, about 5 minutes.

Let gougère stand for 3 to 5 minutes (no longer, or it will stick to foil); pastry may settle some more. Run wide metal spatula under gougère to dislodge it from foil. Ease gougère onto large serving platter or wooden board, cut into wedges and serve warm or at room temperature.

Makes 1 gougère, about 12 servings.

PORK DIM SUM ROLLS

Dim sum, a mid-morning or afternoon snack, have long held an honored position in Chinese cuisine. Instead of making the traditional buns, I form rolls with this pork filling. All the ingredients for the filling go into the food processor at once, and they are chopped and combined with a few quick pulses.

½ **pound (225g) lean boneless pork, cut into 1-inch (2.5cm) pieces and well chilled**
1 **garlic clove, peeled**
1 **scallion, trimmed and cut into 1-inch (2.5cm) lengths**
½ **teaspoon salt, if desired**
½ **teaspoon sugar**
1 **teaspoon Oriental sesame oil**
1 **tablespoon hoisin sauce**
2 **tablespoons water**
1 **tablespoon dry sherry**
¼ **cup canned water chestnuts, rinsed and drained**
1 **package refrigerated buttermilk biscuits (10 biscuits)**
Unbleached all-purpose flour
Watercress or parsley sprigs
6 **tablespoons red-wine vinegar**
3 **tablespoons soy sauce**

Insert *metal blade* and put pork, garlic, scallion, salt, sugar, sesame oil, hoisin sauce, water, sherry, and water chestnuts into work bowl. Pulse very rapidly about 20 times, stopping once or twice to scrape work bowl, until mixture is chopped medium-fine. Do not overprocess.

Separate biscuits and dip both sides of each one into flour to coat lightly. Stretch dough into 3-inch (8cm) circles. Divide pork mixture evenly among biscuits and spread it to edges of dough. Roll up biscuits and place them, seam sides down, on lightly oiled steamer rack. (Rolls may be prepared to this point 1 hour ahead; cover and refrigerate.)

Steam rolls until pork is cooked, about 8 to 10 minutes. Let them cool slightly, then cut each one into thirds. Arrange pieces on serving platter and garnish with watercress or parsley.

Mix vinegar and soy sauce in small bowl and pass with dim sum. Supply toothpicks so your guests can spear rolls and dip them in sauce.

Makes 30 pieces.

NOTE: To make dim sum that are more traditional in shape, place spoonfuls of pork mixture on flattened circles made from 20 biscuits and gather edges of dough together to enclose filling completely. Pinch firmly to seal and steam as directed above. Serve with chopsticks, or knife and fork.

GREEK SPINACH TRIANGLES

Phyllo leaves are wrapped around a filling of spinach, ricotta cheese, and feta cheese to make these crisp and flaky pastries. You can make small triangles to serve as appetizers, or large ones to serve as a main course. You can also make one large pastry in a baking dish and serve it in squares — great for a party! Use fresh spinach if you can. If you must use frozen spinach, buy the leaf variety, not chopped spinach, which is mostly stems.

½ **cup parsley leaves, washed, patted dry and loosely packed**

1 **bunch (about 6) scallions, trimmed and cut into 3-inch (8cm) lengths**

2 **pounds (910g) fresh spinach *or* 2 10-ounce (285g) packages frozen leaf spinach, thawed**

2 **tablespoons olive oil**

¾ **pound (340g) feta cheese, cut into 1-inch (2.5cm) pieces**

1 **1-pound (455g) container ricotta cheese**

¼ **teaspoon freshly ground black pepper**

3 **large eggs**

1 **pound (455g) phyllo leaves, at room temperature**

2 **sticks unsalted butter (8 ounces, 225g), melted**

Insert *metal blade* and process parsley until it is finely chopped, about 30 seconds. Remove and set aside.

Insert *3mm or 4mm slicing disc*, wedge scallion pieces vertically in feed tube and use light pressure to process. Remove and set aside.

If using fresh spinach, remove stems and place leaves in sinkful of cold water. Rinse leaves thoroughly to remove all sand and grit, changing water once or twice if necessary. Lift out handfuls of washed spinach and place leaves in large kettle with just water that clings to them. Cover kettle and place over medium-high heat until water boils and spinach is just wilted, 5 to 10 minutes. Empty spinach into colander and let stand until cool enough to handle. Then squeeze it, a handful at a time, to wring out as much water as possible. (This is important; if filling is too wet, pastry will be soggy.)

With *metal blade* in place, put spinach into work bowl and pulse 4 or 5 times until spinach is chopped. Do not overprocess; you don't want a purée.

If using frozen spinach, thaw it and squeeze water from it. (Frozen spinach is about 75% water; two 10-ounce packages will yield about 5 ounces (140g) when thawed and squeezed to remove water.)

Heat oil in 10-inch (25cm) skillet over medium-high heat. Add scallions and cook, stirring, until tender, about 3 minutes. Add spinach, stir, and cook just long enough to evaporate excess moisture, about 1 minute.

Insert *metal blade*, put feta cheese into work bowl, and pulse a few times until cheese is finely chopped. Add ricotta cheese and process for 10 seconds, stopping to scrape work bowl as necessary. Add pepper and eggs and process for 10 seconds. Scrape work bowl and add spinach mixture and parsley. Pulse a few times to combine thoroughly.

Lay stack of phyllo sheets on work surface and cover with a dry towel, then a damp one. Remove several sheets and cut them in half lengthwise with scissors. Replace sheets under towels. (Sheets can be cut in thirds lengthwise, for very small triangles.)

Remove 1 length of phyllo from beneath towels and position it with a short side toward you. Brush very lightly with butter. Fold both long ends of pastry so they meet in center and brush again with butter. Place rounded teaspoonful of filling in lower left corner of pastry strip. Then flip that corner over to opposite side to form triangle. Continue this flip-flop

Placing filling on dough   *Flipping to form triangle*

folding to end of strip, maintaining triangular shape. Lightly brush entire surface of triangular packet with butter and place on ungreased cookie sheet.

Repeat with remaining pastry, filling, and butter. Place triangles about 1 inch (2.5cm) apart on cookie sheets; they puff up during baking.

Bake in upper third of preheated 375°F. (190°C.) oven until pastries are golden brown, 25 to 30 minutes. Use a wide metal spatula to transfer pastries to cooling rack. Serve hot, warm, or at room temperature. (See NOTE for instructions on making ahead and storing.)

Makes 4 to 5 dozen.

To make large triangles

Lightly brush 2 whole phyllo sheets with butter and arrange them end to end with a 2-inch (5cm) overlap. (Pastry will measure about 12 inches (30cm) wide and 32 inches (80cm) long.) Fold both long ends so they meet in center and brush again with butter. Place ⅓ cup of filling in corner of pastry strip. Then fold over and over to form triangular packet as described above. Brush entire surface with butter and place on ungreased cookie sheet.

Bake as directed above. Serve hot, or transfer to racks and let cool slightly. These are best when warm.

Makes about 18.

To make 1 large spanakopita

Brush sides and bottom of 13 by 9 by 2-inch (33 by 23 by 5cm) baking dish with about 1 tablespoon of the melted butter. Place 1 sheet of phyllo dough into pan and brush lightly with butter. Fold in sides of sheet so it fits pan neatly. Repeat, using 8 to 10 sheets in all. Spread filling over dough. Cover with additional 8 to 10 sheets, brushing each with butter.

Bake in center of preheated 375°F. (190°C.) oven until top is golden brown, 30 to 40 minutes. Allow to cool in pan for 10 to 15 minutes, then cut into squares and serve.

Makes 12 servings.

NOTE: Prepared triangles may be covered and refrigerated up to 24 hours before baking. To freeze unbaked pastries, arrange them on cookie sheets lined with waxed paper. Freeze until firm, then transfer to plastic bags and seal airtight. Pastries will keep up to 2 months. To bake, arrange frozen pastries about 1 inch (2.5cm) apart on ungreased cookie sheets. Bake one sheet at a time in upper third of preheated 375°F. (190°C.) oven until golden brown, 45 to 50 minutes.

To reheat frozen baked pastries, arrange them slightly apart on ungreased cookie sheets and bake in preheated 375°F. (190°C.) oven until they are hot and crisp, about 20 minutes. Pastries may crack a bit on reheating.

SOUPS

Hot or cold, soup is always satisfying. And even more satisfying if you make it yourself! This collection of soups reflects my preference for light, healthful, and colorful food. All the soups are low in calories.

What raises a soup from ordinary to superior is the stock used as its base. My recipe for basic chicken stock, included in this chapter, does not call for salt. When you use this stock as a soup base, you can adjust the salt content of your final soup according to taste or dietary restrictions. Canned chicken broth can be used as a soup base, but remember that most are very salty.

Everyone knows that the food processor is a whiz at puréeing ingredients for soup. Some of the recipes in this chapter will make you also aware of its usefulness in preparing attractive garnishes for soups.

Incidentally, whenever a purée is called for, use the metal blade to process only the solids to the desired consistency. Add the resulting purée to the liquid ingredients and stir to combine them well.

Almost all the soups described in this chapter are quickly made and can be prepared completely or partly in advance.

Cream of Mushroom Soup

BASIC CHICKEN STOCK

The best tasting soups start with homemade stocks. Since chicken stock is so easy to prepare and virtually cooks by itself, you may want to make 2 or 3 quarts at a time. It will keep in the refrigerator for 3 or 4 days, or even longer if you bring it to a boil every few days. And you can freeze it for months, with no loss in quality.

It's also probably the least expensive of meat stocks because you need only necks, backs, and wings. Of course, you can also use a whole chicken, which yields a lot of leftover meat that makes a tasty addition to soups, salads, sandwich fillings or quiches. I usually save the bones from boned chicken breasts as well as the chopped carcasses of roast chickens, and freeze them until I have enough bones to make a stock. A good rule for a well flavored general-purpose stock is 1 pound (455g) of chicken bones and meat to 1 quart (1L) of water.

1 3 to 3½ pound (1.4 to 1.6kg) whole frying chicken or approximately equal weight of chicken backs, necks and wings, in any combination

1 large carrot (4 ounces, 115g), scrubbed and cut into 2-inch (5cm) pieces

1 large onion (8 ounces, 225g), peeled and cut in half

2 celery ribs (4 ounces, 115g total), washed and cut into 3-inch (8cm) pieces

6 black peppercorns

6 parsley sprigs

1 bay leaf

1 1-inch (2.5cm) cube fresh, unpeeled ginger (optional)

3 to 4 quarts (3 to 4L) cold water

Place chicken or chicken parts into 5- to 6-quart (5 to 6L) pot or casserole with heavy bottom. Include giblets; reserve liver for another use. Add remaining ingredients, using enough water to cover chicken completely. (Ginger is not essential, but it does give a wonderfully fresh taste and aroma.)

Set pot over medium heat. As water comes to simmer, scum or foam will rise to surface. Skim off with spoon and discard. Continue skimming as necessary; scum usually ceases to form within half an hour or so.

Never allow liquid to boil. As it gets hot and small bubbles on surface become more numerous, reduce heat to very low and cook slowly, partially covered, for 3 or 4 hours. (If you're confident of your heat source, you need not pay any attention to stock during this period.) Remove from heat and set aside, uncovered, to cool for about 1 hour. Remove chicken and set aside. Strain stock into large container and discard vegetables.

Degrease stock completely. The easiest way is to chill it until all fat rises and solidifies on surface. You can then lift fat off in one or more pieces. If you haven't time for this procedure, let broth sit for about 10 minutes and skim fat from surface with spoon.

Makes 2 to 3 quarts (2 to 3L).

NOTES: Some points to remember in making stock:

1. Use a heavy pot or casserole that distributes heat evenly, allowing the stock to cook gently. Small amounts, like a quart or so, may be cooked overnight in a stoneware slow cooker like the Crock-pot®, (a registered trademark of the Rival Manufacturing Company) at its lowest setting. In this case, no scum will form on the surface.

2. Cook the stock very slowly. Just a bubble or two should break the surface every few seconds. Never boil it or it will become cloudy.

3. Never cover stock completely while it is cooking; the flavor will be adversely affected. Rest the lid of the stock pot on the edge of the pan so air can

circulate freely while the stock simmers.

4. Never cover stock at all while it is cooling; doing so may cause it to turn sour.

You will notice that the above recipe does not call for salt. That is because many recipes using stock require it to be boiled down to concentrate flavor. A salted stock will become excessively salty when reduced. Add salt to taste in individual recipes.

COLD CUCUMBER AND WALNUT SOUP

Low-fat yogurt lends tartness and a light consistency to this smooth, fresh soup, and walnuts give a nice crunch. Appropriate at any time of year, it makes a fine first course for a dinner of roast or grilled chicken. Or make it the main course for lunch, accompanied by pita pockets and an assortment of cheeses.

1 small garlic clove, peeled
¼ cup parsley leaves *or* cilantro leaves, washed and patted dry
½ cup walnuts (2 ounces, 55g)
1 large cucumber (12 ounces, 340g), peeled, halved lengthwise, and seeded
1 large tomato (8 ounces, 225g), with stem removed, halved crosswise
3 cups (720ml) plain low-fat yogurt
2 tablespoons light olive oil
½ teaspoon ground cumin
1½ teaspoons salt, if desired
¼ teaspoon freshly ground black pepper
¾ teaspoon sugar

Insert *metal blade.* With machine running, drop garlic through feed tube and process until it is finely chopped, about 10 seconds. Transfer to large mixing bowl.

With *metal blade* in place, put parsley or cilantro in work bowl and process until finely chopped, 20 to 30 seconds. Remove and set aside, covered.

Insert *medium shredding disc* and use light pressure to process walnuts. Add walnuts to garlic.

Insert *3mm or 4mm slicing disc.* Slice cucumber pieces lengthwise into thirds, then crosswise into 3-inch (8cm) sections. Stand sections vertically in feed tube, wedging them in tightly, and use medium pressure to process. Add cucumber to garlic and walnuts and stir to mix well.

Insert *French-fry disc.* Gently squeeze each tomato half to remove seeds and juice. Place in feed tube, cut sides down, and use light pressure to process. Add processed tomatoes to cucumber mixture, discarding peel if you wish.

With *metal blade* in place, put remaining ingredients into work bowl and process until yogurt is liquefied, about 15 seconds. Add yogurt mixture to cucumber mixture and stir well. Taste for seasoning, cover, and refrigerate until well chilled, at least 1 hour. Soup may be made to this point a day ahead.

Just before serving, taste and adjust seasoning with additional salt, pepper, and sugar, if necessary. Ladle into serving bowls and sprinkle lightly with reserved parsley or cilantro.

Makes about 4 cups (1L), enough for 4 servings.

ROSY GAZPACHO

Like the classic, this is a thick tomato-based soup, which is served cold. What makes this version especially interesting is the vegetables, each processed differently to produce a variety of textures. For best flavor, use only firm, ripe tomatoes.

1 medium onion (5 ounces, 140g) peeled and quartered
2 medium green bell peppers (10 ounces, 285g total), cored, seeded, and cut into 1-inch (2.5cm) squares
2 medium cucumbers (20 ounces, 570g total), peeled, halved lengthwise, and seeded
7 or 8 medium tomatoes (2 pounds, 910g total), with stems removed
2 small garlic cloves, peeled
2 tablespoons fruity olive oil
3 cups (720ml) tomato juice
1/8 teaspoon Tabasco sauce
2 tablespoons red-wine vinegar
2 teaspoons salt, if desired
1/4 teaspoon freshly ground black pepper

Insert *metal blade* and put onion into work bowl. Pulse 5 or 6 times, until onion is chopped medium-fine. Transfer to 5- or 6-quart (5 or 6L) mixing bowl.

With *metal blade* in place, put peppers in work bowl. Pulse quickly 3 times, scrape work bowl, and pulse quickly another 2 or 3 times, until peppers are chopped medium-fine. Add to onions.

Cut cucumber sections in half lengthwise, then crosswise, to get 16 sections, each about 3 inches (8cm) long. Insert *3mm or 4mm slicing disc*, stand cucumber sections vertically in feed tube, wedging them in tightly, and use medium pressure to process. Add to mixing bowl.

Insert *French-fry disc.* Use light pressure to process 6 tomatoes. Remove tomato peel from work bowl and add tomatoes to mixing bowl.

Insert *metal blade* and turn on machine. Drop garlic through feed tube and process until coarsely chopped, about 10 seconds. (Because work bowl and metal blade are wet, garlic will not be finely chopped.) Scrape work bowl. Quarter remaining tomatoes and add them to work bowl with garlic. Process for 2 minutes to make smooth purée. Add to mixing bowl.

Add remaining ingredients to mixing bowl and stir well to combine. Cover and refrigerate for 2 to 3 hours. Taste, adjust seasoning, if necessary, and serve well chilled, accompanied by crusty French or Italian bread.

Makes about 4 quarts (4L).

CHILLED AVOCADO SOUP

This deliciously tangy soup, flecked with bits of green spinach and red tomatoes, is adapted from a recipe in The Vegetarian Epicure, Book Two, *by Anna Thomas. Although usually served cold, it is equally good served hot.*

1 large or 2 medium shallots (1 1/2 ounces, 45g total), peeled
1 jalapeño chile, halved lengthwise and seeded
1 medium cucumber (10 ounces, 285g), peeled, halved lengthwise, seeded, and cut into 1 1/2-inch (4cm) pieces
3 or 4 medium tomatoes (1 pound, 455g total), with stems removed, halved
2 medium ripe avocados (1 pound, 455g total), peeled, pitted, and cut into 2-inch (5cm) pieces
1 cup firmly packed spinach leaves (2 ounces, 55g), washed and patted dry
1/2 teaspoon salt, if desired

⅛	**teaspoon freshly ground black pepper**
¼	**teaspoon ground cumin**
1	**teaspoon sugar**
2 to 3	**tablespoons lemon juice**
1	**tablespoon red-wine vinegar**
1	**cup (240ml) plain yogurt**
¾	**cup (180ml) Half and Half**
1¼	**cups (300ml) chicken stock, homemade or canned**

Garnish

½	**cup cilantro *or* parsley leaves, washed and patted dry**
3	**large scallions (2 ounces, 55g), trimmed and cut into 3-inch (8cm) lengths**
1	**large, ripe avocado (12 ounces, 340g)**
1	**large tomato (8 ounces, 225g), with stem removed, halved crosswise**
	Tortilla chips

Insert *metal blade.* With machine running, drop shallot and chile through feed tube and process until finely chopped, about 10 seconds. Add half each of cucumbers, tomatoes, avocados, and spinach to work bowl and process for 30 seconds. Add remainder of these vegetables and process for 2 minutes, stopping once to scrape work bowl.

Add salt, pepper, cumin, sugar, 2 tablespoons of lemon juice, and vinegar to work bowl and process for 15 seconds. Transfer mixture to large bowl.

With *metal blade* in place, put yogurt and Half and Half in work bowl and process for 15 seconds. Add to avocado mixture along with chicken stock and stir to combine thoroughly. Cover soup and refrigerate until it is well chilled, 2 to 3 hours. Just before serving, stir soup well and taste for seasoning, adding last tablespoon of lemon juice if necessary. While soup is chilling, prepare garnish.

Insert *metal blade.* Put cilantro or parsley into work bowl and process until finely chopped, 20 to 30 seconds. Remove and set aside, covered.

Insert *2mm slicing disc.* Stand scallion sections vertically in feed tube, wedging them in tightly, and use medium pressure to process. Remove and set aside, covered.

Just before serving soup, insert *French-fry disc.* Halve avocado lengthwise and remove pit. Peel each section and halve crosswise. Place avocado pieces in feed tube, last-cut side down, and use light pressure to process. Set aside, covered.

Gently squeeze tomato halves to remove seeds and juice. With *French-fry disc* in place, put tomatoes in feed tube, cut side down, and use light pressure to process. Discard peel and set aside, covered.

To serve, ladle soup into serving bowls and sprinkle lightly and evenly with cilantro or parsley. Place small spoonful of avocado and one of tomato side by side in middle of bowl. Or garnish with alternating thin slices of avocado and tomato arranged in fan. Pass scallions and tortilla chips separately.

Makes about 7 cups (1.7L), 6 to 8 servings.

Chilled Avocado Soup

GARDEN CITY LETTUCE SOUP

This delicately flavored soup takes only minutes to prepare. Although it can be made at any time of year, it is especially good with home-grown garden lettuce.

½ cup parsley leaves, washed and patted dry
2 ounces (55g) Parmesan cheese, cut into 1-inch (2.5cm) pieces
1 medium onion (5 ounces, 140g), peeled and halved vertically
2 tablespoons butter *or* vegetable oil
1 bay leaf
1 1-pound (455g) can peeled tomatoes, well drained
4 cups tender lettuce leaves, washed, dried and loosely packed *or* 1 head red or green leaf lettuce (about ¾ pound, 340g before cleaning), washed and dried
4 cups (1L) chicken stock, homemade or canned
½ teaspoon salt, if desired
Freshly ground black pepper, to taste

Insert *metal blade* and put parsley in work bowl. With machine running, drop cheese through feed tube and process until cheese and parsley are finely chopped, about 20 seconds. Remove and set aside.

Insert *3mm slicing disc.* Stand onion vertically in feed tube and use light pressure to process.

Put butter or oil in 4-quart (4L) pot and set over medium heat. When fat is hot, add onion and bay leaf. Cook, stirring occasionally, until onion is tender but not browned, about 3 minutes.

With *metal blade* in place, put tomatoes into work bowl and pulse rapidly 3 or 4 times to chop tomatoes coarsely. Add to pot with onions.

Cut lettuce into pieces about 1 inch (2.5cm) square and add to tomatoes and onions. Reduce heat to medium-low and cook, stirring occasionally, until lettuce is fully wilted, about 5 minutes.

Add stock, increase heat to medium-high, and bring mixture to boil. Cover pan, reduce heat to low, and let soup simmer slowly for 20 minutes. Taste for seasoning and add salt and pepper if necessary. Remove bay leaf and serve at once. Pass parsley and cheese mixture separately, for sprinkling over each serving.

Soup may be made ahead and reheated.

Makes 4 to 6 servings.

ZUCCHINI AND POTATO SOUP WITH LEEKS

This delicious, low-calorie soup is so simple that a child can prepare it. The processor slices the raw vegetables, then purées them once they are cooked. A hearty restorative when served hot, it's also good when well chilled. Leftover soup takes nicely to reheating.

3 medium zucchini (1 pound, 455g total), trimmed and cut into 3-inch (8cm) lengths
3 medium potatoes (1 pound, 455g total), peeled and quartered lengthwise
½ pound (225g) leeks, trimmed, washed, and cut into 3-inch (8cm) lengths
4 to 6 cups (1 to 1.4L) water
1 teaspoon salt, if desired
1 to 2 cups (240 to 480ml) milk
Freshly ground black pepper, to taste
2 tablespoons snipped fresh chives *or* 1 tablespoon freeze-dried chopped chives

Insert *5mm or 6mm slicing disc.* Wedge zucchini pieces vertically in feed tube and use medium pressure to process. Stand potato quarters vertically in feed tube and use medium pressure to process. Stand leek sections vertically in feed tube and use light pressure to process.

Put vegetables in 4-quart (4L) saucepan and pour in just enough water to cover. Add salt, if using, and stir well. Bring mixture to boil over high heat, then reduce heat to very low. Partially cover pan and simmer until vegetables are very tender, 30 to 40 minutes.

Insert *metal blade.* Use slotted spoon to transfer vegetables to work bowl. Process until very smooth, 1 to 2 minutes, stopping once or twice to scrape work bowl.

Return puréed vegetables to liquid in pan and add 1 to 2 cups of milk, depending on desired consistency. Stir well, taste for seasoning and add pepper and salt, if necessary. Serve hot, sprinkled with chives.

Makes 6 servings.

THICK VENETIAN SOUP

There are dozens of variations of this Italian soup of rice, peas, and Parmesan cheese. All are high in protein and carbohydrates, and low in fat.

2 ounces (55g) Parmesan cheese, cut into 1-inch (2.5cm) pieces
⅓ cup parsley leaves , washed and patted dry
1 medium onion (5 ounces, 140g), peeled and quartered
2 tablespoons butter
¾ cup raw long- or short-grain rice
2 cups fresh peas *or* 1 10-ounce (225g) package frozen peas, thawed
4 cups chicken stock, preferably homemade Salt (see NOTE)
¼ teaspoon freshly ground black pepper

Insert *metal blade.* With machine running, drop cheese through feed tube and process until finely chopped, about 30 seconds. Remove and set aside. Put parsley into work bowl and process until finely chopped, 20 to 30 seconds. Remove and set aside. Add onion to work bowl and pulse rapidly 3 times, then scrape work bowl and pulse quickly 2 or 3 more times, until onion is finely chopped.

Put butter in 3-quart (3L) saucepan over medium heat. When butter is hot, add onion and cook, stirring with wooden spoon, until onion is wilted, 1 to 2 minutes. Add rice and cook another minute or so, stirring until grains begin to turn opaque. Do not allow rice to brown.

If using fresh peas, add them now, stirring to coat them with butter.

Add stock, parsley, salt, and pepper, and stir well to combine them. Increase heat to high and bring mixture to boil, stirring occasionally. Then reduce heat to medium, cover pan, and cook soup at medium boil until rice is tender but still slightly firm to the bite, about 15 minutes.

If using thawed frozen peas, add them after rice has cooked with stock for about 10 minutes. Cover pan and cook until rice is tender, about 5 minutes more.

Just before serving, stir in cheese. Taste and adjust seasoning with more salt and pepper, if necessary.

Makes 4 servings.

NOTE: If using unsalted chicken stock, add 1 to 1½ teaspoons salt. If using canned, salted chicken broth, use about ½ to ¾ teaspoon salt.

VARIATION: Julienned strips of ham make a delicious addition to this soup. Cut 4 ounces (115g) of ham into strips about 1 by ⅛ by ⅛ inch (2.5cm by 3mm by 3mm). Add to soup during last 5 minutes of cooking.

CHICKEN MINESTRONE

Traditional minestrone is a vegetable soup, but the addition of chicken makes this a hearty main course. You may use vegetables other than those suggested, according to what is in season, and you need not stick slavishly to the proportions given here. Supplement fresh vegetables, when necessary, with cooked dried beans or canned Great Northern beans.

This is a soup that may be cooked in leisurely fashion. All the vegetables needn't be ready ahead of time; as you process each one, add it to the others simmering in the casserole.

4 ounces (115g) Parmesan cheese, in 1-inch (2.5cm) pieces
1 medium onion (6 ounces, 170g), peeled and halved vertically
1 large carrot (5 ounces, 140g), trimmed, scrubbed, and cut in 3-inch (8cm) lengths
2 tablespoons olive oil
1 tablespoon butter
2 medium boiling potatoes (12 ounces, 340g total), peeled, cut crosswise into ¾-inch (1.8cm) slices, and reassembled
1 large celery rib (3 ounces, 85g), trimmed and cut into 3-inch (8cm) lengths
1 14- to 16-ounce (400 to 455g) can whole peeled tomatoes, undrained
1 10-ounce (285g) package frozen lima beans, thawed
6 cups (1.4L) chicken stock, preferably homemade
Salt (see NOTE)
¼ teaspoon freshly ground pepper
2 medium zucchini (12 ounces, 340g total), trimmed and cut into 3-inch (8cm) lengths
2 cups cooked chicken, cut into ½-inch (12mm) pieces

Insert *metal blade.* With machine running, drop cheese through feed tube and process until finely chopped, about 30 seconds. Remove and set aside.

Insert *4mm slicing disc,* place onion vertically in feed tube, and use medium pressure to process. Leave onion in work bowl. Stand carrot sections vertically in feed tube, wedging them in tightly, and use firm pressure to process.

Put oil and butter in 5- to 6-quart (5 to 6L) casserole and set over medium heat. When fat is hot, add onions and carrots. Stir well to coat vegetables, then reduce heat to low. Cover pan and cook slowly, stirring occasionally, until onions are golden, about 10 minutes. Carrots should still be crisp.

Insert *French-fry disc.* Place 1 reassembled potato horizontally in feed tube and use firm pressure to process. This will give you diced potatoes. Repeat with second potato. Add to casserole and cook for 2 to 3 minutes, stirring occasionally.

Insert *5mm or 6mm slicing disc.* Stand celery pieces vertically in feed tube, wedging them in tightly, and use medium pressure to process. Add to casserole and cook for 1 minute, stirring constantly.

With *metal blade* in place, put tomatoes in work bowl and rapidly pulse 4 times to chop them coarsely. Add tomatoes and lima beans to casserole, pour in stock, and add salt and pepper. Increase heat to high and bring soup to boil, stirring occasionally. Then reduce heat to medium-low and cover pot. Cook at very slow boil until carrots, potatoes, and celery are almost tender, about 8 to 10 minutes. Watch carefully and adjust heat as necessary to prevent vegetables from overcooking.

Insert *French-fry disc,* stand zucchini pieces vertically in feed tube and use medium pressure to process.

Just before serving, add zucchini and chicken to soup. Stir well and cook at slow boil, uncovered, until zucchini is just tender, 2 to 3 minutes. At this point, all vegetables should be just tender. Serve at once in individual soup bowls, passing cheese separately for sprinkling over each serving.

Makes 8 servings.

NOTE: If using homemade, unsalted, chicken stock, add 1½ teaspoons salt to soup. If using canned, salted, chicken stock, add about ¾ teaspoon salt, adjusting to taste.

CREAMY CARROT SOUP

Jalapeño chiles give bite to this velvety smooth soup, which is equally delicious served hot or cold.

2 jalapeño chiles, halved lengthwise and seeded

1 pound (455g) carrots, scrubbed and cut into 3-inch (8cm) lengths

1 large onion (8 ounces, 225g), peeled and halved vertically

3 tablespoons butter

¼ teaspoon dried thyme leaves

⅛ teaspoon freshly grated nutmeg

⅛ teaspoon white pepper

1 bay leaf

2 cups (480ml) chicken stock, homemade or canned

½ cup (120ml) heavy cream

1½ cups (360ml) milk

1 teaspoon salt, if desired

1 tablespoon chopped fresh dill *or* parsley

Insert *metal blade*. With machine running, drop chiles through feed tube and process until finely chopped, about 10 seconds. Remove metal blade, but leave chiles in work bowl.

Insert *4mm slicing disc*. Stand carrots vertically in feed tube and use firm pressure to process. Leave carrots in work bowl. Place onion vertically in feed tube and use medium pressure to process.

Melt butter in 3- to 4-quart (3 to 4L) saucepan over medium heat. Add chiles, carrots, onion, thyme, nutmeg, pepper and bay leaf. Stir well to coat vegetables and cook for 1 minute. Add 1 cup (240ml) of stock, increase heat to high, and bring mixture to boil, stirring occasionally. Cover pan, reduce heat to medium-low, and cook at slow boil, stirring occasionally, until carrots are very tender, about 30 minutes. Discard bay leaf.

Insert *metal blade*. Put carrot mixture in work bowl and process for 2 minutes, stopping twice to scrape bowl. Mixture will be smooth purée. Return purée to saucepan and add remaining 1 cup (240ml) stock, cream, milk and salt. Stir well.

Set saucepan over medium heat and cook, stirring frequently, until soup is hot; do not allow it to boil. If serving soup hot, taste and adjust seasoning, if necessary. Then pour into serving bowls and sprinkle with about ½ teaspoon chopped dill or parsley for each serving. If serving soup chilled, allow it to come to room temperature in saucepan, then cover and refrigerate for several hours. Taste and adjust seasoning, if necessary; if soup is too thick, thin it with a little milk. Pour into serving bowls and garnish with dill or parsley.

Makes about 6 cups (1.4L), enough for 6 servings.

CREAM OF MUSHROOM SOUP

Cooked and puréed mushroom stems are the special ingredient that gives to this soup a more intense mushroom flavor than the classic Cream of Mushroom soup.

- **5 cups (1.2L) chicken stock, homemade or canned**
- **¼ cup parsley leaves, washed and patted dry**
- **1 small onion (3 ounces, 85g), peeled and halved**
- **3 tablespoons butter**
- **1 pound (455g) fresh mushrooms, with stems removed and caps trimmed flat on opposite sides (reserve stems and trimmings)**
- **3 tablespoons unbleached all-purpose flour**
- **1 tablespoon dry sherry**
- **1 cup (240ml) heavy cream**
- **3 or 4 drops Tabasco sauce**
- **Salt, if desired**

Put stock in 4-quart (4L) saucepan and heat it to simmering.

Insert *metal blade.* With machine running, drop parsley through feed tube and process until finely chopped, about 20 seconds. Remove and set aside, covered.

With *metal blade* in place, turn on machine, drop onion through feed tube, and process until finely chopped, about 10 seconds.

Melt butter in 2-quart (2L) saucepan over medium-low heat. Add onion and stir.

With *metal blade* in place, put mushroom stems and trimmings in work bowl. Pulse 5 times, scrape bowl and pulse 5 more times, until mushroom pieces are very finely chopped. Add to onion and cook slowly, uncovered, stirring occasionally, until mushrooms and onion are very tender, about 10 minutes.

With *metal blade* in place, add cooked mushrooms and onion to work bowl. Process for 2 minutes, stopping once to scrape work bowl. Return purée to saucepan, scraping work bowl well. Stir flour into purée and cook over medium-high heat for 2 to 3 minutes, stirring with wooden spoon. Add ½ cup (120ml) hot chicken stock to mushroom mixture and stir well. Add another ½ cup (120ml) and stir well, then add mushroom mixture to stock remaining in saucepan. Bring mixture to simmer over medium heat, stirring occasionally. Soup should be only slightly thickened.

Insert *2mm slicing disc.* Wedge mushroom caps into feed tube with flat side down and use light pressure to process. Add sliced mushrooms to soup and let simmer until they are tender, a few minutes. Add sherry, cream, and Tabasco sauce. Taste carefully for seasoning, adding salt if necessary. (If you used canned chicken stock, you will probably not need any salt. But if you used homemade, unsalted, chicken stock, you may need about a teaspoon of salt.) Heat thoroughly and serve, sprinkling each portion lightly with parsley.

Makes 6 to 8 servings.

CREAM OF BROCCOLI SOUP

This economical soup makes use of nearly the entire broccoli plant: flowerets, stalks, and leaves. And whether you use whipping cream, light cream, or milk, it is low in calories. I confess to preferring its flavor when I make it with whipping cream, and I like it hot or cold.

1 bunch broccoli (about 1½ pounds, 680g)
2 cups (480ml) chicken stock, homemade or canned
⅛ teaspoon freshly grated nutmeg
½ teaspoon salt, if desired
½ cup (120ml) whipping cream, light cream, or milk

Use small, sharp knife to cut flowerets from broccoli. Strip off leaves and set them aside. Trim off and discard ends of stalks. Peel stalks, cutting into them about ¹⁄₁₆ inch (2mm) to remove tough outer fibers, and cut stalks into 1-inch (2.5cm) pieces.

Insert *metal blade*. Put broccoli stalks into work bowl and pulse several times until coarsely chopped. Remove to 3-quart (3L) saucepan and spread evenly over bottom of pan. Cover with leaves, then with flowerets. Add stock (liquid will not cover broccoli completely), cover, and bring to rapid boil over high heat. Reduce heat to medium, uncover pan, and gently press broccoli with wooden spoon. Liquid should just reach top of broccoli. Cover and cook at slow boil until broccoli is very tender, about 10 minutes. Remove and reserve about ½ cup of cooked flowerets.

With *metal blade* in place, transfer broccoli and cooking liquid to work bowl. Process for 2 minutes, stopping once to scrape bowl. Return mixture to saucepan and add remaining ingredients. Stir well. Soup may be made ahead to this point.

If serving soup hot, bring to simmer over medium heat, stirring occasionally. Pour into serving bowls and garnish with 1 or 2 reserved flowerets.

If serving soup cold, allow it to cool, then cover it and refrigerate for several hours. Taste and adjust seasoning, if necessary. If soup is too thick, thin with a little cream or milk. Pour into serving bowls and garnish with reserved flowerets.

Makes about 4 cups (1L), enough for 4 servings.

PASTA

Although essentially an informal food, pasta takes well to dressing up for more formal occasions. It's perfect for leftovers. I often raid the refrigerator for odds and ends to combine in an impromptu pasta sauce.

Many of the pasta sauces in this chapter are low in calories — in keeping with my campaign to dispel the myth that pasta is fattening. When drowned in butter and cream, of course it is! But a main-dish serving of Pasta with Red Clam Sauce amounts to only about 350 calories. The same is true for Pasta with Tuna Sauce.

You can make pasta with many kinds of flour, but the recipes that follow call for only the more commonly available varieties: unbleached white, bread, whole-wheat, semolina, and buckwheat. The procedure for making pasta dough is essentially the same for any flour; full instructions are given in a section preceding the recipes.

For rolling and cutting pasta dough, a hand-cranked pasta machine does a terrific job, but you can roll and cut the dough by hand. Instructions for both methods are included. Cut pasta can be cooked immediately or dried and stored — although homemade pasta really does taste best if it is cooked and eaten right away.

Straw and Hay Pasta

MAKING PASTA

Mixing the Dough

Always measure flour as described on page 174 or weigh it accurately. Also be sure to use eggs graded "large."

Insert *metal blade* and add flour, salt, oil and water to work bowl. Crack eggs into cup measure. Turn on machine and pour eggs through feed tube all at once. Process for 15 seconds after eggs go in. Pasta mixture will almost form ball. Stop machine and scrape work bowl.

Process for another 30 seconds. By this time, dough should just about gather into mass that barely moves around work bowl. If dough has not completely formed ball at this point, do not be concerned.

Carefully remove all dough from work bowl, scraping metal blade and work bowl clean, and place dough on large sheet of waxed paper. Compress dough into one lump with your hands. Dough should feel slightly moist but firm and not at all sticky. An index finger poked into it should come out clean and dry. Once dough is made, the next step is to knead it with the metal blade.

Kneading the Dough

Insert *metal blade,* and turn on machine. Tear off walnut-size pieces of dough and drop them through feed tube one at a time. After all dough is added, process for another 60 seconds. Dough should form into one large ball on metal blade with a few isolated bits of dough spinning around it. Dough should move freely around work bowl.

If dough does not form ball within 10 or 15 seconds, stop machine. Redistribute dough in work bowl with plastic scraper and add 1 teaspoon of water. Turn on machine and process until ball of dough forms, adding a bit more water through feed tube if necessary. Be careful not to add too much water.

Once ball of dough forms, process for 60 seconds. Carefully remove dough from work bowl and squeeze it briefly between your hands to check its consistency. It should be pliable and slightly moist, but firm and not at all sticky. If dough feels too wet, return it to work bowl with a little flour and process for a few seconds. Once dough is proper consistency, shape it into ball and flatten slightly to form disc. Wrap securely in plastic wrap and set aside at room temperature for at least 30 minutes. During this time, liquid will be absorbed by flour, gluten network (activated by vigorous processing) will relax, and dough will become easy to roll out. (It can sit for hours, but it will be ready to roll out in 30 minutes.)

I think you will be amazed at the difference in consistency between rested dough and just-mixed dough: rested dough feels moister and it is smooth and very supple — ideal for rolling out.

Kneaded pasta dough may be stored in refrigerator, tightly wrapped in plastic, for up to 3 days before rolling. Dough may darken slightly in color, but it will be usable. Bring chilled pasta dough to room temperature before using.

Rolling the Dough by Machine

You can roll dough out by machine or by hand. I use an Italian hand-crank pasta machine made of stainless steel, which does a beautiful job. I also enjoy rolling out dough by hand. I haven't been able to detect any difference in the final result, regardless of the type of pasta, so do what pleases you most.

Divide dough into 6 pieces. Work with one piece at a time, keeping remainder covered with plastic wrap. Flatten piece of dough between your hands until it is about ½ inch (12mm) thick. If dough feels slightly sticky, dust it very lightly with flour. Adjust rollers of pasta-rolling machine to widest opening. Pass dough through as you turn handle.

Decrease setting on rollers by one notch and pass dough through again. Do not fold dough, just pass it through. Reduce setting of rollers one notch each time the dough passes through until you reach the next-to-last setting. At this point, your pasta is probably thin enough.

If dough becomes sticky at any point in rolling, dust it very lightly with flour. Don't overdo it or pasta may become tough. (Ordinarily, you would have to fold dough into thirds after first pass-through and then run dough through widest setting 4 or 5 more times to knead it, folding dough in thirds after each rolling. Since you have already kneaded the dough thoroughly in the food processor, it requires no further kneading with the pasta-rolling machine.)

Set strip of rolled dough (which will be from 2 to 3 feet, 60 to 90cm long) on lightly floured board or towel. Repeat rolling procedure with remaining pieces of dough. Let strips of dough dry, uncovered, for a few minutes, just until they feel smooth and leathery; this makes it easier to cut them with the machine. Be careful not to let them dry too much or dough will crumble and be difficult to work with. If your kitchen is very dry, just work with 1 or 2 strips at a time, rolling them and cutting them before moving on to other pieces of dough.

Cutting the Dough by Machine
Hand-crank pasta-rolling machines come with cutters of different widths. Select the cutting width you want and attach appropriate cutter to machine. Cut long strip of dough crosswise into halves or thirds, depending on how long you like your pasta. Insert one end of strip through cutter and turn handle; support uncut part of dough with other hand. As more of strip comes out, move that hand and place it under the pasta strands to prevent them from collapsing

 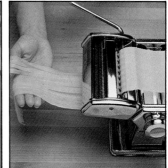

Rolling dough by machine *Cutting dough by machine*

onto each other, while continuing to turn handle with other hand. Lay pasta strands on towel and let them dry for about 5 minutes, at which point they will be ready to cook. If pasta seems sticky, sprinkle it lightly with cornmeal or semolina flour and toss gently to keep strands separate. When you cook pasta, cornmeal or semolina falls to bottom of kettle and pasta will not be gritty. Homemade pasta is best when eaten soon after it is made. Its tenderness disappears after it is completely dry.

If you must store it, form cut strands into coils and let them stand on towel until completely dry. Store in covered container at room temperature.

Rolling the Dough by Hand
The easiest way to roll pasta dough by hand is to roll all the dough at once with a long rolling pin. For those who enjoy adventures in cooking, I recommend this method if time permits. It gives a real sense of satisfaction and accomplishment.

I use a dowel rod that is 3 feet (90cm) long and about 1½ inches (4cm) in diameter. It cost about a dollar at a building-supply store. To condition a dowel, wash it and dry it well. Rub it lightly with olive oil. After the oil is absorbed, rub in a little flour. Repeat this treatment after the first half dozen or so times you use the dowel. To store it, attach a screw with a circle or hook at one end, and hang it in a closet. Don't wash the pin between uses; just wipe it clean. If you don't want to bother with a dowel, use a heavy straight rolling pin.

Divide the dough in half and roll out each piece separately until dough is 1/16-inch (1.5mm) thick; flour dough as necessary to prevent sticking and turn it over from time to time.

The following description of rolling is for the dowel method.

Pasta dough is stretched more than rolled. You should never put downward pressure on the dough, but push the dowel away from you. Sprinkle a large work surface (at least 3 by 3 feet, 90 by 90cm) lightly with flour and place circle of dough on it. Pat dough to flatten it slightly.

Set dowel on dough near edge closest to you, then roll dough out, remembering to push pin away from you rather than exerting downward pressure. Turn dough a quarter turn and repeat movement. Keep rolling and turning dough until it is a circle about 18 inches (45cm) in diameter. Flour dough as necessary, but use flour sparingly; it is important not to use too much flour.

Now stretch and roll dough as described in the following paragraphs until it measures about 3 feet (90cm) in diameter and about 1/16 inch (1.5mm) thick.

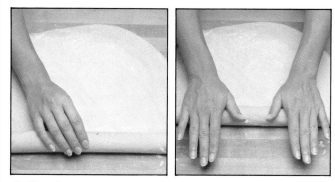

Rolling dough by hand

You must work rapidly so dough will not dry out.

Have circle of dough in front of you and take up about 4 inches (10cm) of its far end on dowel. Place both palms on dowel and roll it back and forth rapidly. As you roll dowel back and forth, slide your hands out to ends of dowel, gently stretching dough sideways in process. Slide your hands gently so as not to tear the dough.

Roll the dowel toward you slightly and take up about 2 more inches (5cm) of dough. Repeat the same motion, rolling the dowel back and forth as your hands slide out to its ends. After you repeat this procedure 5 or 6 times, all of the dough will be taken up on the dowel.

Unroll the dough, turn it over, and rotate the sheet of pasta slightly. Check to see if there are any tears. If so, patch them by pinching the edges together. Roll the dowel over the edges if they are thicker than the rest of the sheet. If dough feels sticky, flour it slightly.

Repeat the rolling and stretching motions as many times as it takes to make the sheet 1/16-inch (1.5mm) thick and about 3 feet (90cm) in diameter. Always remember to check for tears and thick edges; if there are any defects, correct them. All the final stretching should take no more than 10 minutes. The more you do it, the faster and more adept you become.

Cutting Hand-Rolled Pasta
Roll fully stretched sheet of pasta up on dowel, then unroll it onto clean, dry towel set on work surface. Let about 1/3 of sheet hang over edge of counter or table (with no towel underneath). In about 10 minutes, turn sheet and let different portion hang over edge. In 10 minutes more, repeat procedure. Pasta should dry until it feels leathery but pliable. This usually takes about a half hour. If your kitchen is very dry, check pasta every few minutes to prevent

Cutting dough by hand

overdrying. (There have been days when my pasta was ready to cut almost immediately after I stretched it.)

Place pasta sheet on cutting surface and fold a flap of about 3 inches (7cm) over on itself. Keep folding until whole sheet is a flat roll about 3 inches (7cm) wide. Use a heavy knife to trim ends, then cut across roll to make strands as wide as you like — about ⅛ inch (3mm) for linguine and ¼ inch (6mm) for fettuccine. Make 2-inch (5cm) strands for lasagne.

As you cut, keep the knife blade against your knuckles and come down firmly with each cut. Don't raise the knife any higher than your knuckles when cutting. This method almost completely ensures against injury.

When all pasta is cut, open out all strands onto clean, dry towel. If pasta is at all sticky, dust strands lightly with cornmeal or semolina flour. Hand-rolled and cut pasta can be cooked immediately, or within an hour or two. Or it may be dried completely, wrapped airtight, and stored at room temperature. But homemade pasta is best when eaten soon after being made.

Cooking Fresh Pasta
Fresh pasta cooks in practically no time at all. Bring 6 quarts (6L) of water to boil over high heat. There is no need to add salt or oil to water. Drop in pasta and give it a stir. Allow water to come back to boil and start testing pasta for doneness in about 1 minute. Test pasta frequently, and drain when it is "al dente" — firm to the bite but tender. Serve it at once with pasta sauce of your choice.

Making Pasta with Food-Processor Attachment
Several food-processor manufacturers offer pasta attachments. You make the pasta mixture in the work bowl of the food processor and the attachment extrudes it into any one of several shapes. The method is quick and the results are good. To make pasta with a pasta attachment for a food processor, follow the manufacturer's directions.

BASIC PASTA

This is an all-purpose pasta — tender, delicious and slightly chewy. It is easy to roll out by hand or by machine.

2 cups (10 ounces, 285g) unbleached all-purpose flour
¾ **teaspoon salt, if desired**
1 **tablespoon oil**
1 **tablespoon water**
3 **large eggs**

Follow procedures on pages 34 to 37.
Makes about 1 pound (455g) uncooked dough.

WHOLE-WHEAT PASTA

This hearty pasta is particularly good when served with a robust, flavorful sauce, such as a Tuna Sauce with Anchovies and Capers (see page 42), or a Bolognese sauce (see page 44).

> 1 cup whole-wheat flour (5 ounces, 140g)
> 1 cup unbleached all-purpose flour (5 ounces, 140g)
> ¾ teaspoon salt, if desired
> 1 tablespoon oil
> 1 tablespoon water
> 3 large eggs

Follow procedures on pages 34 to 37.
   Makes 1 pound (455g) uncooked dough.

BREAD-FLOUR PASTA

Bread flour has a very high gluten content and makes an especially chewy pasta. It is very good in soups, as it keeps its texture well on reheating.
   Roll this dough by machine, if possible; it retracts too much when rolled out by hand.

> 2 cups bread flour (10 ounces, 285g)
> ¾ teaspoon salt, if desired
> 1 tablespoon oil
> 1 tablespoon water
> 3 large eggs

Follow procedures on pages 34 to 37.
   Makes 1 pound (455g) uncooked dough.

WATER PASTA

Because it contains no eggs and no oil, this pasta is virtually fat-free. It is bland on its own, but excellent in well-flavored soups or with spicy sauces.

> 2 cups unbleached all-purpose flour (10 ounces, 285g)
> ¾ teaspoon salt, if desired
> ½ cup (120ml) water

Insert *metal blade* and put flour and salt into work bowl. Start machine and add water rapidly through feed tube.
   Follow procedures on pages 34 to 37.
   Makes 1 pound (455g) uncooked dough.

EGG-YOLK PASTA

This is the tenderest pasta of all. The raw dough is very beautiful — intensely gold in color — but the color fades during cooking.

> 1¾ cups unbleached all-purpose flour (8¾ ounces, 250g)
> ¾ teaspoon salt, if desired
> 2 tablespoons oil
> 2 tablespoons water
> 8 large egg yolks
> Additional water

Insert *metal blade* and put flour, salt, oil, 2 table-spoons water, and yolks into work bowl. Process for 15 seconds, scrape work bowl, and process for another 30 seconds. Mixture will appear crumbly.

Turn mixture out onto large sheet of waxed paper and shape it firmly into a mass. With *metal blade* in place, start machine. Tear off walnut-size pieces of dough and drop them one at a time through feed tube. When all dough is included, gradually add water through feed tube, 1 teaspoon at a time, until dough forms a ball on blade with only a few stray bits. Once ball is formed, process for 60 seconds.

Remove dough from work bowl, shape it into a cake, and wrap it securely in plastic wrap. Let dough rest at room temperature for at least 30 minutes, then roll and cut dough as described on pages 34 to 37.

Makes about 18 ounces (510g) uncooked dough.

EGG-WHITE PASTA

This pasta has no cholesterol, because only egg whites are used as the liquid—no yolks and no oil. The cooked pasta is tender and chewy, but slightly firm and bland, so it takes well to characterful sauces.

2 cups unbleached all-purpose flour (10 ounces, 285g)
¾ **teaspoon salt, if desired**
⅔ **cup (160ml) egg whites (from 5 or 6 large eggs)**

Insert *metal blade* and put flour and salt into work bowl. Start machine and pour egg whites through feed tube. Process for 15 seconds, scrape work bowl, and process for 30 seconds. Dough will form a ball on metal blade.

Remove dough and shape it into a single mass. To knead, tear off walnut-size pieces and proceed as described on pages 34 to 37. At end of kneading, this dough will be a bit moister and softer than other doughs, and may feel slightly sticky.

Makes 1 pound (455g) uncooked dough.

SEMOLINA PASTA

Semolina flour, made from durum wheat, has a granular texture; it gives this pasta a rich flavor.

1¼ cups unbleached all-purpose flour (6¼ ounces, 180g)
1 cup semolina flour (5 ounces, 140g)
¾ **teaspoon salt, if desired**
1 tablespoon oil
1 tablespoon water
3 large eggs

Insert *metal blade* and put both flours, salt, oil, and water into work bowl. Crack eggs into cup. Start machine, pour eggs through feed tube, and process until dough gathers into a ball, 15 to 20 seconds. Dough will feel moist and slightly sticky.

Remove dough and place on sheet of waxed paper. With *metal blade* in place, start machine. Tear off walnut-size pieces of dough and drop them one at a time through feed tube. When all dough is included, it will form a ball (with a few stray bits) that will tend to stick to sides of work bowl. Process for 60 seconds, then proceed as described on pages 34 to 37.

Makes about 18 ounces (510g) uncooked dough.

100% SEMOLINA PASTA

This recipe produces an especially rich-tasting pasta. The dough is quite firm; it is hard to roll out by hand, but a pasta machine can handle it very easily.

2½ cups semolina flour (12½ ounces, 355g)
1 teaspoon salt, if desired
1 tablespoon oil
3 large eggs
2 tablespoons water

Insert *metal blade* and put semolina, salt, and oil into work bowl. Crack eggs into cup. Start machine, add eggs through feed tube, and process for 15 seconds. Scrape work bowl (dough will be gathered into several large masses) and process for another 30 seconds; dough should almost be gathered into one large mass. Scrape blade and bowl and transfer dough onto large sheet of waxed paper. Press dough into a cake; it will feel very firm.

With *metal blade* in place, start machine. Tear off walnut-size pieces of dough and drop them one at a time through feed tube. After all dough is included, add water through feed tube and process until dough forms one large ball on blade with a few stray bits.

Since this is a firm, heavy pasta dough, you will have to stop machine a few times to redistribute dough in work bowl. Do not add more water; just stop machine periodically, scrape work bowl, and continue processing. Dough will soon form a ball on blade and will move freely around work bowl. Once ball forms, process for 75 to 90 seconds more.

Remove dough and press it into a cake; it will feel firm and slightly moist. Wrap securely in plastic wrap and let dough rest at room temperature for at least 30 minutes.

Proceed as described on pages 34 to 37.

Makes about 1¼ pounds (570g) uncooked dough.

SPINACH PASTA

Spinach gives pasta a beautiful green color without flavoring it intensely. Spinach pasta is especially attractive served with a tomato-based sauce, and it is wonderful combined with golden pasta for Straw and Hay Pasta (see page 45).

2 cups unbleached all-purpose flour (10 ounces, 285g)
1 cup tightly packed spinach leaves (2 ounces, 55g), washed and thoroughly dried
¾ teaspoon salt, if desired
1 tablespoon oil
2 large eggs

Red Clam Sauce on Bread-Flour Pasta

Insert *metal blade*. Put 1 cup of flour and all of spinach into work bowl and process until spinach is finely chopped, about 30 seconds. Add remaining flour, salt, and oil to work bowl. Crack eggs into cup. Start machine, pour eggs through feed tube, and process for 15 seconds.

Proceed as described on pages 34 to 37.

Makes 1 pound (455g) uncooked dough.

BUCKWHEAT PASTA

Buckwheat flour supplements all-purpose flour to make a soft and supple dough that produces a tender pasta. Its rich flavor goes well with strong sauces.

1½ cups unbleached all-purpose flour (7½ ounces, 215g)
½ cup buckwheat flour (2½ ounces, 70g)
¾ teaspoon salt, if desired
1 tablespoon oil
1 tablespoon water
3 large eggs

Insert *metal blade* and put both flours, salt, oil, and water into work bowl. Crack eggs into cup. Start machine, add eggs through feed tube, and process for 20 seconds. Dough should almost be gathered into a ball. Remove dough, place on sheet of waxed paper, and shape into a ball.

With *metal blade* in place, start machine. Tear off walnut-size pieces of dough and drop them one at a time through feed tube. When all dough is included, it should gather into a ball within a few seconds. Process for 60 seconds, adding small amount of water if necessary.

Proceed as described on pages 34 to 37.

Makes 1 pound (455g) uncooked dough.

RED CLAM SAUCE

This is one of the tastiest and easiest sauces of all, with a mild clam flavor. It is especially pretty with spinach pasta.

1 small garlic clove, peeled
½ cup parsley leaves, washed and patted dry
1 tablespoon olive oil
2 1-pound (455g) cans whole plum tomatoes, drained
2 6½-ounce (185g) cans chopped clams
¼ teaspoon freshly ground black pepper
1 teaspoon dried oregano leaves
1 teaspoon sugar, if desired
1 pound (455g) fresh pasta, cut into ¼-inch (6mm) strips

Insert *metal blade*. With machine running, drop garlic and parsley through feed tube and process until finely minced, about 10 seconds.

Put oil in 12-inch (30cm) skillet and set over medium heat. Add garlic and parsley, stir well, and cook for 1 to 2 minutes without browning garlic.

With *metal blade* in place, put tomatoes into work bowl and pulse rapidly 4 times. Add tomatoes to skillet. Drain clam liquid into skillet, reserving clams. Add pepper and oregano.

Cook over medium heat, stirring occasionally, until sauce is reduced to about 2½ cups (600ml). Stir in clams. Taste sauce and add sugar if necessary.

To serve, cook pasta in 6 quarts (6L) of boiling water until tender but firm to the bite. Drain well and turn into heated serving dish. Pour sauce over pasta and serve at once.

Makes 4 servings.

TUNA SAUCE

This robust tomato sauce from Sicily is rich with the flavors of tuna, anchovies, and capers.

½	cup parsley leaves, washed and patted dry
2	small garlic cloves, peeled
1	medium onion (5 ounces, 140g), peeled and quartered
1	8-inch (20cm) celery stalk, cut into 6 pieces
2	tablespoons olive oil
2	1-pound (455g) cans whole plum tomatoes, undrained
	Pinch cayenne
¼	teaspoon freshly ground black pepper
2	teaspoons dried basil leaves
1	1¾-ounce (50g) can anchovies, drained on paper towels
20	pitted medium black olives, drained
1	7-ounce (200g) can tuna in oil, drained
1	tablespoon small capers, rinsed and drained
1 to 2	teaspoons sugar
½	cup (120ml) tomato sauce
1	pound (455g) fresh pasta, cut into ¼-inch (6mm) strips

Insert *metal blade*, put parsley into work bowl, and process until finely chopped, about 20 seconds. Remove and set aside.

With *metal blade* in place, start machine and rapidly drop garlic, onion, and celery through feed tube. Process until vegetables are very finely chopped, about 10 seconds.

Put oil in 3-quart (3L) saucepan, add garlic, onion, and celery, and set over medium-low heat. Stir well, cover pan, and cook slowly, stirring occasionally, until vegetables are very tender, 10 to 15 minutes.

With *metal blade* in place, put tomatoes (with juice), cayenne, pepper, and basil into work bowl and pulse rapidly 4 times, to chop tomatoes coarsely. Add to saucepan.

With *metal blade* in place, put anchovies into work bowl and process until they are almost puréed, about 5 seconds. Add to tomato mixture. Increase heat to high and bring mixture to boil, then reduce heat to medium-low and let sauce bubble slowly, uncovered, until it is slightly thickened, 20 to 30 minutes. There will be about 4 cups (1L) of sauce.

With *metal blade* in place, put olives into work bowl and process for 3 seconds, just to chop them coarsely. Add to sauce. Add tuna to sauce and stir to break it into chunks. Stir in capers, 1 teaspoon of sugar, and tomato sauce and simmer for 2 or 3 minutes longer. Taste and add more sugar if necessary. There will be about 5 cups (1.2L) of sauce. (Sauce may be made ahead and refrigerated for up to 2 days; reheat slowly.)

To serve, cook pasta in 6 quarts (6L) of boiling water until tender but firm to the bite. Drain well and turn into heated individual serving dishes. Top with sauce and sprinkle with reserved parsley.

Makes 4 to 6 servings.

MONTANA MEAT SAUCE

This sauce is tangy, hearty, and delicious. The following recipe makes a double batch, enough for 12 to 15 servings. You can cut it in half.

1½ pounds (680g) beef chuck *or* round steak, trimmed and cut into 1-inch (2.5cm) pieces

½ cup (½ ounce, 15g) parsley leaves, loosely packed

2 small garlic cloves, peeled

2 large onions (1 pound, 455g total), peeled and cut into eighths

1 small green bell pepper (4 ounces, 115g), cored, seeded, and cut into 1-inch (2.5cm) pieces

¼ cup (60ml) olive oil

1 cup (240ml) canned beef broth

3 1-pound (455g) cans whole plum tomatoes, undrained

1 6-ounce (170g) can tomato paste

1 tablespoon dried basil leaves

1 teaspoon dried oregano leaves

½ teaspoon dried thyme leaves

¼ teaspoon freshly ground black pepper

1 teaspoon salt, if desired

1 teaspoon sugar, or to taste, if desired

2 pounds (910g) fresh pasta, cut into ¼-inch (6mm) strips

Additional ground pepper, if desired

Freshly grated Parmesan cheese

Line baking sheet with foil. Arrange pieces of beef on sheet in single layer and place in freezer until beef is very cold but not at all firm, about 30 minutes.

Insert *metal blade* and put parsley into work bowl. Start machine, drop garlic through feed tube, and process until parsley and garlic are finely chopped, about 10 seconds. Add half the onion and half the green pepper to work bowl. Pulse 3 times, scrape bowl, and pulse 2 more times, until onion and pepper are chopped medium-fine.

Put oil in deep 12-inch (30cm) skillet or wide 5-quart (5L) Dutch sauté pan. Set pan over medium heat and add onion mixture.

With *metal blade* in place, put remaining onion and green pepper into work bowl. Pulse 3 times, scrape bowl, and pulse 2 more times. Add this mixture to skillet and stir well, then cover and cook over medium heat, stirring once or twice, until vegetables are very tender but not brown, 8 to 10 minutes. Uncover pan during last 2 minutes of cooking.

With *metal blade* in place, put half the beef into work bowl. Pulse 12 to 15 times to chop meat into small pieces, then add to skillet and stir well. Repeat with remaining meat. Cook, stirring occasionally, until meat loses its pink color.

Add broth and increase heat to high. Cook, stirring often, until broth is almost absorbed and meat mixture is very thick. Remove from heat.

With *metal blade* in place, put half the tomatoes (with juice) into work bowl and pulse quickly 4 times to chop them coarsely.

Add tomatoes to meat mixture and put skillet back over medium heat. Process remaining tomatoes and add them to skillet. Stir in tomato paste, basil, oregano, thyme, pepper, and salt, mixing well. When mixture comes to a boil, reduce heat to very low. Simmer very slowly, uncovered, stirring occasionally, until sauce is thickened, about 1 hour. There should be 9 to 10 cups (2.2 to 2.4L) of sauce. Taste and adjust seasoning; add sugar if needed.

Sauce may be refrigerated for several days or frozen. To serve, pour sauce over pasta and toss well. Grind black pepper over individual servings and pass grated cheese separately.

Makes 12 to 15 servings.

BOLOGNESE SAUCE WITH BEEF, CHICKEN, AND HAM

The traditional sauce from Bologna, Italy, is characterized by finely chopped meat simmered with tomatoes and vegetables. This recipe is an untraditional variation, combining beef, chicken, and ham. It may be made days ahead, and its flavor improves on standing.

½ pound (225g) beef round steak, trimmed and cut into 1-inch (2.5cm) pieces

½ pound (225g) boneless, skinless chicken breasts, cut into 1-inch (2.5cm) pieces

4 ounces (115g) Parmesan cheese, cut into 1-inch (2.5cm) pieces

1 small onion (2 to 3 ounces, 55 to 85g), peeled and quartered

1 small garlic clove, peeled

1 small carrot (2 ounces, 55g), scrubbed and cut into 1-inch (2.5cm) pieces

1 stalk celery (2 ounces, 55g), cut into 1-inch (2.5cm) pieces

2 tablespoons butter

2 ounces (55g) cooked lean ham, chilled and cut into 1-inch (2.5cm) pieces

¼ teaspoon freshly ground black pepper

½ teaspoon freshly grated nutmeg

1 teaspoon salt, if desired

1 cup (240ml) dry white wine

2 1-pound (455g) cans whole plum tomatoes, undrained

3 tablespoons tomato paste

1 to 2 teaspoons sugar

1 pound (455g) fresh pasta, cut into ¼-inch (6mm) strips

Line baking sheet with foil. Arrange pieces of beef and chicken on sheet in single layer and place in freezer until meat is well chilled but not at all firm, about 30 minutes.

Insert *metal blade*. With machine running, drop cheese through feed tube and process until very finely chopped, about 45 seconds. Remove and set aside.

With *metal blade* in place, start machine, drop onion, garlic, carrot, and celery through feed tube, and process until vegetables are finely chopped, about 10 seconds.

Put butter in 4-quart (4L) saucepan over medium heat. Add vegetables, stir well, and cover.

With *metal blade* in place, put ham into work bowl and pulse 5 or 6 times, until ham is finely chopped. Add ham to saucepan and stir, then cover pan and cook, stirring occasionally, until vegetables are tender, about 10 minutes.

With *metal blade* in place, add chilled beef and chicken to work bowl. Pulse about 15 times to chop meat fine, stopping to scrape work bowl once or twice. Add meat to saucepan and cook over medium heat, stirring, until beef loses its pink color, about 5 minutes. Mixture will be very thick.

Add pepper, nutmeg, salt, and wine. Increase heat to high and cook, stirring occasionally, until wine has almost evaporated, 5 to 10 minutes.

With *metal blade* in place, put 1 can (1 pound, 455g) of tomatoes (with juice) into work bowl and pulse rapidly 4 times to chop tomatoes coarsely. Add to saucepan and stir in tomato paste. When sauce begins to boil, reduce heat to medium-high and cook, stirring frequently, until sauce is slightly thickened, about 10 minutes. Remove from heat.

With *metal blade* in place, put remaining tomatoes and juice into work bowl and pulse 4 times to chop tomatoes coarsely. Add tomatoes and 1 teaspoon of sugar to sauce, set pan over medium-low heat, and bring sauce to a simmer. Taste carefully and add more sugar, salt, pepper, or nutmeg if necessary. There will be about 6 cups (1.4L) of sauce.

(Sauce can be made ahead and refrigerated for a few days or frozen for longer storage.)

To serve, cook pasta in 6 quarts (6L) of boiling water until tender but firm to the bite. Drain well and turn into large warm serving dish. Pour sauce over pasta, add half the cheese, and toss well. Serve at once, passing remaining cheese separately.

Makes 4 to 6 servings.

STRAW AND HAY PASTA

Paglia e fieno, as it is called in Italian, is a beautiful dish of yellow and green pasta in a creamy sauce with mushrooms, peas, ham, and cheese.

¾ **pound (340g) fresh spinach fettuccine**

¾ **pound (340g) fresh basic or semolina fettuccine**

4 **ounces (115g) Parmesan cheese, cut into 1-inch (2.5cm) pieces**

½ **medium onion (2 to 3 ounces, 55 to 85g), peeled and cut into 2 pieces**

5 **tablespoons butter**

1 **pound (455g) fresh mushrooms, cleaned, with stems separated from caps**

1 **teaspoon salt, if desired**

½ **teaspoon freshly ground black pepper**

1 **cup thawed frozen peas (5 ounces, 140g)**

1¼ **cups (300ml) heavy cream**

6 **ounces (170g) baked or boiled ham, cut into 1 by ⅛ by ⅛-inch (2.5cm by 3mm by 3mm) strips**

Spread each kind of pasta on a separate towel.

Insert *metal blade*. With machine running, drop cheese through feed tube and process until very finely chopped, about 45 seconds. Remove and set aside.

With *metal blade* in place, start machine and drop onion through feed tube. Process until onion is finely chopped, about 10 seconds.

Melt 3 tablespoons of butter in 12-inch (30cm) skillet over medium-low heat. Add onion and cook slowly, stirring occasionally, until onion is tender but not browned, 6 to 8 minutes.

Insert *French-fry disc*. Wedge mushroom caps into feed tube on their sides and use medium pressure to process. When caps are processed, put stems into feed tube and use medium pressure to process.

Add mushrooms, salt, and pepper to skillet and raise heat to high. Stir and toss mixture almost constantly until mushrooms begin to release their juices, about 3 minutes.

Reduce heat to medium, add peas, and cook 1 minute longer, tossing frequently. Pour in ½ cup (120ml) of cream and cook until liquid is slightly thickened, about 2 minutes. (Sauce may be prepared to this point an hour ahead.)

Bring 6 quarts (6L) of water to a boil. Put remaining cream in small saucepan over low heat to keep it warm, and reheat mushroom mixture over medium heat. Melt remaining butter in 10-inch (25cm) skillet over medium-low heat and add ham. Cook for 2 to 3 minutes just to heat ham through, tossing frequently. Warm large serving dish.

Drop yellow pasta into boiling water and stir. When water returns to a boil, add spinach pasta. (Spinach pasta is moister and cooks faster than plain pasta, so it is added later.) Allow water to return to boil and start testing pasta for doneness after 1 minute.

Drain pasta immediately and turn into serving dish. Add warm cream and toss to coat pasta well. Then add half of ham, half of mushroom sauce, and half of cheese and toss again. Make a depression in center of pasta and fill with remaining mushroom sauce; distribute remaining ham on top. Serve at once, passing remaining cheese separately.

Makes 6 servings.

TURKEY TETRAZZINI

Luisa Tetrazzini was a famous Italian coloratura soprano at the turn of the century; a pasta and chicken dish was created in her honor. The substitution of turkey for chicken is a latter-day invention.

- 10 ounces (285g) fresh pasta cut into ⅛-inch (3mm) strips
- 1 tablespoon oil
- ¼ cup parsley leaves, tightly packed, washed and patted dry
- 4 ounces (115g) Parmesan cheese, cut into 4 pieces
- ½ pound (225g) mushrooms, cleaned and trimmed flat on 2 opposite sides (reserve trimmings)
- 1 medium red or green bell pepper (5 ounces, 140g), cored, seeded, and cut into 1-inch (2.5cm) pieces
- 2 cups (480ml) turkey stock
- 1½ cups (360ml) Half and Half *or* milk
- 5 tablespoons butter
- ½ cup unbleached all-purpose flour (2½ ounces, 70g)
- ¼ cup (60ml) dry sherry
- 2 teaspoons salt, if desired
- ½ teaspoon freshly ground black pepper
- ⅛ teaspoon Tabasco sauce
- 2 cups diced cooked turkey (10 ounces, 285g)

Cook pasta in large pot of unsalted boiling water just until it is tender. Drain and rinse well in large basin of cold water until pasta is cool. Drain thoroughly, place in large plastic bag, and add oil. Mix well, seal bag, and set aside until ready to use. (Pasta may be made hours ahead and refrigerated.)

Insert *metal blade,* put parsley into work bowl, and process until finely chopped, 20 to 30 seconds. Remove and set aside.

With *metal blade* in place, start machine, drop cheese through feed tube, and process until finely chopped, 45 to 60 seconds. Remove and set aside.

Insert *4mm slicing disc.* Place single layer of mushrooms in feed tube, flat side down, and use light pressure to process. When all mushrooms are sliced, remove from work bowl, add trimmings, and set aside.

With *metal blade* in place, add red or green pepper to work bowl and pulse 4 or 5 times to chop pepper coarsely.

Combine stock and Half and Half in 2-quart (2L) saucepan and set over medium heat. Add mushrooms and simmer until they are just tender, about 5 minutes. Add chopped pepper and cook another 30 seconds. Remove vegetables with slotted spoon and set them aside, keeping liquid over medium-low heat.

Melt butter in 3-quart (3L) saucepan over medium heat. Add flour and cook, whisking constantly, until mixture becomes quite thick and pasty, about 2 minutes. Remove from heat and pour in stock mixture all at once. Whisk briskly to smooth sauce, then return pan to heat and boil for about 1 minute, whisking constantly. Remove from heat and stir in sherry, salt, black pepper, and Tabasco sauce.

Adjust oven rack to upper third position and preheat oven to 350°F. (175°C.).

Turn 2½ cups (600ml) of sauce into large mixing bowl and add pasta, mushrooms, red or green pepper, and half the cheese. Mix well. Put mixture into 2- to 2½-quart (2 to 2.5L) ovenproof round or oval serving dish. Make well in center of pasta.

Add parsley and turkey to remaining sauce, mix thoroughly, and pour into well in pasta. Sprinkle remaining cheese evenly over top. (Dish may be made ahead to this point; bake within 1 hour or cover loosely with plastic wrap and refrigerate.)

Bake uncovered until dish is bubbly and top is

lightly browned, about 25 minutes (35 minutes if refrigerated).

Makes 6 to 8 servings.

PASTA CARBONARA

This classic dish is rich with the flavors of bacon, cheese, and cream.

8 slices bacon (8 ounces, 225g), cut crosswise into ¼-inch (6mm) strips
2 tablespoons parsley leaves, patted dry
4 ounces (115g) Parmesan cheese, cut into 1-inch (2.5cm) pieces
3 large eggs, at room temperature
¼ cup butter (2 ounces, 55g)
¾ cup (180ml) heavy cream
Large pinch cayenne pepper
¼ teaspoon salt, if desired
1 pound (455g) fresh pasta, cut into ⅛-inch (3mm) strips

Cook bacon in 10-inch (25cm) skillet over medium-low heat, stirring frequently, until bacon is crisp and browned. Drain on paper towels and set aside.

Insert *metal blade*. With machine running, drop parsley through feed tube and process until finely minced, about 20 seconds. Remove and set aside.

With *metal blade* in place, start machine, drop cheese through feed tube, and process until finely chopped, about 45 seconds. Remove half of cheese and set aside. Crack eggs into work bowl with remaining cheese and process for 5 seconds.

Melt butter in 1-quart (1L) saucepan over medium heat. Add the cream, cayenne, and salt and keep mixture hot over low heat.

Have warm serving bowl and serving dishes ready.

Cook pasta in 6 quarts (6L) of boiling water until it is tender but firm to the bite. Just before pasta is ready, add bacon to hot cream mixture. Turn cooked pasta into heated serving bowl. Quickly add cream mixture and egg mixture and toss well. Heat of pasta and cream will cook eggs. Serve immediately, sprinkling each portion lightly with parsley. Pass reserved cheese separately.

Makes 4 servings.

PASTITSIO

Pastitsio is a festive Greek dish in which two layers of pasta in an eggy white sauce conceal a very tangy tomato and meat mixture. Served with a green salad and dry red wine or retsina, it is a very satisfying meal. Commercial pasta is used in this recipe.

Meat Filling

- 1 pound (455g) lean beef, trimmed and cut into 1-inch (2.5cm) pieces
- 4 ounces (115g) Parmesan cheese, cut into 1-inch (2.5cm) pieces
- 1 slice firm-textured white bread (1½ ounces, 45g), torn into pieces
- 2 small garlic cloves, peeled
- 1 large onion (8 ounces, 225g), peeled and cut into eighths
- 3 tablespoons olive oil
- 2 1-pound (455g) cans whole tomatoes, drained
- 1 cup (240ml) tomato sauce
- 1 teaspoon dried oregano leaves
- ¼ teaspoon cinnamon
- ½ teaspoon salt, if desired
- ¼ teaspoon freshly ground black pepper
- 1 large egg

Pasta and Sauce

- 2 cups elbow spaghetti or salad macaroni (½ pound, 225g)
- 3 cups (720ml) milk
- 1 stick unsalted butter (4 ounces, 115g)
- ½ cup unbleached all-purpose flour (2½ ounces, 70g)
- 5 large eggs
- 1½ teaspoons salt, if desired
- ¼ teaspoon freshly grated nutmeg

Line shallow pan with foil and arrange meat on pan in single layer. Place in freezer until meat is very cold, about 30 minutes.

Insert *metal blade*. With machine running, drop cheese through feed tube and process until finely chopped, about 45 seconds. Remove and set aside.

With *metal blade* in place, put bread into work bowl and process for 20 to 30 seconds. Measure and set aside ½ cup of crumbs.

With *metal blade* in place, start machine, drop garlic through feed tube, and process until garlic is finely minced, about 10 seconds. Add onion and pulse 3 times. Scrape work bowl and pulse 2 or 3 more times, until onion is finely chopped.

Heat oil in 12-inch (30cm) skillet over medium-low heat. Add onion and garlic and stir well. Cook slowly, stirring occasionally, until onion is very tender but not browned, about 8 minutes.

Meanwhile, with *metal blade* in place, put meat into work bowl and pulse about 15 times, stopping once to scrape work bowl. Meat should be finely chopped; pulse a few times more if necessary.

Add meat to skillet. Cook, stirring occasionally, until meat loses its pink color.

With *metal blade* in place, put tomatoes, tomato sauce, oregano, cinnamon, salt, and pepper into work bowl and pulse 4 times, just to chop tomatoes coarsely. Add tomato mixture to skillet, stir well, and simmer slowly, uncovered, over medium-low heat for 30 to 40 minutes. Mixture should be quite thick; it should measure about 4 cups (1L). Remove from heat and taste for seasoning.

With *metal blade* in place, crack egg into work bowl and process for 5 seconds. Add egg and bread crumbs to skillet, mix well, and set aside.

Bring 6 quarts (6L) of water to a rapid boil, drop in pasta, and cook, uncovered, until pasta is tender but still has some bite. (Commercial pasta takes about 6 minutes.) Drain well and transfer to large bowl of cold water; let stand until needed.

Put milk in 1-quart (1L) saucepan and bring

almost to a boil over medium-high heat. Reduce heat to low and keep milk hot.

Melt butter in 3-quart (3L) saucepan over medium heat. Add flour, whisk well, and cook for 2 minutes, whisking constantly. Remove from heat and let bubbling subside for a few seconds, then immediately add milk and whisk rapidly. Bring mixture to a boil over medium-high heat, whisking constantly. Once boil is reached, cook for about 2 minutes, whisking vigorously. Sauce should be thick. Remove from heat and set aside for 5 minutes.

Use *metal blade* to process remaining 5 eggs for 10 seconds. Stop machine and quickly add about 1 cup (240 ml) of hot white sauce. Process for 5 seconds. Gradually whisk egg mixture into remaining sauce. Stir in salt and nutmeg.

Drain pasta thoroughly. Mix half the pasta with 1½ cups (360ml) of white sauce.

Adjust oven rack to center position and preheat oven to 350°F. (175°C.).

Butter a 13 by 9 by 2-inch (33 by 23 by 5cm) baking pan. Spread pasta and white-sauce mixture into pan and sprinkle with half the cheese, then spread all of meat filling on top. Combine remaining pasta with remaining sauce and spread over meat mixture. Finally sprinkle remaining cheese evenly on top. Pan will be almost full. May be made to this point one day ahead; cover loosely with plastic and refrigerate.

Bake until pasta mixture is set and top of *pastitsio* is light golden brown, 40 to 45 minutes (1 hour if refrigerated). Cool in pan for 15 to 20 minutes, then cut into rectangles to serve.

Makes 6 to 8 servings.

NOTE: To freeze baked pastitsio, refrigerate until is sets and is very cold, then cut into individual servings, wrap each in foil, and freeze for up to 2 months. To reheat, place frozen wrapped pastitsio on baking sheet in center of preheated 350°F. (175°C.) oven until heated through, 30 to 45 minutes.

ORIENTAL NOODLE CAKE

In this noodle cake, homemade egg noodles are cooked as usual, then fried like a pancake in a large skillet. This is an excellent accompaniment to stir-fried meat or poultry.

10 ounces (285g) fresh pasta, cut into ⅛-inch (3mm) strips, preferably Basic or Semolina

1 tablespoon Oriental sesame oil

1 large egg

3 tablespoons oil

Cook pasta, drain well, and return to pot filled with cold water. Let stand until completely cool, then drain well and place in large bowl with sesame oil. Toss to coat well. (Pasta may be prepared to this point one day ahead; cover and refrigerate.)

Crack egg into pasta and mix well with hands. Heat 2 tablespoons of oil in 12-inch (30cm) skillet over medium-high heat. When oil is hot, swirl pan to run oil all over bottom and part way up sides. Add pasta to pan, coiling it into an even layer. Press top firmly with spatula and cover pan.

Reduce heat to medium and cook, shaking pan occasionally, until pasta is browned on bottom, 5 to 7 minutes. Uncover and put 12-inch (30cm) pizza pan on top of skillet. Holding skillet and pan together securely, invert them and turn noodle cake onto pan. Put skillet back on burner and gently slide noodle cake back into skillet with cooked side up. Pour remaining oil down side of skillet and shake to distribute oil underneath noodle cake. Cover pan and cook until cake is browned, 5 to 7 minutes. If it sticks, shake pan and add a little more oil.

To serve, slide noodle cake from skillet onto large oven-proof serving platter. Cover loosely with foil and keep warm in an oven set at lowest temperature until ready to serve.

Makes one 12-inch (30cm) cake, about 8 servings.

SHRIMP AND NOODLES WITH GINGER-FLAVORED BROTH

This is a light but very satisfying dish. Chicken broth is flavored with ginger, soy sauce, sherry, and sesame oil; shrimp and carrots are added; and finally, noodles, black mushrooms, scallions, and watercress are mixed in for a quick heating.

¾ **pound (340g) fresh pasta, cut into ⅛-inch (3mm) strips (see NOTE)**
1 **¼-inch (6mm) slice fresh ginger, peeled**
1 **large carrot (4 to 5 ounces, 115 to 140g), peeled, cut in half lengthwise, and cut into 3-inch (8cm) lengths**
4 **large scallions (2⅔ ounces, 75g total), trimmed and cut into 3-inch (8cm) lengths**
4 **large dried shiitake mushrooms, soaked in boiling water for 30 minutes, drained, and squeezed of excess moisture, stems removed**
3 **cups (720ml) chicken stock**
3 **tablespoons soy sauce**
2 **tablespoons dry sherry**
1 **tablespoon Oriental sesame oil**
¾ **pound (340g) shrimp, peeled and cut into ½-inch (12mm) pieces**
2 **cups watercress leaves (1½ ounces, 45g), loosely packed**
Additional soy sauce

Bring 6 quarts (6L) of water to a boil over high heat. Add pasta and cook just until tender, then drain well, return to cooking pot, and fill pot with cold water. Let stand until needed.

Insert *metal blade*. With machine running, drop ginger through feed tube and process until finely chopped, about 10 seconds. Leave in work bowl.

Insert *2mm slicing disc*. Wedge carrots upright in feed tube and use firm pressure to process. Transfer ginger and carrots to 5-quart (5L) pan and set aside.

Insert *4mm slicing disc*. Wedge scallions upright in feed tube and use medium pressure to process. Leave scallions in work bowl.

Insert *medium shredding disc*, place mushrooms in feed tube, and use firm pressure to process. Remove scallions and mushrooms and set aside, covered.

Add stock, soy sauce, sherry, and sesame oil to carrots and ginger. Bring to boil over medium-high heat, then reduce heat to medium-low and cook at slow boil until carrots are tender but still have some crunch, 2 to 3 minutes. Add shrimp and cook just until they turn opaque, 1 to 2 minutes.

Drain pasta. Add it to broth mixture, then add scallions, mushrooms, and watercress. Mix well and cook briefly just until dish is heated through and watercress is wilted. Taste and season with more soy sauce if necessary.

Makes 4 servings.

NOTE: Pasta made with egg whites or water is particularly good in this dish; do not use whole-wheat or buckwheat pasta. The dish is also good when allowed to cool to room temperature. The pasta absorbs most of the liquid, so you can eat it with chopsticks.

COLD SESAME CHICKEN WITH NOODLES

This spicy dish should be made at least a few hours ahead, to allow the flavors to blend.

2 **large boneless, skinless chicken breast halves (about 8 ounces, 225g total)**
1 **bunch scallions (4 ounces, 115g total), trimmed and cut into 3-inch (8cm) lengths**
2 **tablespoons sesame seeds**
2 **quarts (2L) water**

12 ounces (340g) fresh pasta, cut into ⅛-inch (3mm) strips (see NOTE)

2 tablespoons Oriental sesame oil

3 large garlic cloves, peeled

½ cup (120ml) tahini (sesame-seed paste)

½ cup (120ml) chicken stock

1 tablespoon sugar

⅓ cup (80ml) soy sauce

⅓ cup (80ml) red-wine vinegar

Put each chicken breast half on sheet of plastic wrap, skinned side down. Fold ends in slightly, then

Cold Sesame Chicken and Shrimp and Noodles

roll to form long cylinder. Wrap tightly in plastic wrap and place in freezer until chicken is firm but easily pierced with tip of sharp knife. Unwrap and cut breasts in half crosswise.

Insert *3mm slicing disc.* Wedge chicken breasts upright in feed tube and use firm pressure to process. Remove and set aside; wipe work bowl with paper towels.

With *3mm slicing disc* in place, wedge scallions upright in feed tube and use light pressure to process. Remove, wrap in plastic wrap, and set aside.

Put sesame seeds in shallow baking pan and toast in 350°F. (175°C.) oven until they are golden brown, 7 to 10 minutes. Remove and set aside.

Bring 2 quarts (2L) of water to boil in 4-quart (4L) saucepan over high heat. Add chicken and stir to separate slices. Cook until chicken turns opaque and is cooked through, about 1 minute. Drain and set aside in large bowl.

Cook pasta, drain well, and return to pot filled with cold water. Let stand until completely cool, then drain thoroughly and put into large bowl. Add 1 tablespoon of sesame oil and mix well. Cover and set aside.

Insert *metal blade.* With machine running, drop garlic through feed tube and process until finely chopped, about 10 seconds. Scrape work bowl, add tahini, stock, sugar, remaining sesame oil, soy sauce, and vinegar, and process until smooth, about 15 seconds.

Add sauce to chicken. Then add pasta and mix well. Cover and refrigerate for at least a few hours or as long as 2 days.

To serve, turn mixture out onto large serving platter, sprinkle sesame seeds over center, and sprinkle scallions around edge.

Makes 6 to 8 servings.

NOTE: Use any of the egg pastas except spinach, whole-wheat, or buckwheat for this dish.

QUICHES

Quiches make excellent appetizers, first courses, or main dishes. They are so simple to prepare with the food processor that you can make one, bake it and serve it within an hour.

All these recipes use either a crust made from classic pastry or quick pastry. Both are made with all-purpose white flour. I have experimented with quiche pastries made with whole-wheat flours and been disappointed; the flavor of the crust dominates the filling.

All these quiches may be prepared ahead and frozen, following directions given at the end of the chapter. You can take one straight from the freezer and bake it for about an hour. If you prepare a salad while the quiche bakes, you can serve a balanced homemade meal in a little time with almost no effort.

Fontina Quiche with Roasted
Red Peppers

ABOUT QUICHE PASTRY

Pastry bases for quiches should be tender and flaky, never soggy. The flakiness of a pastry is determined to a large extent by the size of the fat particles in it: very large particles make a very flaky pastry, very small particles result in a "short," crumbly pastry. A good quiche pastry should be of medium flakiness, with fat particles about the size of small peas. And that is exactly what the food-processor method gives us. Instructions for two kinds of quiche pastry follow: one quick pastry, to be made and filled with no preliminary baking, and another, classic pastry, to be partially baked before being filled.

QUICK QUICHE PASTRY

This pastry may be used as soon as it is made, provided the butter and water are very cold. Wheat germ adds a bit of texture and a nice nutty taste.

For one 9-inch (23cm) Shell

1 cup unbleached all-purpose flour (5 ounces, 140g)

¼ teaspoon salt, or to taste

2 tablespoons raw (untoasted) wheat germ

1 stick unsalted butter (4 ounces, 115g), chilled and cut into 6 pieces

4 tablespoons ice water

For one 11-inch (28 cm) Shell

1½ cups unbleached all-purpose flour (7½ ounces, 215g)

¼ teaspoon salt, or to taste

3 tablespoons raw (untoasted) wheat germ

1½ sticks unsalted butter (6 ounces, 170g), chilled and cut into 9 pieces

6 tablespoons ice water

Insert *metal blade* and put flour, salt, wheat germ, and butter into work bowl. Pulse 3 or 4 times, just to start chopping butter. Then begin pulsing rapidly and pour water through feed tube all at once. Pulse 20 to 30 times, just until dough begins to mass and looks as though it will hold together when pressed. (Do not overprocess; dough should not gather into ball on blade.) If necessary, add a bit more water.

Carefully remove dough from work bowl, press together into ball, and then flatten slightly. Dough should be moist and only slightly sticky; dust very lightly with flour. (Dough may be prepared to this point, wrapped and refrigerated for up to 3 days or frozen for longer storage.)

Roll out dough on lightly floured surface to large circle (12-inch, 30cm diameter for 9-inch, 23cm pan; 14-inch, 35cm diameter for 11-inch, 28cm pan). Use light strokes and roll outward from center. Flour pastry only as necessary; too much flour will make pastry tough.

Fold pastry circle in half and place into pie pan or quiche pan. Then unfold and carefully fit pastry into pan. (Do not stretch it.) Ease some of overhanging edge of pastry into pan to make it fit snugly all over the bottom and sides of pan. Trim off excess pastry with a sharp knife or make fluted rim. Shell is now ready to be filled and baked.

CLASSIC QUICHE PASTRY

Traditionally, a pastry shell for quiche is given a preliminary baking so it will remain crisp and flaky. Some of the quiche recipes in this section call specifically for a partially baked shell.

This pastry recipe uses a mixture of butter and lard or vegetable shortening, a combination of fats that makes a particularly tasty and flaky pastry.

For 9-inch (23cm) Shell

1 **cup unbleached all-purpose flour (5 ounces, 140g)**
¼ **teaspoon salt, or to taste**
½ **stick unsalted butter (2 ounces, 55g), chilled and cut into 4 pieces**
2 **tablespoons lard or vegetable shortening (1 ounce, 30g), chilled and cut into 2 pieces**
3 **tablespoons ice water**

For 11-inch (28cm) Shell

1½ **cups unbleached all-purpose flour (7½ ounces, 215g)**
¼ **teaspoon salt, or to taste**
¾ **stick unsalted butter (3 ounces, 85g), chilled and cut into 6 pieces**
3 **tablespoons lard or vegetable shortening (1½ ounces, 45g), chilled and cut into 3 pieces**
5 **tablespoons ice water**

Make pastry as directed for Quick Quiche Pastry above. Wrap dough in plastic wrap and refrigerate for at least 1 hour, then roll it out as in recipe above. (If pastry is too firm to roll, rap it a few times with rolling pin to make it malleable.) Fit pastry into pan and trim away edge or form fluted rim.

Prick pastry bottom several times with fork and freeze shell for 15 minutes (or refrigerate for 30 minutes to an hour) until firm. Line shell with aluminum

Lining shell with foil   *Filling with weights*

foil, pressing foil over bottom and into corners, and fill with dried beans, rice, or pie weights to prevent pastry from rising unevenly (see NOTE).

For a partially baked shell, place in center of preheated 400°F. (205°C.) oven and bake just until pastry is set, 12 to 15 minutes. Then carefully remove foil and weights, return pan to oven, and bake just until pastry starts to color and pull away from pan, another 3 to 5 minutes. (If pastry puffs up during baking, prick gently with fork or cake tester.) Remove from oven and set aside to cool.

For fully baked shell, to be used for tarts, pies, or frozen quiches (see page 65), place in center of preheated 400°F. (205°C.) oven and bake just until pastry is set, 12 to 15 minutes. Then carefully remove foil and weights, return pan to oven, and bake until pastry is golden brown all over with darker edges, 8 to 9 minutes. Remove from oven and cool completely.

NOTE: If using metal pie weights, preheat them before baking pastry shell; otherwise they retard baking of crust.

THREE-CHEESE QUICHE

This savory quiche may be baked in a 9-inch (22cm) quiche pan and served as a main dish, or baked in an 11-inch (28cm) tart pan (1-inch, 2.5cm deep) and served as an appetizer.

- 1 9-inch (23cm) or 11-inch (28cm) pastry shell, uncooked (page 54), or partially baked (page 55)
- 1 ounce (30g) Parmesan cheese
- 6 ounces (170g) imported Gruyère or Emmenthaler cheese (or a combination), chilled
- 2 ounces (55g) feta cheese
- 2 teaspoons Dijon mustard
- 4 large eggs
- ¾ cup (180ml) whipping cream
- ¼ cup (60ml) milk
- ⅛ teaspoon freshly grated nutmeg
- ⅛ teaspoon white pepper *or* pinch of cayenne

Prepare pastry shell and set it aside. Adjust oven rack to center position and place heavy baking sheet on rack. Preheat oven to 375°F. (190°C.).

Insert *metal blade,* turn on machine, and drop Parmesan cheese through feed tube. Process until finely chopped, about 30 seconds. Remove and set aside.

Insert *medium shredding disc* and use light pressure to process Gruyère cheese. Remove and set aside.

Insert *metal blade.* Coarsely crumble feta cheese into work bowl and process until finely chopped, 5 to 10 seconds.

Spread mustard over bottom of pastry. Sprinkle feta evenly into shell, then sprinkle Gruyère cheese on top.

With *metal blade* in place, put remaining ingredients into work bowl and process just to blend well,

about 5 seconds. Carefully pour mixture over cheeses in pastry shell, then sprinkle Parmesan cheese evenly over top.

Set pan on baking sheet and bake until filling is puffed and set and top is golden brown, 35 to 40 minutes. Let stand for 10 minutes before serving. (Filling will settle as quiche cools.) This is good hot, warm, or at room temperature.

Makes 4 to 6 main-course, 12 appetizer servings.

FONTINA QUICHE WITH ROASTED RED PEPPERS

Fontina cheese and roasted red peppers go together beautifully in this quiche, which makes an excellent appetizer, first course, or main course.

- 1 9-inch (23cm) pastry shell, uncooked (page 54) or partially baked (page 55)
- 1 ounce (30g) Parmesan cheese
- 8 ounces (225g) Fontina cheese, chilled
- 4 large eggs
- ½ cup (120ml) whipping cream
- ½ cup (120ml) milk
- ⅛ teaspoon freshly grated nutmeg
- ⅛ teaspoon white pepper
- ½ cup roasted red peppers (4 ounces, 55g; see NOTE), cut into ¼-inch (6mm) strips

Prepare pastry shell and set aside. Adjust oven rack to center position and place heavy baking sheet on rack. Preheat oven to 375°F. (190°C.).

Insert *metal blade.* Turn on machine, drop Parmesan cheese through feed tube and process until finely chopped, about 20 seconds. Remove and set aside.

Insert *medium shredding disc* and use light pressure to process Fontina cheese. Sprinkle into pastry shell.

Insert *metal blade,* put eggs, cream, milk, nutmeg, and pepper into work bowl, and process just to blend them well, about 5 seconds. Pour mixture over cheese in pastry shell. Arrange red-pepper strips on top and sprinkle with Parmesan cheese.

Set pan on baking sheet and bake until filling is puffed and set and top is golden brown, 35 to 40 minutes. Let stand for 10 minutes before serving.

Makes 4 main-course, 8 appetizer servings.

NOTE: Roasted red peppers (sweet red bell peppers, not pimientos) are commonly sold in 7- or 8-ounce (200 or 225g) jars. Progresso is a good brand. This recipe requires only half the peppers in a jar; the remainder will keep up to 1 week, covered, in the refrigerator.

SPINACH QUICHE
This quiche is beautifully layered, with a green spinach base and a creamy white topping.

1 9-inch (23cm) pastry shell, partially baked (page 55)
2 teaspoons Dijon mustard
4 ounces (115g) Swiss cheese, cut into 1-inch (2.5cm) pieces
1 10-ounce (285g) package frozen leaf spinach, thawed
½ teaspoon lemon juice
½ teaspoon salt, if desired
¼ teaspoon freshly ground black pepper
¼ teaspoon dried tarragon leaves, crushed, or 1 tablespoon chopped fresh tarragon leaves
¾ cup (180ml) whipping cream
4 large eggs
½ cup (120ml) Half and Half
⅛ teaspoon freshly grated nutmeg

Prepare pastry shell and set aside. Adjust oven rack to center position and place heavy baking sheet on rack. Preheat oven to 375°F. (190°C.).

Spread Dijon mustard over bottom of prepared pastry.

Insert *metal blade* and put cheese into work bowl. Pulse 3 times, then process continuously until cheese is finely chopped, about 20 seconds. Remove and set aside.

Squeeze as much moisture as possible from spinach. With *metal blade* in place, put spinach, lemon juice, salt, pepper, and tarragon into work bowl and process until spinach is finely chopped, about 30 seconds, stopping once to scrape work bowl. Add ¼ cup (60ml) cream and 1 egg to work bowl and process until mixture is smooth, about 15 seconds, stopping to scrape work bowl as necessary. Spread mixture into quiche shell and sprinkle evenly with cheese. Rinse work bowl and blade.

With *metal blade* in place, process remaining cream, remaining eggs, Half and Half, and nutmeg just to blend them well, about 5 seconds. Pour carefully into quiche shell.

Place pan on baking sheet and bake until filling is puffed and set and top is light golden brown, 35 to 40 minutes. Let stand for 10 minutes before serving.

Makes 4 to 6 servings as main course.

TOMATO AND BASIL QUICHE

This recipe was given to me by Ruth Moreau, a student in one of my classes. It makes a very full quiche, one with more vegetables and less custard than most. If you cannot get fresh basil, use dried—but only if the leaves have a sweet, basil aroma when crushed between the fingers.

Tomato and Basil Quiche

1 11-inch (28cm) pastry shell, partially baked (page 55)
3 medium tomatoes (1 pound, 455g total)
4 ounces (115g) Emmenthaler cheese, cut into 1-inch (2.5cm) pieces
4 ounces (115g) Gruyère cheese, cut into 1-inch (2.5cm) pieces
2 tablespoons flour
2 medium onions (¾ pound, 340g total), peeled and cut into quarters
2 tablespoons butter
3 tablespoons olive oil
1 teaspoon dried basil leaves, crushed, *or* 2 tablespoons chopped fresh basil
3 large eggs
1 cup (240ml) whipping cream
⅛ teaspoon white pepper
¼ teaspoon salt, if desired

Prepare pastry shell and set it aside.

Drop tomatoes into 2 quarts (2L) of boiling water, leave for 10 seconds, then drain and rinse under cold water. Use small sharp knife to cut out stems and remove peels. Cut tomatoes crosswise into ½-inch (12mm) slices and set aside.

Adjust oven rack to center position and place heavy baking sheet on rack. Preheat oven to 350°F. (175°C.).

Insert *metal blade* and put cheeses and flour into work bowl. Pulse 3 times, then process continuously until cheese is very finely chopped, about 20 sec-

onds. Remove mixture from work bowl and sprinkle 1 cup into pastry shell. Reserve remaining cheese mixture.

With *metal blade* in place, put onions into work bowl. Pulse 3 times, scrape bowl, and pulse 3 more times until onions are finely chopped. Melt butter with 2 tablespoons of oil in 12-inch (30cm) skillet over medium-low heat. Add onions and cook, stirring occasionally, until onions are very tender and golden, about 30 minutes. (Do not let onions brown.) Cool slightly, then distribute onions evenly and loosely over cheese in pastry shell.

Heat remaining tablespoon of oil in same skillet over medium-high heat. Add tomato slices and cook just to heat tomatoes through and brown them lightly, less than 1 minute on each side. Remove from heat and sprinkle evenly with basil. Arrange slices in single layer over onions in pastry shell and sprinkle remaining cheese over top. Shell will be quite full.

With *metal blade* in place, put remaining ingredients into work bowl and process just to blend them well, about 5 seconds. Pour custard slowly into pastry shell.

Place pan on baking sheet and bake until filling is puffed and set and top is golden brown, 35 to 40 minutes. Let stand for 10 minutes before serving.

Makes 6 main-course servings.

MUSHROOM QUICHE

Sour cream, added to the custard mixture, is a nice counterbalance to the sweetness of the cream sherry.

1 9-inch (23cm) pastry shell, partially baked (page 55)
1 medium onion (5 ounces, 140g), peeled and quartered
2 tablespoons butter
½ pound (225g) fresh mushrooms, cleaned and trimmed flat on 2 opposite sides (reserve trimmings)
¼ teaspoon dried tarragon leaves, crushed
½ teaspoon salt, if desired
⅛ teaspoon freshly ground black pepper
4 large eggs
¾ cup (180ml) whipping cream
½ cup (120ml) sour cream
1 tablespoon cream sherry
⅛ teaspoon white pepper

Prepare pastry shell and set aside. Adjust oven rack to center position and place heavy baking sheet on rack. Preheat oven to 375°F. (190°C.).

Insert *metal blade.* Turn on machine, drop onion through feed tube and process until minced, about 10 seconds. Melt butter in 10-inch (25cm) skillet over medium heat, add onions, and cook, stirring frequently, until onions are just tender, 4 to 5 minutes. Set aside.

Insert *2mm slicing disc.* Arrange mushrooms in feed tube flat side down and use light pressure to process. Add mushrooms (including trimmings), tarragon, salt, and black pepper to skillet, return to medium heat, and cook, stirring occasionally, until mushrooms begin to release their juices, 3 to 4 minutes. Cook 2 or 3 minutes more, stirring frequently, to evaporate excess liquid. Set aside to cool slightly, then turn into pastry shell.

Insert *metal blade,* put remaining ingredients into work bowl, and process just to blend them well, about 10 seconds. Pour over mushrooms.

Set pan on baking sheet and bake until filling is puffed and set and top is lightly browned, 35 to 40 minutes. Let stand for 10 minutes before serving.

Makes 4 to 6 main-course servings.

ONION QUICHE

Use the sweetest onions you can get—Walla Walla sweet onions, Vidalia onions, or any mild-flavored yellow onion. Use a 9-inch (23cm) deep pastry shell to prepare as a main dish, an 11-inch (28cm) shell for an appetizer.

1 9-inch (23cm) or 11-inch (28cm) pastry shell, uncooked (page 54) or partially baked (page 55)
3 ounces (85g) Swiss cheese, cut into 1-inch (2.5cm) pieces
5 medium onions (1½ pounds, 680g total) peeled and cut into eighths
2 tablespoons butter
1 tablespoon olive oil
3 large eggs
¼ cup (60ml) plain yogurt
¾ cup (180ml) whipping cream
½ teaspoon salt, if desired
Dash of freshly grated nutmeg
⅛ teaspoon freshly ground black pepper

Prepare pastry shell and set aside.

Insert *metal blade.* Put cheese into work bowl, pulse 3 times, then process continuously until cheese is finely chopped, about 20 seconds. Remove and set aside.

With *metal blade* in place, put half of the onions into work bowl. Pulse 3 times, scrape work bowl, then pulse 3 more times, just until onions are minced. Remove and repeat with remaining onions.

Melt butter with oil in 12-inch (30cm) heavy-bottomed skillet over medium heat. Add onions and stir well, then reduce heat to very low and cook onions slowly, uncovered, stirring occasionally, until very tender and pale gold, about 1 hour (or slightly longer). Onions will be reduced to about 1½ cups (360ml) when cooked. Cool slightly or completely.

(Onions may be prepared to this point a day or two ahead; cover and refrigerate.)

Adjust oven rack to center position and place heavy baking sheet on rack. Preheat oven to 375°F. (190°C.).

With *metal blade* in place, put remaining ingredients into work bowl and process just to blend them well, about 10 seconds. Add to cooled onions in skillet along with two-thirds of cheese. Stir to mix well.

Spread onion mixture in pastry shell and sprinkle evenly with remaining cheese.

Place pan on baking sheet and bake until filling is puffed and set and top is golden brown, 35 to 40 minutes. Let stand for 10 minutes before serving.

Makes 4 main-course, 12 appetizer servings.

LEEK AND BACON QUICHE

Leeks, bacon, and Gruyère cheese make this a quiche of distinctive flavors.

1 9-inch (23cm) pastry shell with high fluted rim, partially baked (page 55)
1¼ pounds (570g) leeks, trimmed of roots and greens, thoroughly washed, and cut into 3-inch (8cm) lengths
3 tablespoons butter
4 ounces (115g) sliced bacon, cut crosswise into ⅛-inch (3mm) strips
4 ounces (115g) Gruyère cheese, chilled
4 large eggs
1½ cups (360ml) heavy cream
⅛ teaspoon white pepper
⅛ teaspoon freshly grated nutmeg
½ teaspoon salt, if desired

Prepare pastry shell and set aside.

You should have 8 ounces (225g) of trimmed and washed leeks. Insert *2mm slicing disc.* Stand leeks vertically in feed tube and use medium pressure to process. Melt butter in 10-inch (25cm) skillet over medium-low heat and add leeks. Stir with wooden spoon and cook slowly, covered, stirring occasionally, until leeks are very tender but not browned, about 30 minutes. Uncover and set aside.

Cook bacon in small skillet over medium-low heat, stirring frequently, until browned and crisp. Set on paper towels to drain.

Insert *medium shredding disc* and use light pressure to process cheese. Remove and set aside.

Adjust oven rack to center position and place heavy baking sheet on rack. Preheat oven to 350°F. (175°C.).

Sprinkle half the cheese into pastry shell. Spread leeks loosely over cheese, then distribute bacon evenly over leeks. Sprinkle remaining cheese on top.

Insert *metal blade*, put remaining ingredients into work bowl, and process for 10 seconds. Carefully pour mixture into pastry shell.

Set pan on baking sheet and bake until filling is puffed and set and top is golden brown, 40 to 45 minutes. Let stand for 10 minutes before serving. This is best when hot.

Makes 6 servings.

HAM AND BROCCOLI QUICHE
The pastry for this colorful and tangy quiche should have a high fluted rim. The quiche makes a hearty main dish.

1 9-inch (23cm) pastry shell with fluted rim, partially baked (page 55)
2 ounces (55g) sharp Cheddar cheese, chilled
1 cup cooked broccoli flowerets and stems (4 ounces, 115g), very well drained and cut into ¼- to ½-inch (6 to 12mm) pieces (see NOTE)
4 ounces (115g) cooked ham, cut into 1-inch (2.5cm) pieces
4 large eggs
1 cup (240ml) light cream
1 tablespoon lemon juice
¼ teaspoon dried oregano leaves
Pinch of cayenne
½ teaspoon salt, if desired

Prepare pastry shell and set aside. Adjust oven rack to center position and place heavy baking sheet on rack. Preheat oven to 375°F. (190°C.).

Insert *medium shredding disc* and use light pressure to process cheese. Sprinkle cheese into pastry shell. Distribute broccoli evenly over cheese.

Insert *metal blade* and put ham into work bowl. Pulse 5 or 6 times, stopping once to scrape work bowl, until ham is coarsely chopped. Sprinkle over broccoli in pastry shell.

With *metal blade* in place, put remaining ingredients into work bowl and process just to blend them well, about 10 seconds. Pour carefully into pastry shell.

Set pan on baking sheet and bake until filling is puffed and set and top is lightly browned, 35 to 40 minutes. Let stand for 10 minutes before serving.

Makes 4 to 6 main-course servings.

NOTE: Thawed frozen broccoli is fine for this quiche. A 10-ounce (285g) package of broccoli spears (flowerets and stems) when drained thoroughly will yield almost 7 ounces (200g) of broccoli. Be sure to pat broccoli thoroughly dry.

PINEAPPLE AND HAM QUICHE

Eileen Conwell created the original version of this recipe for the National Pineapple Cooking Classic in 1979, and she won a first prize for it. The pineapple provides an effective counterpoint to the sharpness of the onions.

1 9-inch (23cm) pastry shell, uncooked (page 54) or partially baked (page 55)
1 8-ounce (225g) can crushed pineapple in juice
4 ounces (115g) Swiss cheese, chilled
4 ounces (115g) sharp Cheddar cheese, chilled
4 ounces (115g) cooked ham, cut into 1-inch (2.5cm) pieces
½ medium green pepper (2½ ounces, 70g), cored, seeded, and cut into 1-inch (2.5cm) pieces
1 small onion (2½ ounces, 70g), peeled and quartered
4 tablespoons butter
4 large eggs
1 cup (240ml) whipping cream
1½ tablespoons Dijon mustard
¼ teaspoon white pepper
½ teaspoon powdered chicken-broth base
¾ teaspoon prepared horseradish

Prepare pastry shell and set aside. Adjust oven rack to center position and place heavy baking sheet on rack. Preheat oven to 375°F. (190°C.).

Set wire strainer over bowl and turn pineapple into strainer, pressing fruit with spoon. Pineapple should yield about ½ cup (120ml) juice. Set pineapple and juice aside.

Insert *medium shredding disc* and use light pressure to process both cheeses. Remove and set aside.

Insert *metal blade* and put ham into work bowl.

Pineapple and Ham Quiche

Pulse 4 to 6 times until ham is finely chopped, scraping work bowl as necessary. Remove and set aside.

With *metal blade* in place, put green pepper and onion into work bowl. Pulse 3 times, scrape work bowl, and pulse 3 more times, until vegetables are finely chopped.

Melt 2 tablespoons of butter in 10-inch (25cm) skillet over medium heat. Add onion and green pepper and cook, stirring occasionally, until vegetables are tender but not browned, 3 to 4 minutes. Add pineapple juice, increase heat to high, and cook, stirring frequently, until liquid is absorbed. Remove from heat and stir in pineapple and ham. Set aside to cool to room temperature.

Reserve ¼ cup of pineapple and ham mixture for topping, and spread remainder into quiche shell. Sprinkle shredded cheese on top.

With *metal blade* in place, put remaining ingredients into work bowl and process just to blend them well, about 5 seconds. Pour over pineapple mixture in quiche shell. Sprinkle reserved pineapple and ham mixture on top and dot with remaining 2 tablespoons of butter.

Bake until filling is puffed and set and top is golden brown, 35 to 40 minutes. Let stand for 10 minutes before serving.

Makes 4 to 6 main-course servings.

CRAB QUICHE

It's always a luxury to have crabmeat, and it is beautifully presented in this delicious quiche, which makes an elegant lunch or first course.

1	9-inch (23cm) pastry shell, partially baked (page 55)
½	ounce (15g) Parmesan cheese
2	tablespoons parsley leaves, washed and patted dry
1	large shallot (1 ounce, 30g), peeled
2	tablespoons butter
½	pound (225g) lump crabmeat, picked over to remove cartilage
2	tablespoons dry sherry
2	large eggs plus 2 large egg yolks
1¼	cups (300ml) whipping cream
¼	teaspoon salt, if desired
⅛	teaspoon white pepper
⅛	teaspoon freshly grated nutmeg

Prepare pastry shell and set aside. Adjust oven rack to center position and place heavy baking sheet on rack. Preheat oven to 375°F. (190°C.).

Insert *metal blade*, turn on machine and drop cheese through feed tube. Process until finely chopped, about 20 seconds. Remove and set aside. Put parsley into work bowl and process until finely chopped, about 20 seconds. Remove and set aside.

With *metal blade* in place, turn on machine, drop shallot through feed tube, and process until minced, about 15 seconds.

Melt butter in 10-inch (25cm) skillet over medium heat. Add shallot and cook, stirring, for 1 minute. Add crab, toss, and cook for 1 minute. Add sherry and cook, tossing, until wine is absorbed, 30 to 60 seconds. Remove from heat and stir in parsley. Set aside.

With *metal blade* in place, put eggs and yolks into work bowl and process until mixture is slightly thickened, about 90 seconds. Add remaining ingredients and process for 5 seconds.

Spread crab mixture loosely in prepared pastry shell; do not pack it down. Pour cream mixture over crab and sprinkle top evenly with cheese.

Place pan on baking sheet and bake until quiche is puffed and set and top is lightly browned, 35 to 40 minutes. Let stand for 10 minutes before serving.

Makes 4 to 6 main-course servings.

CLAM QUICHE

Paprika sprinkled on the top just before baking gives this flavorful quiche a beautiful golden-brown color.

1 11-inch (28cm) pastry shell with high fluted rim, partially baked (page 55)
3 6½-ounce (185g) cans minced clams
4 ounces (115g) sliced bacon, cut crosswise into ¼-inch (6mm) strips
1 medium onion (5 ounces, 140g), peeled and quartered
½ medium green bell pepper (2 ounces, 55g), cored, seeded, and cut into 1-inch (2.5cm) pieces
2 tablespoons butter
⅛ teaspoon Tabasco sauce
5 large eggs
1¼ cups (300ml) heavy cream
¼ teaspoon white pepper
⅛ teaspoon freshly grated nutmeg
¾ teaspoon salt, if desired
Paprika

Prepare pastry shell and set aside.

Set large wire strainer over bowl and turn clams into strainer; set aside to drain. Reserve ½ cup (120ml) of clam juice.

Cook bacon in 10-inch (25cm) skillet over medium-low heat, stirring occasionally, until bacon is lightly browned but not crisp. Remove and set on paper towels to drain. Discard bacon fat but do not wash skillet.

Insert *metal blade* and put onion and green pepper into work bowl. Pulse 3 times, scrape work bowl, and pulse 2 more times, until vegetables are chopped medium-fine.

Melt butter over medium heat in skillet used to cook bacon, add onion and pepper, and cook, stir-ring frequently with wooden spoon, until vegetables are tender but not browned, about 5 minutes. Add reserved clam juice and increase heat to high. Cook, stirring almost constantly, until liquid is nearly absorbed and mixture resembles a purée, about 4 minutes. Add clams and cook, stirring, for 1 minute longer. Remove from heat and stir in Tabasco. Set aside to cool.

Adjust oven rack to center position and place heavy baking sheet on rack. Preheat oven to 325°F. (160°C.).

Insert *metal blade,* put eggs, cream, pepper, nut-meg, and salt into work bowl, and process for 5 seconds. Distribute bacon evenly in pastry shell. Add about ½ cup (120ml) of egg mixture to cooled clam mixture. Stir well and spread evenly over bacon. Carefully pour remaining egg mixture into shell. Sprinkle top lightly with paprika.

Place pan on baking sheet and bake until filling is puffed and set and top is golden brown, 40 to 45 minutes. Let stand for 10 minutes before serving.

Makes 6 main-course, 12 appetizer servings.

FREEZING A QUICHE

You can enjoy the luxury of reaching into the freezer and taking out a quiche that will be just as flaky and delicious as if it were freshly made, and ready to serve within an hour. The secret is to freeze the uncooked custard mixture in a fully baked pastry shell. The custard will not become watery nor will the crust become soggy.

Any quiche in this chapter can be prepared in this way. Make the quiche shell and bake it completely, as described in the recipe for Classic Quiche Pastry (page 55). About 5 minutes before the pastry is done, remove it from the oven, brush the shell lightly with beaten egg and return it to the oven. Remove the shell after 5 minutes and allow it to cool completely before continuing with the recipe. (The cooked egg wash acts as a sealant, protecting the pastry from its liquid filling.)

Spoon the prepared filling into the baked shell and freeze the quiche. When it is frozen solid, wrap it airtight in plastic wrap and aluminum foil. Store it in the freezer, where it will keep up to 4 weeks.

To bake a frozen quiche, unwrap it and place it promptly in the center of an oven preheated to 375°F. (190°C.). Do not allow it to thaw. Bake it until the filling is puffed and set, about 1 hour. Allow it to cool for about 10 minutes before serving it.

SALADS

While many of these salads are meant to be served with meals, others are meals in themselves. The Potato, Ham and Cheese Salad or the Oriental Chicken Salad could well serve as main courses. Since they require no last-minute fussing, they are excellent party dishes. The Crab and Avocado Salad makes a fine main course for a light supper as well as an excellent start to a meal.

All these salads are tailored to today's taste for light and fresh food. The most nutritious is Tabbouleh, which is made from whole grain and fresh herbs; it has a tangy flavor and a tender, slightly chewy texture.

For those watching their intake of cholesterol, I have developed a very convincing Eggless Egg Salad that substitutes bean curd for eggs, and is virtually cholesterol-free. People who have tested it for me are hard pressed to tell it from the real thing.

Spinach and Mushroom Salad
with Red Peppers

SPINACH AND MUSHROOM SALAD WITH RED PEPPERS

Strips of red pepper add color and texture to the tender greens and mushrooms.

- 2 pounds (910g) fresh spinach
- 2 hard-cooked eggs, halved, with yolks separated from whites
- 2 large red bell peppers (¾ to 1 pound, 340 to 455g total)
- 1 large shallot (1 ounce, 30g), peeled
- ½ cup (120ml) olive oil
- ½ cup (120ml) safflower oil
- ⅓ cup (80ml) plus 1 tablespoon cider vinegar
- 1 tablespoon plus 1 teaspoon sugar
- ¾ teaspoon freshly grated nutmeg
- Freshly ground black pepper, to taste
- ½ pound (225g) large mushrooms, cleaned, trimmed, and cut flat on opposite sides

Wash spinach thoroughly, discard stems and blemished leaves, and spin or pat leaves dry. There should be 1 pound (455g) of cleaned spinach. Wrap in plastic and refrigerate.

Insert *metal blade.* Put egg whites into work bowl and pulse several times to chop them fine. Remove and set aside. Add yolks to work bowl and process until they are finely chopped, about 2 seconds. Remove and set aside. Wipe out work bowl.

Stand peppers upright on cutting board and use sharp knife to cut 3 or 4 vertical slices from each, leaving only cores and seeds. Remove seeds and ribs from slices.

Insert *2mm slicing disc.* Wedge pepper slices on their sides in feed tube and use light pressure to process. Transfer to 1-quart (1L) bowl.

Insert *metal blade.* Turn on machine and drop shallot through feed tube. Process until minced, about 10 seconds. Scrape work bowl, add oils, vinegar, sugar, nutmeg, and pepper, and process for 5 seconds. Remove 1 tablespoon of dressing and add to peppers; mix well and set aside. Leave remaining dressing in work bowl.

With *2mm slicing disc* in place, wedge mushrooms in feed tube, one layer at a time, flat side down. Use light pressure to process. Leave mushrooms in work bowl.

Insert *6mm slicing disc.* Put spinach into feed tube in batches, packing leaves loosely. Use light pressure to process. Repeat until all spinach is processed. Empty work bowl into salad dish as necessary.

Empty contents of work bowl into large salad dish and toss thoroughly. Sprinkle chopped yolk over center of salad and spoon ring of chopped white around it. Garnish outer edge with pepper strips and serve immediately.

Makes 8 servings.

VARIATION: If red peppers are not available, omit them. Process eggs whole, pulsing 4 or 5 times until they are coarsely chopped, then sprinkle them over center of salad.

CARROTS AND TURNIPS WITH CAPER VINAIGRETTE

This zesty salad is best made an hour or so ahead, but will keep well for 2 or 3 days when refrigerated.

- ½ cup parsley leaves, washed and patted dry
- ¼ cup (60ml) olive oil
- 2 tablespoons lemon juice
- ½ teaspoon salt, if desired
- ⅛ teaspoon freshly ground black pepper
- 2 teaspoons Dijon mustard
- 1 tablespoon capers, rinsed and drained
- 2 large carrots (½ pound, 225g total), peeled and cut into 2 to 3-inch (5 to 8cm) lengths

1 medium turnip (6 ounces, 170g), peeled and quartered vertically
2 large scallions (1½ to 2 ounces, 45 to 55g total), trimmed and cut into 3-inch (8cm) lengths
Lettuce leaves

Insert *metal blade* and put parsley into work bowl. Process until finely chopped, about 20 seconds. Add oil, lemon juice, salt, pepper, mustard, and capers and process for 5 seconds. Remove metal blade, leaving dressing in work bowl.

Insert *medium shredding disc.* Place carrot sections vertically in feed tube and use firm pressure to process. Leave in work bowl. Place turnips vertically in feed tube and use firm pressure to process. Remove shredding disc, leaving vegetables and dressing in work bowl.

Insert *1mm or 2mm slicing disc.* Place scallions horizontally in feed tube and use light pressure to process.

Empty work bowl into medium mixing bowl and toss salad well, then cover and refrigerate it for at least 1 hour. Mix again just before serving in salad bowls lined with lettuce.

Makes 4 to 6 servings.

THREE-TONE COLESLAW

In this simple preparation, the dressing is made in the work bowl and the cabbage is shredded right into it. The whole salad is then turned out into a serving dish. If your food processor is larger than the standard size, you can shred all the cabbage without emptying the work bowl.

2 large egg yolks
¼ cup (60ml) cider vinegar
1½ tablespoons Dijon mustard

½ teaspoon white pepper
Dash of Tabasco
1 teaspoon celery seed
1½ tablespoons sugar
½ teaspoon salt, if desired
1¼ cups (300ml) vegetable oil
⅓ cup (80ml) plain yogurt
1 small head green cabbage (1¼ pounds, 570g)
1 small head red cabbage (1¼ pounds, 570g)
1 large carrot (5 ounces, 140g), peeled and cut into 3-inch (8cm) lengths

Insert *metal blade* and put yolks, vinegar, mustard, pepper, Tabasco, celery seed, sugar, salt, and 1 tablespoon of oil into work bowl. Process for 1 minute. With machine running, drizzle remaining oil through feed tube in very slow, steady stream, to make a mayonnaise. Scrape work bowl. Add yogurt and pulse rapidly 2 or 3 times to combine well. Remove metal blade but leave dressing in work bowl.

Rest green cabbage on its side and use sharp heavy knife to slice off about 1 inch (2.5cm) of top; set top aside. Cut 3-inch (8cm) slice from midsection of cabbage. Lay this piece flat and cut it into wedges to fit feed tube, removing any core. Repeat with red cabbage.

Insert *1mm slicing disc.* Wedge cabbage sections tightly into feed tube and use medium pressure to process. Cut reserved cabbage tops in half to form 4 half circles. Place them in feed tube 2 at a time, with broad cut surfaces together and narrow cut surfaces against disc. Use medium pressure to process and leave cabbage in work bowl.

Insert *fine shredding disc.* Lay carrots on their sides in feed tube and use firm pressure to process.

Invert work bowl over large serving dish and toss salad thoroughly. Cover and refrigerate until serving time.

Makes 8 servings.

TOMATOES AND CUCUMBERS WITH FETA VINAIGRETTE

This is quick, easy, and delicious. These instructions apply to a food processor that is larger than the standard size. If you own a standard machine, process the lettuce first, using the thickest slicing disc you have, and set it aside. Process everything else into the work bowl and toss everything together just before serving.

> 2 tablespoons parsley leaves, washed and patted dry
>
> ¼ cup (60ml) safflower or sunflower oil
>
> ¼ cup (60ml) olive oil
>
> 1 tablespoon red-wine vinegar
>
> 1 tablespoon lemon juice

Tomatoes and Cucumbers with Feta Vinaigrette

> ½ teaspoon dried oregano leaves
>
> 1 teaspoon Dijon mustard
>
> Pinch of freshly ground black pepper
>
> 2 ounces (55g) feta cheese, cut into 2 pieces
>
> 4 medium tomatoes (1 pound, 455g total), with stems removed
>
> 1 medium cucumber (8 to 10 ounces, 225 to 285g), peeled and cut into 3-inch (8cm) lengths
>
> 14 pitted medium black olives, drained
>
> 1 medium head romaine lettuce, cut into 3-inch (8cm) sections

Insert *metal blade* and put parsley into work bowl. Process until finely chopped, about 20 seconds. Remove and set aside. With metal blade in place, put oils, vinegar, lemon juice, oregano, mustard, and pepper into work bowl and process for 3 seconds. Add cheese and pulse a few times to chop cheese medium-fine. Remove metal blade, leaving dressing in work bowl.

Insert *6mm slicing disc* and use light pressure to process tomatoes. Leave in work bowl.

Insert *2mm slicing disc*, stand cucumber upright in feed tube, and use medium pressure to process. Leave in work bowl.

Insert *3mm slicing disc* and use light pressure to process olives. Leave in work bowl.

Insert *8mm slicing disc*, wedge romaine sections upright in feed tube, and use light pressure to process them.

Invert work bowl over large serving platter, toss salad gently, and sprinkle with reserved parsley. (Salad may be assembled an hour before serving; cover work bowl with plastic wrap and refrigerate. Tomatoes will release some of their juices into dressing, but romaine will remain crisp because it is on top of other vegetables.)

Makes 6 servings.

JERUSALEM ARTICHOKE REMOULADE

In addition to the traditional gherkins, capers, and mustard, this remoulade contains horseradish to give it a sharper edge. The salad, a variation of the classic made with celery root, is crunchy and refreshing. It is especially good with grilled meats.

1	pound (455g) Jerusalem artichokes
1	quart (1L) water mixed with 2 tablespoons lemon juice
1/4	cup parsley leaves, washed and patted dry
1	large scallion (2/3 ounce, 20g), trimmed and cut into 1-inch (2.5cm) lengths
2	2-inch (5cm) sweet gherkins (1 ounce, 30g total), drained and halved crosswise
1	large egg
1	tablespoon Dijon mustard
1	teaspoon prepared horseradish
2	teaspoons lemon juice
1/8	teaspoon white pepper
1/2	cup (120ml) plus 1 tablespoon sunflower or safflower oil
2	teaspoons capers, drained
1	large carrot (4 ounces, 115g), peeled and cut into 2-inch (5cm) lengths
	Boston lettuce leaves (optional)

Use sharp paring knife to peel Jerusalem artichokes; drop them immediately into water and lemon-juice mixture. There should be 3/4 pound (340g) of peeled Jerusalem artichokes. Set aside.

Insert *metal blade* and put parsley into work bowl. Turn on machine and drop scallions through feed tube. Process until parsley and scallions are chopped medium-fine, about 10 seconds. With machine running, drop gherkins through feed tube and process until finely chopped, about 10 seconds.

Remove mixture and set aside.

With *metal blade* in place, put egg, mustard, horseradish, lemon juice, pepper, and 1 tablespoon of oil into work bowl. Process for 1 minute. With machine running, drizzle remaining oil through feed tube in very slow, steady stream to make a creamy mayonnaise. Add capers and process for 5 seconds, then add gherkin mixture and process with 2 pulses, each lasting about a second. Remove metal blade but leave remoulade in work bowl.

Insert *2mm square julienne disc.* Stand carrots upright in feed tube and use firm pressure to process. Drain Jerusalem artichokes, pat them dry, and use firm pressure to process.

Turn salad into bowl and mix well. Cover and chill for about 30 minutes before serving. (Salad may be made well ahead; its flavor actually improves over time. But Jerusalem artichokes begin to discolor after 2 or 3 days in refrigerator.)

Makes 6 to 8 servings.

RED ONIONS WITH CUCUMBERS AND OLIVES

This robust salad is for those who like their onions raw. Soaking the onions in ice water removes some of their bitter flavor. The salt used to remove excess moisture from the cucumbers is washed away when they are rinsed. The entire salad can be prepared two or three days before it is served.

¼ cup parsley leaves, washed and patted dry
1 large red onion (8 ounces, 225g), peeled and halved vertically
3 or 4 medium cucumbers (2 pounds, 910g total), peeled and halved lengthwise
2 teaspoons salt
14 medium pitted black olives, rinsed, drained, and patted dry
¼ cup (60ml) olive oil
¼ cup (60ml) safflower oil
2 tablespoons cider vinegar
1 large egg yolk
⅛ teaspoon dried thyme leaves
¼ teaspoon dry mustard
¼ teaspoon prepared horseradish
¼ teaspoon salt, if desired
⅛ teaspoon freshly ground black pepper
1 teaspoon sugar

Insert *metal blade.* Put parsley into work bowl and process until finely chopped, about 20 seconds. Remove and set aside.

Insert *1mm slicing disc.* Stand onion halves vertically in feed tube and use medium pressure to process. Transfer to large bowl and cover with water and ice cubes; let stand for 30 to 60 minutes. Drain onions well, pat dry, and place in large mixing bowl.

Remove seeds from cucumbers with spoon and discard. Cut cucumbers into 3-inch (8cm) lengths.

Insert *3mm slicing disc.* Wedge cucumber sections vertically in feed tube and use light pressure to process. Place sliced cucumbers in colander and sprinkle with 2 teaspoons of salt. Mix well and let stand for 30 to 60 minutes. Then rinse under cold running water, drain well, and pat dry. Add cucumbers to onions.

Insert *2mm slicing disc.* Stand olives in feed tube in one layer and use light pressure to process. Add to onions and cucumbers.

With *metal blade* in place, put remaining ingredients into work bowl and process for 3 seconds. Pour dressing over vegetables, add parsley, and toss gently to mix salad well. Cover and chill for 1 to 2 hours, and stir well before serving.

Makes 6 servings.

POTATO SALAD WITH HAM AND CHEESE

This colorful salad is dressed with a vinaigrette, which brings out the full flavor of potatoes better than the more commonly used mayonnaise. Try to use red boiling potatoes, and be sure to add the vinaigrette while the potatoes are warm and can absorb it readily. Finally, serve the salad warm or at room temperature; chilling it dulls the flavors.

3 large scallions (2 ounces, 55g total), trimmed and cut into 3-inch (8cm) lengths

3 large celery ribs (9 ounces, 255g total), trimmed and cut into 3-inch (8cm) lengths

6 ounces (170g) boiled ham, cut into 1 by ⅛ by ⅛-inch (2.5cm by 3mm by 3mm) pieces

1 8-ounce (225g) piece Swiss cheese, preferably Gruyère, chilled

9 or 10 small boiling potatoes (2 pounds, 910g total)

¼ cup (60ml) dry white vermouth

½ cup (120ml) salad oil

1 tablespoon red-wine vinegar

1 tablespoon lemon juice

1 tablespoon Dijon mustard

½ teaspoon dried oregano

½ teaspoon salt, if desired

¼ teaspoon freshly ground black pepper

2 medium tomatoes (8 ounces, 225g total), cut into 12 wedges

Insert *2mm slicing disc.* Stand scallion sections vertically in feed tube, wedging them in tightly, and use light pressure to process. Remove and set aside.

With *2mm slicing disc* in place, stand celery sections vertically in feed tube, wedging them in tightly, and use medium pressure to process. Transfer to large bowl. Add ham to celery.

Cut cheese into three pieces about 3 by 1 by 1 inches (8 by 2.5 by 2.5cm).

Insert *medium shredding disc.* Stand pieces of cheese upright in feed tube and use light pressure to process. Add to ham and celery and mix gently. (Salad may be made ahead to this point. Cover and refrigerate, but bring to room temperature before proceeding.)

Boil or steam unpeeled potatoes until they are easily pierced by sharp knife, 15 to 18 minutes. (It is important that they be completely cooked.) Drain potatoes and cover them with ice and water, letting them sit for 7 to 8 minutes. Then drain and pat dry. (Ice water firms potatoes a bit, but they should still be warm inside.) Do not peel potatoes.

Insert *6mm slicing disc.* Place potatoes in feed tube and use light pressure to process. Transfer to large mixing bowl and use rubber spatula to fold in scallions and vermouth. Let potatoes stand for 10 minutes. Wipe work bowl with paper towels.

Insert *metal blade.* Put oil, vinegar, lemon juice, mustard, oregano, salt, and pepper into work bowl and process for 5 seconds.

Add ham and cheese mixture to potatoes and pour dressing over salad. Use rubber spatula to fold ingredients gently but thoroughly, let stand for 15 to 30 minutes, then fold again. Turn salad out onto large serving platter and decorate with border of tomato wedges.

Makes 4 main-dish servings, 8 to 10 side-dish servings.

EGGLESS EGG SALAD

Anyone wishing to cut back on cholesterol will enjoy this salad, made with tofu instead of eggs. Turmeric gives it an appealing yellow color.

¼ **cup parsley leaves, washed and patted dry**
1 **small garlic clove, peeled**
2 **scallions (1⅓ ounces, 40g total), trimmed and cut into 1-inch (2.5cm) lengths**
1 **celery rib (1½ ounces, 45g), cut into 1-inch (2.5cm) lengths**
¼ **cup (60ml) mayonnaise, preferably homemade (page 78)**
1 **tablespoon Dijon mustard**
½ **teaspoon prepared horseradish**
½ **teaspoon salt, if desired**
¼ **teaspoon freshly ground black pepper**
3 **drops Tabasco sauce**
⅛ **teaspoon turmeric**
1 **pound (455g) firm tofu, cut into 3 by 1 by 1-inch (8 by 2.5 by 2.5cm) pieces**

Insert *metal blade* and put parsley into work bowl. With machine running, drop garlic, scallions, and celery through feed tube. Process until vegetables are finely chopped, about 10 seconds.

Add mayonnaise, mustard, horseradish, salt, pepper, Tabasco, and turmeric to work bowl and process for 5 seconds. Scrape work bowl and process for 2 seconds more. Remove metal blade, leaving mixture in work bowl.

Insert *French-fry disc.* Stand tofu pieces upright in feed tube and use very light pressure to process.

Transfer salad to serving bowl and fold everything together, being careful not to crumble tofu; it should resemble pieces of chopped egg white. Serve the salad immediately, or cover and refrigerate for up to 2 or 3 days.

Makes about 2 cups (480ml).

VARIATION: For a pungent flavor, substitute ¼ cup cilantro leaves for parsley. And for a little more bite, add a seeded fresh jalapeño chile along with garlic, scallions, and celery.

TABBOULEH

This Middle Eastern classic has cracked wheat, or bulgur, as its main ingredient. Fresh mint, lemon juice, and plenty of parsley contribute refreshing flavors that balance the heartiness of the wheat.

1 **cup bulgur, preferably coarse**
2 **cups (480ml) boiling water**
1 **cup parsley leaves, washed and patted dry**
2 **tablespoons fresh mint leaves, firmly packed**
6 **large scallions (4 ounces, 115g total), trimmed and cut into 3-inch (8cm) lengths**
⅓ **cup (80ml) olive oil**
¼ **cup (60ml) lemon juice**
¼ **teaspoon salt, if desired**
⅛ **teaspoon freshly ground black pepper**
2 **medium tomatoes (10 ounces, 285g total), stems removed, halved crosswise**
Romaine lettuce leaves from heart of lettuce
Black olives, green bell pepper strips or rings, cucumber slices, parsley sprigs, for garnish (if desired)

Place bulgur in medium bowl, pour boiling water over it, and let it stand at least 2 hours. Drain well in strainer, pressing out excess water, and turn bulgur into mixing bowl.

Insert *metal blade.* Put parsley and mint into work bowl and process until finely chopped, about

Tabbouleh and Eggless Egg Salad

20 seconds. Remove metal blade but leave parsley and mint in work bowl.

Insert *2mm slicing disc.* Wedge scallions upright in feed tube and use medium pressure to process. Leave parsley, mint, and scallions in work bowl.

With *metal blade* in place, add oil, lemon juice, salt, and pepper to work bowl and process for 3 seconds. Add mixture to bulgur and mix well.

Insert *French-fry-disc.* Put each tomato half, cut side down, into feed tube and use light pressure to process. Remove any peel from work bowl. Add tomatoes to bulgur mixture.

Fold all ingredients together and cover. When ready to serve, line salad bowl with lettuce leaves, standing them upright, and pile tabbouleh in center; garnish as you wish.

Tabbouleh is best at room temperature. Though it will keep well in the refrigerator for several days, it should be brought to room temperature before serving.

Makes 6 servings.

ORIENTAL CHICKEN SALAD WITH RICE-STICK NOODLES

A superb choice for a party. It makes an impressive presentation, and all the components can be prepared ahead of time, in stages to fit your schedule. Only the final assembly needs to be done just before serving.

4 or 5 boneless, skinless chicken-breast halves (1 pound, 455g total)

2 cups (480ml) chicken stock, homemade or canned

1 layer rice-stick noodles (about 5 ounces, 140g; see page 177)

Oil for frying

¼ cup roasted peanuts (1 ounce, 30g)

⅓ cup (80ml) red-wine vinegar

2 tablespoons dry sherry

⅓ cup (80ml) vegetable oil, preferably peanut oil

1 tablespoon oyster sauce

2 tablespoons soy sauce

1½ tablespoons Oriental sesame oil

2 teaspoons light brown sugar, firmly packed

Freshly ground black pepper, to taste

½ medium head iceberg lettuce (8 ounces, 225g), cut to fit feed tube

1 8-ounce (225g) section Chinese cabbage

1 4-ounce (115g) section romaine lettuce

6 large scallions (4 ounces, 115g total), trimmed and cut into 3-inch (8cm) lengths

1 large red bell pepper (7 to 8 ounces, 200 to 225g), cut into quarters vertically, cored, and seeded

Cooking Chicken

Put chicken breasts and stock into 10-inch (25cm) skillet. Cover pan and bring stock to simmer over medium heat. Turn chicken over, reduce heat to low, and poach at simmer until chicken is just done, about 6 minutes total cooking time. Meat should spring back when pressed with fingertip. Remove chicken from stock and set aside until cool enough to handle. (Save stock for another use.) Shape each breast portion into a roughly cylindrical form, wrap securely in plastic wrap, and refrigerate for several hours, until chicken is very cold. (Chicken may be prepared a few days ahead and frozen; thaw in refrigerator before using.)

Preparing Noodles

Heat 1 inch (2.5cm) of oil in Dutch skillet or deep-fat fryer to 400°F. (205°C.). Break up noodles into 2-inch (5cm) sections and drop half into oil. Stir rapidly with chopsticks; rice sticks will puff to crispy, curly threads in just a few seconds. Drain noodles immediately on paper towels and repeat with remaining noodles. Set aside at room temperature. (Noodles may be made several hours ahead.)

Processing Peanuts and Making Dressing

Insert *metal blade*. Turn on machine and drop peanuts through feed tube. Process for 5 seconds, remove and set aside.

With *metal blade* in place, put vinegar, sherry, vegetable oil, oyster sauce, soy sauce, sesame oil, brown sugar, and pepper into work bowl and process for 5 seconds. Transfer dressing to small bowl and set aside. Do not wash work bowl. (Dressing may be made an hour or two ahead and covered.)

Processing Chicken and Vegetables

Insert *6mm slicing disc*. Cut well chilled chicken breasts in half crosswise and wedge pieces tightly in feed tube, one layer at a time, with cut sides down. Use medium pressure to process. Transfer chicken to medium bowl and mix with ⅓ cup (80ml) of prepared dressing. (Chicken may be processed and dressed 1 or 2 hours ahead; cover tightly and set aside.)

Insert *4mm slicing disc.* Use light pressure to process vegetables, one after the other, in the following order; leave them in work bowl: lettuce, cabbage, romaine, scallions (stood upright in feed tube), and pepper (pieces wedged in feed tube with longest edge against disc). Place vegetables on large serving platter. (Vegetables may be prepared 2 to 3 hours ahead; cover and refrigerate.)

Assembling Salad

This should be done just before serving, to preserve crispness of rice-stick noodles.

Add remaining dressing to vegetables and toss gently to coat them well. Add chicken with its dressing, half the peanuts, and half the noodles; toss to combine them well. Mound salad in center of platter, arrange remaining noodles around border, and sprinkle remaining peanuts over center. Serve at once.

Makes 6 main-course servings or 10 to 12 side-dish servings.

CRAB AND AVOCADO SALAD

This luxurious and substantial salad may be served as a luncheon dish or as the first course of a formal dinner.

1 tablespoon parsley leaves, washed and patted dry

1 hard-cooked egg yolk

1 small shallot (½ ounce, 15g), peeled, *or* 1 inch (2.5cm) from white parts of 3 scallions

2 large ripe but firm avocados (1 pound, 455g total)

¼ cup (60ml) sour cream

¼ cup (60ml) mayonnaise, preferably homemade (page 78)

¼ teaspoon salt, if desired

⅛ teaspoon white pepper

½ teaspoon prepared horseradish

2 teaspoons lemon juice

8 ounces (225g) fresh crab meat, picked over to remove cartilage

Insert *metal blade* and put parsley into work bowl. Process until finely chopped, about 20 seconds. Add yolk and process for 3 or 4 seconds. Remove and set aside, covered.

With *metal blade* in place, turn on machine and drop shallot or scallions through feed tube. Process until minced, about 15 seconds. Scrape work bowl.

Cut 1 avocado in half lengthwise and remove pit. Scoop out flesh, being careful to leave skin intact. Add avocado to work bowl with shallot, then add sour cream, mayonnaise, salt, pepper, horseradish, and lemon juice. Process until mixture is very smooth, about 1 minute, stopping once or twice to scrape work bowl. Remove *metal blade* but leave avocado mixture in bowl.

Cut second avocado in half lengthwise and remove pit. Carefully cut flesh of each half in half crosswise, without cutting through skin. Gently run small, sharp knife around each half to loosen flesh, then use grapefruit spoon to ease 2 pieces of avocado out of each shell.

Insert *French-fry disc.* Stand avocado quarters upright in feed tube and use light pressure to process. Scrape mixture into small mixing bowl and gently fold in crab meat. (Salad may be prepared to this point 1 hour ahead; cover and refrigerate.)

When ready to serve, divide crab and avocado mixture among 4 avocado shells. Sprinkle lightly with parsley and egg-yolk mixture and serve cold.

Makes 4 servings.

MAYONNAISE

The simplest homemade mayonnaise, made with fresh eggs, high-quality oil, and real lemon juice, is beyond comparison with commercial brands. And certainly the food processor has made mayonnaise making a lot simpler. To make it by hand, you must be very careful to beat in the oil drop by drop until the mayonnaise has begun to thicken properly, a procedure that takes about 10 minutes. With the food processor, a mayonnaise can be ready in 2 to 3 minutes.

1 large egg plus 2 large egg yolks (see NOTE)
1 tablespoon Dijon mustard
2 teaspoons lemon juice
1/8 teaspoon white pepper
2 cups (480ml) best-quality oil
Salt, if desired
Additional lemon juice and pepper, if desired

Insert *metal blade.* Put egg, yolks, mustard, lemon juice, pepper, and 1 tablespoon of oil into work bowl and process for 1 full minute. Drizzle remaining oil through feed tube in very slow, steady stream. When about a third of oil is added, mayonnaise will begin to thicken and sound of machine will become deeper. After this point, add oil in dollops, waiting a few seconds between additions. When all oil is added, taste mayonnaise for seasoning and adjust with salt, more lemon juice, and more pepper, if needed. Transfer to airtight container and refrigerate. Mayonnaise will keep for at least 1 week in refrigerator.

Makes about 2½ cups (600ml).

VARIATIONS: Process 1 tablespoon of drained capers with 1 cup (240ml) of mayonnaise for a delicious accompaniment to grilled or pan-fried fish. Use 1 teaspoon of wine vinegar and 1 teaspoon of lemon juice (instead of only lemon juice) for a different flavor. Increase mustard (up to ¼ cup, 60ml), or eliminate it altogether.

NOTE: Using egg yolks only will make a very thick mayonnaise; using a whole egg will make a thinner mayonnaise.

GREEN MAYONNAISE

This is especially tasty with eggs, fish, and grilled meats. The fresh greens could be a mixture of spinach, watercress, parsley, scallions, and chervil.

1 cup firmly packed fresh greens
1 large egg plus 2 large egg yolks
½ teaspoon salt, if desired
Freshly ground black pepper, to taste
1 tablespoon lemon juice
2 cups (480ml) best-quality oil

Put greens in small saucepan with small amount of water and cook, covered, until they are wilted, about 2 minutes. Drain, cool, and squeeze out as much water as possible, compressing greens into small nugget. Set aside.

Insert *metal blade.* Put egg, yolks, salt, pepper, lemon juice, and 1 tablespoon of oil into work bowl and process for 1 full minute. With machine running, add remaining oil through feed tube in very thin, steady stream. After about a third of oil is added, mixture will begin to thicken and sound of machine will become deeper. After this point, add oil in dollops, waiting a few seconds between additions. When all oil has been added, drop greens through feed tube and process a few seconds more. Taste and adjust seasoning as necessary. Mayonnaise will keep at least a week covered tightly in refrigerator.

Makes about 2½ cups (600ml).

YOGURT CHEESE DRESSING

This is a nice chunky salad dressing. It can also be served as a vegetable dip or heaped onto a split baked potato.

1 small garlic clove, peeled
½ cup (120ml) plain yogurt
½ cup (120ml) mayonnaise
⅓ cup crumbled feta cheese *or* 3 to 4 tablespoons crumbled blue cheese

Insert *metal blade.* Turn on machine, drop garlic through feed tube and process until minced, 10 to 15 seconds. Scrape work bowl and add remaining ingredients. Pulse rapidly a few times just to combine everything well.

Makes about 1 cup (240ml).

VARIATION: Substitute 2 ounces (55g) of Parmesan cheese for feta or blue cheese. Cut it into 1-inch (2.5cm) pieces, add to work bowl with garlic, and process until very finely chopped, about 45 seconds.

MAIN DISHES

The main dish is the core of a well planned meal. I have tried to include something for every occasion — from casual to formal. Many of the recipes feature chopped or thinly sliced meat or poultry, which are easier than ever to prepare in the food processor.

Vegetables figure prominently in most of the recipes, as accompaniments to meat in stir-fries and soufflés or on their own in pizza and egg rolls. Sliced, chopped or shredded, they can be made ready very quickly in the processor, allowing you to present attractive and healthy meals without spending hours in the kitchen.

Feta Soufflé

CLASSIC PIZZA

This pizza is exceptionally good and very versatile: you may substitute 1 cup of whole-wheat flour for white flour in the crust, make almost any variation in the topping, and double or triple the amount of spices in the sauce.

The pizza can be baked directly on tiles, or in a pizza pan. The former is preferable; it imparts a desirable crunchiness to the crust. Line the oven rack with quarry tiles (available at building supply stores) or a large baking stone. Allow the oven to heat 30 minutes before baking the pizza.

1½ teaspoons active dry yeast
1¼ teaspoons sugar
¾ cup (180ml) warm water
2 tablespoons olive oil
2 cups unbleached all-purpose flour (10 ounces, 285g)
½ teaspoon salt, if desired
6 ounces (170g) mozzarella cheese, well chilled
4 ounces (115g) pepperoni, well chilled
4 ounces (115g) fresh mushrooms, cleaned and trimmed flat on opposite sides
1 medium green pepper (5 ounces, 140g), cored, seeded, and cut flat at stem end
1 medium onion (5 ounces, 140g), peeled, and quartered
½ cup parsley leaves, washed and patted dry
1 garlic clove, peeled
1 1-pound (455g) can peeled Italian plum tomatoes, undrained
1 teaspoon crumbled dried oregano
1 teaspoon crumbled dried basil
¼ teaspoon freshly ground black pepper

Stir yeast and ¼ teaspoon sugar into water and let stand until yeast dissolves and mixture is foamy, about 10 minutes. Stir in 1 tablespoon oil. Reserve remaining sugar for sauce.

Insert *metal blade*, put flour and salt in work bowl and turn machine on. While machine is running, pour yeast mixture through feed tube in slow steady stream. Process until dough gathers into ball on blades, then continue processing another 30 seconds to knead. Carefully remove dough and knead briefly in your hands to check consistency; it should be moist but only very slightly sticky. If necessary, add another tablespoon of flour and process briefly.

Place dough in large ungreased bowl, cover, and set aside at room temperature until dough has at least tripled in volume, 2 to 3 hours. (It does dough no harm to let it rise longer. It may rise all day if bowl is large enough. It may also be made the day before and allowed to rise in refrigerator.)

Wipe out work bowl and insert *medium shredding disc.* Use light pressure to process cheese; remove and set aside.

Insert *2mm slicing disc.* Use firm pressure to process pepperoni; remove and set aside. Use light pressure to process mushrooms; remove and set aside.

Insert *3mm or 4mm slicing disc,* insert pepper in feed tube vertically and use light pressure to process. Remove and set aside.

Insert *metal blade*, put onion in work bowl and pulse 3 times, until onion is coarsely chopped.

Heat 1 tablespoon of olive oil in 2-quart (2L) saucepan over medium heat. Add onion and cook until tender but not browned, about 5 minutes.

With metal blade in place, process parsley and garlic until coarsely chopped, about 10 seconds. Add to saucepan.

Add undrained tomatoes to work bowl and pulse 3 or 4 times, just to break them up. Add to saucepan. Stir in oregano, basil, pepper, and 1 teaspoon sugar. Reduce heat and allow sauce to simmer, uncovered,

Classic Pizza

until it thickens, 20 to 30 minutes. It should hold its shape in a spoon but it should not be a thick paste. Set sauce aside to cool to room temperature; it will thicken further as it cools. (Sauce may be made ahead and refrigerated for a few days or frozen for longer storage.)

Preheat oven to 450°F. (235°C.) and set rack in middle position.

Turn risen dough out onto lightly floured surface and gently shape into ball. Cover and let stand 10 minutes. Roll dough out to 13- to 14-inch (33 to 35cm) circle, turning frequently so it doesn't stick.

If baking pizza on tiles, have on hand a pizza peel or other instrument (rimless cookie sheet or piece of plywood) for transferring pizza to oven. Sprinkle cornmeal lightly over peel. Fold circle of pizza dough in half, gently place onto peel, then unfold and reshape into circle, arranging dough very near far edge of peel. Spread dough with cooled tomato sauce to within ½ inch (12mm) of edge. Arrange pepperoni, mushrooms, and pepper on top and sprinkle with cheese. Gently shake peel to be sure dough is not sticking. Open oven and insert peel all the way to back of oven. Gently ease peel out from under pizza, sliding pizza onto tiles. Bake pizza until crust is golden brown, about 15 to 20 minutes. Slide peel under pizza to remove it from oven.

If baking pizza in pan, place heavy baking sheet on oven rack to preheat. Brush 13- or 14-inch (33 or 35cm) pizza pan lightly with olive oil and fold dough into it. Cover with sauce, toppings and cheese. Set pan on baking sheet in oven and bake as directed above.

Makes 1 large pizza, 8 generous servings.

NOTE: People on low-sodium diets can enjoy this pizza, altered as follows. Omit salt in dough. Omit pepperoni and use more mushrooms instead. Use low-sodium mozzarella cheese and low-sodium canned tomatoes.

STIR-FRIED CHICKEN WITH VEGETABLES

This colorful dish, seasoned with Oriental fish sauce and lime juice, can be served with steamed rice, but it is more interesting when served over an Oriental Noodle Cake (see page 49).

Chicken

1 pound (455g) boneless, skinless chicken breast halves
2 tablespoons Oriental fish sauce (nuoc mam)
2 tablespoons dry sherry
Freshly ground black pepper to taste

Sauce

1 tablespoon cornstarch
1½ teaspoons sugar
1 tablespoon Oriental fish sauce (nuoc mam)
½ cup (120ml) chicken stock

Vegetables

3 large leeks, with stem ends, tough outer leaves and about 3 inches (8cm) of green tops removed (about 8 ounces, 225g total trimmed weight)
1 large red bell pepper (about 8 ounces, 225g)
1 1-inch (2.5cm) cube fresh ginger, peeled
4 tablespoons oil
3 cups small broccoli flowerets (about 10 ounces, 280g)
8 ounces (225g) carrots, peeled and cut into 4-inch (10cm) lengths
8 ounces (225g) peeled jicama, cut to fit feed tube
1 teaspoon salt, or to taste
3 tablespoons fresh lime juice
1 cup loosely packed fresh bean sprouts (about 4 ounces, 115g)

Place each chicken piece on sheet of plastic wrap, with original skin side down. Fold about 1 inch (2.5cm) of each end toward center and roll breast to form cylinder. Wrap securely in plastic to maintain cylindrical shape. Freeze on baking sheet until flesh resists when squeezed but can easily be pierced with sharp knife, about 60 minutes. (If chicken is frozen solid, let it sit at room temperature for 15 to 20 minutes before testing with knife.) Remove plastic wrap and cut breasts in half crosswise.

Insert *4mm slicing disc.* Place chicken pieces into large feed tube, cut side down, putting in as many as will fit snugly. Use firm pressure to process. Transfer slices to medium mixing bowl and add fish sauce, sherry, and pepper. Mix well and set aside. Chicken may be prepared 1 or 2 hours before cooking; cover and refrigerate.

Mix all sauce ingredients in small bowl, stirring to dissolve cornstarch. Set aside.

Cut leeks into 4-inch (10cm) lengths and rinse thoroughly of all grit and sand. Pat dry and set aside. Stand pepper upright on work surface and cut flesh from core in 4 pieces.

Insert *metal blade*, turn on machine and drop ginger through feed tube; process until minced. Leave in work bowl.

Insert *2mm slicing disc.* Place leeks horizontally in feed tube and use light pressure to process.

Heat 2 tablespoons oil in 12-inch (30cm) skillet over medium-high heat. When hot, add ginger and leeks. Stir well with 2 wooden spatulas, then add broccoli and mix gently. Cover pan, reduce heat to medium, and cook until leeks are tender, about 2 minutes.

With *2mm slicing disc* in place, stack pieces of pepper in feed tube and use light pressure to process. Remove and set aside.

Insert *medium shredding disc,* put carrots horizontally in feed tube and use firm pressure to process. Add carrots to skillet and mix well; leave skillet uncovered.

Insert *3mm slicing disc,* put jicama in feed tube and use firm pressure to process. Remove slices, stack them, and reinsert them in feed tube at right angle to first cut. Use medium pressure to process again. Add jicama to skillet, toss well, and add salt and lime juice. Toss again briefly, remove from skillet and set aside.

Heat remaining 2 tablespoons oil in skillet over medium-high heat. Stir chicken mixture, add to skillet and stir-fry until chicken is just cooked, about 2 minutes. Stir sauce mixture and add to chicken. Cook, stirring, until sauce thickens, about 1 minute.

Add pepper and bean sprouts, toss well, and cook 30 seconds. Return jicama mixture to skillet and mix well to heat through.

Taste for seasoning, adding more salt, sugar or lime juice, if necessary. Remove skillet from heat and let stand 1 to 2 minutes. Pour over noodle cake (see NOTE) and serve. This dish tastes better warm rather than very hot.

Makes 6 generous servings.

NOTE: Cook noodle cake only after all ingredients for stir-fry are ready. When noodle cake is done, transfer it to large oven-proof serving platter, cover it loosely with foil, and keep it warm in an oven set at its lowest temperature.

Stir-Fried Chicken with Vegetables

STEAK AND VEGETABLE STIR-FRY

Several vegetables, cut in different ways, contribute flavor and texture to this beautiful stir-fry dinner. Be sure to have all ingredients assembled before you begin to cook.

1 pound (455g) flank steak, trimmed
1 tablespoon cornstarch
1 teaspoon sugar
4 tablespoons oil
2 tablespoons soy sauce
1 tablespoon Oriental fish sauce (nuoc mam) or 1 additional tablespoon soy sauce
3 tablespoons oyster sauce
1 tablespoon dry sherry
2 large red bell peppers (1 pound, 455g total)
6 scallions (4 ounces, 115g), trimmed and cut into 3-inch (8cm) lengths
½ pound (225g) peeled jicama *or* ½ pound (225g) peeled turnips, cut to fit feed tube
1 1-inch (2.5cm) cube fresh ginger, peeled
2 garlic cloves, peeled
Black mushrooms, for garnish (optional, see NOTE)

Cut steak lengthwise (with grain) into 3 strips, then cut each strip crosswise into 3-inch (8cm) sections. Place on foil-lined baking sheet and freeze until meat is firm but can be easily pierced with a sharp knife, about 60 minutes.

Insert *6mm slicing disc.* Wedge pieces of meat upright in feed tube so meat will be cut across grain. Use firm pressure to process. Transfer meat to large mixing bowl, add cornstarch and sugar, and toss to coat meat well. Add 1 tablespoon oil, soy sauce, fish sauce, oyster sauce, and sherry. Mix well and let meat stand at least 30 minutes. Meat may be prepared hours ahead to this point; cover and refrigerate.

Place peppers upright on work surface. With sharp knife, cut 3 or 4 vertical slices from each one, leaving core. Trim any seeds or membrane from slices.

Insert *4mm or 6mm slicing disc.* Wedge pepper slices horizontally in feed tube and use light pressure to process. Stand scallions vertically in feed tube and use light pressure to process. Remove peppers and scallions and set aside.

Insert *French-fry disc* and use firm pressure to process jicama or turnips. Remove and set aside.

Insert *metal blade* and turn machine on. Drop ginger and garlic through feed tube and process until minced, about 30 seconds.

Heat 1 tablespoon oil in 12-inch (30cm) skillet over medium-high heat. When oil is hot, add ginger and garlic and cook, stirring, for a few seconds. Add jicama or turnip and cook for 2 minutes, tossing with 2 broad spatulas. Do not overcook; vegetable should be tender but still slightly crisp. Add peppers and scallions and stir-fry for 30 seconds. Remove from skillet and set aside.

Heat remaining 2 tablespoons oil in skillet. Stir meat mixture lightly and add to pan. Stir-fry, tossing almost constantly, just until meat loses its pink color, 3 to 4 minutes. Return jicama mixture to skillet and toss everything together for just a few seconds to heat through. Transfer to serving dish and garnish with mushrooms, if using. Serve hot, with boiled rice.

Makes 4 to 6 servings.

NOTE: Black mushrooms not only make an attractive garnish for this dish, they add a wonderful flavor. Soak 1 ounce (30g) of Oriental black mushrooms (such as shiitake) in enough hot water to cover for 30 minutes or until the mushrooms are tender. Squeeze them out, but do not discard the liquid. Remove and discard tough stems. Heat ¼ cup (60ml) mushroom liquid, ¼ cup (60ml) oyster sauce, and 1 tablespoon oil in 10-inch (25cm) skillet over low heat. Add mushrooms and let them steep in this liquid, turning them over once or twice, until the liquid is absorbed and the mushrooms are heated through, about 15 minutes. The mushrooms may be prepared in advance; reheat them before using.

STIR-FRIED SHRIMP WITH BLACK BEANS AND HOISIN SAUCE

This exotic dish is not only delicious and easy to make, it's also low in calories! The shrimp, which become spiral shaped during cooking, are especially attractive.

1 **pound (455g) medium shrimp in shells (about 22 to 24)**
1½ **cups (360ml) water**
3 **large scallions (2 ounces, 55g total), trimmed and cut into 3-inch (8cm) lengths**
2 **tablespoons fermented black beans (see page 174)**
2 **small garlic cloves, peeled**
2 **tablespoons oil**
1 **piece peeled fresh ginger, about 1 inch (2.5cm) in diameter and ⅓ inch (8mm) thick**
1½ **tablespoons cornstarch**
2 **tablespoons hoisin sauce**
1 **tablespoon dry sherry**
¾ **teaspoon salt, if desired**
2 **teaspoons sugar**
Hot cooked rice
1 **lemon, cut into 4 wedges**

Peel shrimp and cut them in half lengthwise. Put them in bowl, cover and refrigerate them. Put shells in 2-quart (2L) saucepan and add water. Bring to boil over high heat, pressing shells with wooden spoon. (Watch carefully or liquid may boil over.) Reduce heat to low and simmer slowly for 5 to 10 minutes. Strain liquid and discard shells. You should have 1 to 1⅓ cups (240 to 320ml). Set it aside to cool to room temperature.

Insert *4mm slicing disc*, wedge scallions vertically in feed tube and use medium pressure to process. Remove scallions and set them aside.

Insert *metal blade* and put beans in work bowl. Turn on machine and drop garlic through feed tube. Process until beans and garlic are very finely chopped, about 20 seconds. Scrape work bowl and its cover and add 1 tablespoon of oil. Process 5 seconds; you will have a pasty mixture. Add it to shrimp, mix very well and set aside. (May be prepared to this point hours ahead; cover and refrigerate.) Wipe work bowl and its cover with paper towels.

Insert *metal blade*, turn on machine and drop ginger through feed tube. Process 10 seconds, scrape work bowl and process another 5 to 10 seconds. Add cornstarch, hoisin sauce, sherry, salt, sugar, and shrimp liquid (which may still be warm). Process 10 seconds and leave mixture in work bowl.

Heat remaining 1 tablespoon of oil in 12-inch (30cm) skillet over medium-high heat. Add shrimp mixture and cook, tossing constantly with 2 broad spatulas, for 15 seconds. Add scallions and keep tossing just until shrimp turn pink, about 1 to 2 minutes. Remove skillet from heat.

Reprocess cornstarch mixture for 3 seconds and add it to shrimp mixture. Return skillet to medium-high heat and toss everything together until mixture comes to boil and sauce thickens slightly. Serve immediately with hot rice and lemon wedges. Squeeze a few drops of lemon juice over each serving before eating.

Makes 4 servings.

STIR-FRIED MUSHROOMS, PEPPERS, AND TOFU

This is one of the easiest and best tasting stir-fry dishes I know. It is delicious warm, but even better when chilled and served cold. Before you begin cooking this, or any stir-fry dish, assemble all the ingredients close to the skillet or wok.

2 to 3	**tablespoons hoisin sauce**
2	**tablespoons soy sauce**
⅓	**cup (80ml) canned chicken broth *or* water**
2	**tablespoons dry sherry**
1	**tablespoon Oriental sesame oil**
½	**teaspoon salt, if desired**
½	**pound (225g) tofu, cut into ½-inch (12mm) cubes**
1	**tablespoon cornstarch**
2	**tablespoons water**
¾	**pound (340g) fresh, firm mushrooms, cleaned, with 2 opposite sides trimmed flat**
1	**piece peeled fresh ginger, about 1 inch (2.5cm) in diameter and ¼ inch (6mm) thick**
6	**large scallions (about 4 ounces, 115g total), trimmed and cut into 3-inch (8cm) lengths**
1	**large green bell pepper (8 ounces, 225g)**
1	**large red bell pepper (8 ounces, 225g)**
2	**tablespoons oil**
6	**ounces (170g) fresh bean sprouts (about 3 cups)**
½	**cup salted or unsalted roasted cashews (2½ ounces, 70g)**
	Hot cooked white or brown rice, if desired

Mix hoisin sauce, soy sauce, chicken broth, sherry, sesame oil and salt in medium bowl. Add tofu and mix gently with rubber spatula to coat with sauce; set aside. (May be prepared several hours ahead; cover with plastic wrap and refrigerate.)

Mix cornstarch with 2 tablespoons water in small bowl and set aside.

Insert *4mm slicing disc* and wedge mushrooms into feed tube, one layer at a time, flat side down. Use light pressure to process. Remove and set aside.

Insert *metal blade,* turn on machine, and drop ginger through feed tube while machine is running. Process until finely chopped, about 10 seconds. Remove metal blade and leave ginger in work bowl.

Insert *2mm or 3mm slicing disc,* wedge scallions vertically in feed tube and use medium pressure to process. Leave scallions in work bowl.

Stand peppers upright on cutting surface and cut flesh away from cores, producing 4 rectangles from each pepper.

Insert *4mm slicing disc,* wedge pepper rectangles into feed tube, long sides down, and use light pressure to process, making strips of pepper.

Heat oil in 12-inch (30cm) skillet over medium-high heat. Add sliced mushrooms (and their trimmed ends) and cook for 1 to 2 minutes, tossing constantly with 2 broad spatulas. At first, all oil will be absorbed. As mushrooms cook, they will release their juices and begin to sound squeaky when tossed. At that point, increase heat to high and add peppers, scallions and ginger. Continue tossing until pepper strips are heated through, about 1 minute. Add tofu mixture and toss gently to combine everything well, about 1 minute. Stir up cornstarch mixture and add it to skillet along with bean sprouts and nuts. Fold everything together well and toss with 2 spatulas until sauce thickens and bean sprouts are heated through, about 1 minute. Peppers and bean sprouts should be tender, but still crisp; do not overcook. Serve warm over hot cooked rice. Or let cool completely, cover and refrigerate. Stir well and serve cold as a salad or side dish.

Makes 4 to 6 servings.

FETA CHEESE SOUFFLE

Although this soufflé contains 4 ounces of feta cheese, it has a wonderfully mild flavor. Serve it as a first course at dinner, or make it the main course at lunch, complemented by a crisp green salad and followed by fruit for dessert.

3 tablespoons butter
¼ cup unbleached all-purpose flour (1¼ ounces, 35g)
1 cup (240ml) hot milk
¼ teaspoon salt, if desired
⅛ teaspoon white pepper
⅛ teaspoon freshly grated nutmeg
1 tablespoon distilled white vinegar
1 tablespoon water
6 large egg whites
4 ounces (115g) feta cheese, cut into 1-inch (2.5cm) pieces
4 large egg yolks
2 tablespoons snipped fresh chives *or* 1 tablespoon freeze-dried chopped chives

Butter 6-cup (1.5L) soufflé dish and dust it lightly with fine dry unseasoned bread crumbs. Tap out excess crumbs. Set oven rack in lower third and preheat oven to 400°F. (205°C.).

Melt butter in 1-quart (1L) saucepan over medium heat. When bubbling, add flour and stir with small wire whisk, reaching all over bottom and sides of pan. Cook 2 minutes, whisking frequently. Remove pan from heat and pour in hot milk. Return pan to medium heat and whisk constantly until mixture comes to boil and thickens to medium paste, about 2 minutes. Remove pan from heat, whisk in salt, pepper, and nutmeg, and place a piece of buttered waxed paper or plastic wrap directly on surface of sauce, to prevent skin from forming. Keep sauce warm until needed.

Combine vinegar and water in small cup. Insert *metal blade*, put egg whites in work bowl, turn on machine and process 10 seconds. With machine running, pour vinegar mixture through feed tube and process until whites are thick and hold their shape, about 45 seconds. Remove metal blade and use rubber spatula to transfer whites to 1-quart (1L) mixing bowl. Return metal blade to work bowl and pulse once to spin whites off blade. Remove blade and scrape remaining whites out of work bowl. Do not wash work bowl.

With *metal blade* in place, process feta cheese and egg yolks until smooth, about 1 minute, stopping machine once to scrape work bowl. Taste mixture and add more salt if necessary. (Some brands of feta cheese are saltier than others. Add only as much salt as suits your taste.) Remove waxed paper or plastic wrap from sauce and whisk briefly. (If sauce is not warm, reheat it over medium heat.) Add sauce to cheese mixture in work bowl and process for 3 seconds only. Scrape work bowl. Sprinkle chives over sauce and spoon egg whites in a ring over chives. Pulse twice. Scrape work bowl well and pulse 1 or 2 more times, just until egg whites are incorporated. Some streaks of egg white may remain; do not overprocess.

Turn mixture into prepared dish and place in oven, immediately reducing heat to 375°F. (190°C.). Bake until soufflé is puffed and golden brown, 35 to 40 minutes. (Center should still be slightly soft.) Serve immediately.

Makes 4 servings.

BROCCOLI AND HAM SOUFFLE PIE

The "crust" of this delicious pie is a very special (and very easily made) soufflé mixture.

- **3 cups broccoli flowerets (about 10 ounces, 285g)**
- **4 large eggs, separated**
- **1 tablespoon distilled white vinegar**
- **1 cup (240ml) sour cream, for soufflé**
- **¼ teaspoon salt, if desired**
- **⅛ teaspoon white pepper**
- **½ cup unbleached all-purpose flour (2½ ounces, 70g)**
- **4 ounces (115g) boiled ham, cut into 1-inch (2.5cm) pieces**
- **4 ounces (115g) sharp Cheddar cheese, chilled**
- **2 large eggs**
- **⅓ cup sour cream (80ml), for filling**
- **2 teaspoons Dijon mustard**
- **⅛ teaspoon freshly ground black pepper**
- **¾ teaspoon oregano**
- **¼ teaspoon salt, if desired**

Bring about 4 quarts (4L) of water to boil over high heat. Add broccoli and cook, uncovered, until broccoli turns brilliant green and is just barely tender, about 5 minutes. Drain well, then plunge into large pan of very cold water and let stand until cool. Drain, then set broccoli on paper towels to drain completely. Gently squeeze to release liquid. Broccoli may be prepared to this point 1 day ahead; wrap in paper towels and plastic wrap and refrigerate.

Set oven rack in center position and preheat oven to 375°F. (190°C.). Butter ovenproof glass pie plate with 11-inch (28cm) top diameter and dust lightly with fine, unseasoned bread crumbs. Tap out excess crumbs.

Insert *metal blade*, put egg whites in work bowl, and process for 10 seconds. While machine is running, add vinegar through feed tube and process until whites are very thick and hold their shape, about 45 seconds. Remove metal blade and use rubber spatula to scrape whites into 1-quart (1L) bowl. Return metal blade to work bowl and pulse once to spin off any whites. Remove blade and scrape any remaining whites out of work bowl. Do not wash work bowl.

With *metal blade* in place, process 4 yolks, 1 cup sour cream, ¼ teaspoon salt, and white pepper for 5 seconds. Pour flour in ring over sour-cream mixture and spoon egg whites in ring on top of flour. Pulse twice, then scrape work bowl and pulse once more. Do not overprocess. Transfer mixture to 1-quart (1L) measure, scraping work bowl thoroughly. There should be about 4 cups (1L) of batter. Do not wash work bowl. Pour half of batter into prepared pan; cover remaining batter and keep at room temperature. Tilt pan to level batter and to run it partway up sides.

Bake this bottom crust for 15 minutes, remove from oven and let cool for 10 minutes. (While cooling, crust will sink slightly.) Do not turn oven off. With metal blade in place, add ham to work bowl. Pulse 3 times, then process continuously until ham is chopped medium-fine, about 5 seconds. Transfer ham to large mixing bowl.

Insert *medium shredding disc* and use light pressure to process cheese. Add half of cheese to ham, reserving remainder.

Divide broccoli into 2 batches. Insert *metal blade*, add 1 batch of broccoli and pulse 3 times, just to chop broccoli coarsely. Remove and set aside. Repeat with second batch; you will need 2 cups of chopped broccoli altogether. Add broccoli to ham and cheese.

With *metal blade* in place, process 2 eggs, ⅓ cup

sour cream, mustard, black pepper, oregano, and ¼ teaspoon salt for 5 seconds. Add to broccoli mixture and fold in gently.

Spread broccoli mixture over crust, smoothing it to edges of pie plate and mounding it slightly in center. Pour remaining soufflé mixture on top, covering filling. (You might not use all the batter; see NOTE.)

Return pie to oven and bake for 20 minutes. Sprinkle remaining cheese over top and bake until cheese is melted and top of pie is puffed and golden brown, about 5 minutes. Let stand at room temperature 15 to 30 minutes before serving; it's best when not too hot.

Makes 6 servings.

NOTE: A pie plate with a top diameter of 11 inches (28cm) will hold all the batter. Some glass pie plates have a top diameter of 10 inches (25cm). Such pans may not hold all the batter.

HAMBURGER PATTIES

Any beef that is ground and sold in markets can contain up to 30% fat, according to federal regulations. About 15 to 20% fat is ideal for making tasty and juicy hamburgers; less than 15% fat gives dry hamburgers.

Before chopping beef in a food processor, trim off all membrane, gristle, and fat; reserve the fat. Cut the beef into 1-inch (2.5cm) pieces, and the fat into ½-inch (12mm) pieces. Arrange the meat on a foil-lined tray and place it in the freezer until well chilled, about 30 minutes.

In any food processor that is larger than the standard size, you can process up to 1½ pounds (680g) of lean beef, or 3 solidly packed cups, with 6 ounces (170g) of fat, or ¾ cup. This makes almost 2 pounds (910g) of beef with about 20% fat. In a standard-size food processor, process the meat and fat in batches. Once you've made your own hamburger in the food processor, you'll probably do it whenever you need ground beef.

1½ pounds (680g) fully trimmed lean beef, cut into 1-inch (2.5cm) pieces and well chilled

6 ounces (170g) beef fat, cut into ½-inch (12mm) pieces (see NOTE)

1 teaspoon salt, if desired

¼ teaspoon freshly ground black pepper

¼ to ½ cup (60 to 120ml) cold water

Insert *metal blade* and put beef, fat, salt, pepper, and ¼ cup (60ml) of water in work bowl. Pulse 5 times, then process continuously for 10 seconds. Check consistency; if meat is dry, add more water and pulse a few times until desired texture is reached. Do not overprocess.

Remove work bowl from processor base and carefully lift out metal blade. Divide meat mixture into 6 portions and shape into round patties at least ¾ inch (18mm) thick. Use as little pressure as possible in shaping patties. Hamburger must be handled lightly.

Pan-broil over medium-high heat or broil over charcoal. Cooking for about 2 minutes per side produces a rare and juicy interior.

Makes 6 servings.

NOTE: Brisket is the only cut of beef I know that makes excellent hamburger with no added fat. The meat itself contains enough fat. Use either the thick or thin boneless cut, but trim off the top layer of fat. Cut the brisket into 1-inch (2.5cm) pieces, chill it, then chop it with the metal blade. Shape and cook the meat as described above.

PARTY HAMBURGERS

You can dress up hamburgers for company with this recipe that combines elements of Chinese and French cuisines. The patties are seasoned with oyster sauce and dressed with a cream sauce that is flavored with tarragon.

1½ **pounds (680g) beef round, with all membrane, fat, and gristle removed, cut into 1-inch (2.5cm) pieces**

6 **ounces (170g) beef fat, preferably from kidney, at room temperature and cut into ½-inch (12mm) pieces**

1 **medium onion (5 ounces, 140g), peeled and quartered**

2 **tablespoons butter**

1 **large egg**

3 **tablespoons oyster sauce**

¼ **teaspoon freshly ground black pepper**

2 **tablespoons water**

1 **tablespoon oil**

Flour

⅓ **cup (80ml) white wine *or* dry vermouth**

1 **cup (240ml) heavy cream**

¾ **teaspoon dried tarragon, crumbled**

¼ **teaspoon salt, if desired**

½ **teaspoon lemon juice**

Parsley sprigs for garnish

Arrange pieces of meat on foil-lined baking sheet and place in freezer until well chilled, about 30 minutes. Divide meat and fat into 2 batches.

Insert *metal blade.* Put 1 batch of combined meat and fat in work bowl, pulse 5 times, then process continuously for 10 seconds. Scrape work bowl and pulse a few more times, until meat is very finely chopped. Transfer meat to large mixing bowl. Process remaining meat and fat in same way.

With *metal blade* in place, add onion to work bowl. Pulse 3 times, scrape work bowl, and pulse 2 or 3 more times, until onion is finely chopped.

Melt 1 tablespoon of butter in 12-inch (30cm) skillet. Add onion and cook over medium heat until onion is tender but not browned, about 5 minutes.

Add onion, egg, oyster sauce, pepper, and water to meat. Mix gently with wooden spoon.

Just before cooking, shape meat mixture into 6 patties, at least ¾ inch (18mm) thick. Heat oil and remaining butter over medium heat in same skillet used to cook onion. Lightly coat 3 patties with flour, dusting off excess. (Do this just before cooking or flour will become pasty.) Add patties to hot oil and butter and cook them for 3 to 5 minutes per side. (Medium-rare patties take about 6 minutes total cooking time.) Transfer patties to platter, cover loosely with foil, and place in warm oven. Flour and cook remaining patties, adding more oil and butter to pan if necessary.

Pour off cooking fat, but leave browned bits of meat in skillet. Add wine and cream to skillet and turn to high. Boil rapidly, stirring with wooden spoon to scrape up bits of meat. Add tarragon and cook 2 to 3 minutes, stirring constantly, until sauce is reduced to about half and is thick enough to coat a spoon lightly. Remove from heat and taste for seasoning, adjusting with salt, pepper, and lemon juice, if necessary. Spoon sauce over patties, garnish platter with parsley, and serve at once.

Makes 6 servings.

TACOS

Tacos, always a favorite with the young set, taste better than ever when you chop your own meat.

2 **pounds (910g) lean beef, trimmed and cut into 1-inch (2.5cm) pieces**

2 **tablespoons oil**

Tacos

| 3 tablespoons tomato paste |
| 1/2 cup (120ml) water |
| 2 teaspoons chili powder |
| 1/2 teaspoon ground cumin |
| 1 teaspoon dried oregano |
| 1 teaspoon salt, if desired |
| 1/2 teaspoon freshly ground black pepper |
| 2 medium onions (10 ounces, 285g total), peeled and quartered |
| 4 ounces (115g) Monterey Jack cheese, chilled |
| 4 ounces (115g) Cheddar cheese, chilled |
| 1/2 head iceberg lettuce (3/4 pound, 340g), cut to fit feed tube |
| 3 medium tomatoes (1 pound, 455g total), stem ends removed |
| Taco sauce |
| Taco shells |

Place pieces of meat on foil-lined baking sheet and freeze until well chilled, about 30 minutes.

Divide meat into 3 batches. Insert *metal blade* and put 1 batch of meat in work bowl. Pulse 5 times, then process continuously until meat is chopped medium-fine, about 10 seconds. Scrape work bowl and check texture of meat; if necessary, pulse a few more times. Transfer chopped meat to large bowl. Process remaining batches of meat in same way, then wipe out work bowl with paper towels, carefully wipe metal blade, and reinsert it.

Heat oil in 12-inch (30cm) skillet over medium-high heat. Add meat and cook, tossing with two broad spatulas, until meat loses its pink color, 5 to 10 minutes. Add tomato paste, water, chili powder, cumin, oregano, salt, and pepper. Stir well, cover pan, and reduce heat to low. Simmer for 20 minutes, stirring occasionally; mixture will be thick. Meat may be prepared ahead to this point. When reheating, adjust consistency with additional tomato paste and water, if necessary.

With *metal blade* in place, put onions in work bowl. Pulse 3 times, then scrape work bowl and pulse 2 or 3 more times, until onions are finely chopped. Remove and set aside.

Insert *medium shredding disc* and use light pressure to shred both cheeses. Remove and set aside.

Insert *4mm slicing disc* and use light pressure to process lettuce. Remove and set aside.

Insert *French-fry disc* and use light pressure to process tomatoes. Remove and set aside.

To serve, reheat meat mixture, and heat taco shells according to manufacturer's directions. Bring everything to the table in separate dishes and let your guests assemble their own tacos.

Makes 16 to 18 tacos.

MEAT LOAF

This meat loaf is especially moist because of two unconventional ingredients: carrots and potatoes. You can use any cut of beef, but chuck or round is best. Be sure to remove all fat and membrane. Leftovers are wonderful in sandwiches

2 pounds (910g) lean beef, trimmed and cut into 1-inch (2.5cm) pieces
8 ounces (225g) beef fat, preferably from kidney, at room temperature and cut into ½-inch (12mm) pieces
1 large onion (8 ounces, 225g), peeled and cut into sixths
1 medium carrot (3 ounces, 85g), peeled and cut into 1-inch (2.5cm) pieces
1 medium potato (5 ounces, 140g), peeled and cut into quarters
2 tablespoons ketchup
¾ cup fine, dry, unseasoned bread crumbs (6 ounces, 170g)
1 teaspoon salt, if desired
½ teaspoon freshly ground black pepper
1 teaspoon dried oregano
¼ teaspoon dried thyme
1 tablespoon Worcestershire sauce
2 large eggs

Arrange pieces of meat on foil-lined baking sheet and place in freezer until meat is well chilled, about 30 minutes.

Set oven rack in lower third and preheat oven to 350°F. (175°C.).

Divide meat and fat into 3 batches. Insert *metal blade*, and put 1 batch each of meat and fat into work bowl. Pulse 5 times, then process continuously until meat is very finely chopped, about 10 seconds. Transfer meat to large mixing bowl. Process remaining batches of meat and fat in same way. Wipe out work bowl with paper towels.

With *metal blade* in place, put onion in work bowl. Pulse 3 times, scrape work bowl, and pulse 2 or 3 more times, until onion is finely chopped. Add to meat.

With *metal blade* in place, add carrot and potato to work bowl. Pulse 3 times, then process continuously for 15 seconds. Scrape work bowl, add ketchup and process until vegetables are puréed, about 1 minute. Stop to scrape work bowl as necessary. Add remaining ingredients, pulse 5 times, then process continuously for 30 seconds. Add mixture to meat and mix well with hands or wooden spoon.

Transfer mixture to shallow baking pan and shape into free-form loaf measuring about 10 by 5 by 3 inches (25 by 13 by 8cm). Meat loaf may be prepared to this point several hours ahead; cover loosely with plastic wrap and refrigerate.

Bake until loaf is browned, about 1 hour. Let stand 10 minutes before slicing.

Makes about 8 servings.

SPICY LAMB PILAF

This spicy and delicious lamb dish has a decided Indian flavor, which you can emphasize by serving it with Indian condiments like chopped peanuts, mango chutney, and shredded coconut. Chopped fresh tomatoes also complement the dish nicely. Despite the number of ingredients, it is quick and easy to prepare.

1 pound (455g) lean lamb, fully trimmed and cut into 1-inch (2.5cm) pieces
5 tablespoons olive oil
1 teaspoon ground cumin
¼ teaspoon ground turmeric
½ teaspoon ground coriander
2 teaspoons salt, if desired

¼	**teaspoon freshly ground black pepper**
1	**cup converted rice (7 ounces, 200g)**
2	**cups (480ml) water**
2	**small garlic cloves, peeled**
1	**1-inch cube fresh ginger, peeled**
1	**large onion (8 ounces, 225g), peeled and cut into eighths**
1	**large green bell pepper (8 ounces, 225g), cored, seeded, and cut into 1-inch (2.5cm) squares**
1	**large carrot (4 ounces, 115g), peeled, trimmed, and cut into 3-inch (8cm) lengths**
6	**large scallions (4 ounces, 115g total), trimmed and cut into 3-inch (8cm) lengths**
2	**tablespoons lemon juice**
4	**ounces (115g) firm, fresh, medium mushrooms (about 8), wiped clean and cut flat at opposite sides**

Arrange lamb on foil-lined baking sheet and freeze until well chilled, about 30 minutes.

Insert *metal blade*, put lamb in work bowl and pulse 5 times. Scrape work bowl and process continuously for 10 seconds. Lamb should be finely chopped; if necessary, pulse a few more times to achieve proper texture.

Heat 2 tablespoons of oil in 12-inch (30cm) skillet over medium-high heat. Add lamb and cook, stirring frequently with wooden spoon, until meat loses its pink color. Add cumin, turmeric, coriander, 1 teaspoon salt, and pepper. Stir well and cook mixture for 1 or 2 minutes. Remove to large bowl. Do not wash skillet.

Heat 1 tablespoon of oil in 2-quart (2L) saucepan over medium-high heat. Add rice and remaining 1 teaspoon salt. Cook, stirring constantly with wooden spoon, until most rice grains turn milky. Do not allow rice to brown. Add water. Bring rice mixture to vigorous boil without stirring. Stir well once or twice, cover pan, and reduce heat to very low. Cook, without stirring, until rice is tender, about 20 minutes. Meanwhile, prepare vegetables.

With *metal blade* in place, turn on machine and drop garlic and ginger through feed tube. Process until finely chopped, about 15 seconds. Scrape work bowl, add onion and green pepper, and pulse 3 times. Scrape work bowl and pulse 2 or 3 more times; onion and pepper should be chopped medium-fine. Leave vegetables in work bowl and remove metal blade.

Insert *medium shredding disc*, lay carrot sections horizontally in feed tube, and use firm pressure to process.

Heat remaining 2 tablespoons of oil over medium-high heat in same skillet used to cook lamb. Add contents of work bowl and cook, stirring with wooden spoon or spatula, for about 2 minutes.

Insert *3mm or 4mm slicing disc*, wedge scallion sections vertically in feed tube and use medium pressure to process. Add scallions to skillet, stir well and cover pan. Reduce heat to medium and cook for 4 to 5 minutes, stirring once or twice. Carrots should be slightly crisp. Uncover pan, add lemon juice and stir well. Add to lamb.

When ready to serve, put vegetables and lamb mixture in skillet and reheat gently over medium-low heat.

Insert *1mm slicing disc*, wedge mushrooms in feed tube with flat side down and use light pressure to process. Put mushrooms (and their trimmed ends) on top of lamb and put hot rice on top of mushrooms. (Heat of rice and lamb will cook mushrooms.) Toss gently but thoroughly with 2 broad spatulas. Turn into serving dish and serve at once.

Makes about 6 servings.

INTERNATIONAL FLANK STEAK CURRY

This spicy one-dish meal is refreshing, but not hot. It combines elements of several cuisines: the stir-fry cooking method and the marinade for the meat are Chinese; the onion purée is from India; and French cuisine provides the inspiration for blanching the vegetables and using wine.

Even though the dish is called a curry, you'll notice that there is no curry powder in the list of ingredients. Indian cooks rarely, if ever, use the curry powder so familiar to Westerners. Instead, they devise a different mixture of spices for each dish; the result is great flexibility and subtlety in flavoring.

Although there are several steps to making the curry, everything can be prepared ahead of time, and the cooking itself takes only a few minutes.

Please note, however, that it is essential to add the tomatoes and lemon juice at the very last minute before serving. This contributes greatly to the fresh taste of the dish. Serve the curry with boiled rice.

1¼ pounds (570g) flank steak	
1 tablespoon soy sauce	
1 tablespoon oyster sauce	
1 tablespoon dry sherry	
4 tablespoons oil	
1 1½-inch (4cm) cube fresh ginger, peeled	
3 medium onions (about 15 ounces, 425g total), peeled and quartered	
4 large garlic cloves, peeled	
1 medium Granny Smith apple (about 5 ounces, 140g), quartered, cored, but not peeled	

International Flank Steak Curry

- $^{1}/_{2}$ cup (120ml) dry vermouth
- 1 tablespoon ground coriander
- 1 teaspoon ground cumin
- $^{1}/_{2}$ teaspoon turmeric
- $^{1}/_{2}$ teaspoon salt, if desired
- $^{1}/_{4}$ teaspoon freshly ground black pepper
- 2 medium tomatoes (about 12 ounces, 340g)
- 4 cups cauliflower flowerets (about 12 ounces, 340g), cut into 1-inch (2.5cm) pieces
- 1 package (10 ounces, 285g) frozen peas, thawed
- 2 to 3 tablespoons lemon juice
- Chopped peanuts, flaked coconut, mango chutney, for condiments (optional)

Trim steak of fat and surface membranes. Cut lengthwise into thirds, then crosswise into 3-inch (8cm) lengths. Put pieces of meat on foil-lined baking sheet and freeze until meat is firm but can be easily pierced with a sharp knife, about 60 minutes.

Insert *6mm slicing disc*, wedge pieces of meat upright in feed tube, and use firm pressure to process. Transfer slices to medium mixing bowl and add soy sauce, oyster sauce, sherry, and 1 tablespoon of oil. Mix well and set aside. (Meat may be prepared to this point several hours before cooking; cover with plastic wrap and refrigerate.) Wipe out work bowl.

Insert *metal blade*, put ginger, onions, garlic, and apple in work bowl, pulse 3 times, then process continuously for 20 seconds. With machine running, pour vermouth through feed tube and continue processing until mixture is smooth purée, about 1 minute. Add coriander, cumin, turmeric, salt, and pepper and process 5 seconds. Remove from work bowl, cover, and set aside. Purée may be made several hours before cooking.

Remove stem ends of tomatoes with sharp paring knife. Bring 6 quarts (6L) of water to rolling boil over high heat. Drop in tomatoes and leave them for 20 seconds, then quickly transfer them to large bowl of very cold water and let stand until completely cool. Remove peels with sharp knife, cut tomatoes in half crosswise, and gently squeeze each half to remove seeds and juice.

Insert *French-fry disc*. Stand tomato halves on their sides in feed tube, wedging them in, and use light pressure to process. Set tomatoes aside. (Tomatoes may be prepared up to 2 hours before cooking.)

Drop cauliflower into boiling water used for tomatoes and cook just until translucent and tender but still crisp, 3 to 4 minutes. Do not overcook. Drain flowerets immediately, plunge into basin of cold water and let stand until completely cool. Drain well and set aside. (Cauliflower may be prepared to this point up to a day before cooking; drain well on paper towels, wrap in dry paper towels and then plastic wrap, and refrigerate.)

Heat 2 tablespoons of oil in 12-inch (30cm) skillet over high heat. Stir steak mixture. When oil is very hot, add meat and stir fry, tossing constantly with 2 broad spatulas, until meat loses its pink color. Transfer meat and juices to dish and set aside.

Add remaining tablespoon of oil to skillet and set pan over medium-high heat. Add onion purée and cook, stirring until purée thickens slightly, 2 to 3 minutes. Add cauliflower and stir well. Cover pan, reduce heat to medium, and cook, stirring once or twice, until cauliflower is tender, but still slightly crisp, about 5 minutes.

Add meat, meat juices, and peas to skillet. Stir well, cover pan, and cook 2 minutes longer. Just before serving, add tomatoes and 2 tablespoons lemon juice. Mix well and taste for seasoning; add third tablespoon of lemon juice if necessary. Transfer to serving platter and serve at once with boiled rice. Pass condiments separately.

Makes 4 to 6 servings.

EGG ROLLS WITH SEVEN VEGETABLES

These egg rolls are so tasty and substantial that you will not miss the meat.

2 cups cold cooked brown rice
1 tablespoon firmly packed light-brown sugar
1 tablespoon soy sauce
1 tablespoon hoisin sauce
1 tablespooon dry sherry
Freshly ground black pepper, to taste
2 or 3 garlic cloves, peeled
1 medium onion (5 ounces, 140g), peeled and cut in half vertically
2 large celery ribs (4 ounces, 115g total), cut into 2-inch (5cm) lengths
2 tablespoons oil
1 pound (455g) green cabbage, cut to fit feed tube
½ pound (225g) peeled jicama or turnip, cut to fit feed tube
½ pound (225g) fresh bean sprouts
1 tablespoon Oriental sesame oil
½ cup loosely packed watercress leaves
1 large egg
2 tablespoons cold water
14 or 15 egg-roll wrappers, 7 inches (17cm) square
Oil, for frying
Lime Dipping Sauce (recipe follows)

Mix rice, sugar, soy sauce, hoisin sauce, sherry, and pepper in small bowl and set aside.

Insert *metal blade.* Turn machine on, drop garlic through feed tube, and process until finely chopped, about 10 seconds. Leave in work bowl.

Insert *2mm slicing disc.* Use medium pressure to process onion. Leave in work bowl.

Shaping cylinder of filling

Folding nearest corner

Folding two side corners

Shaping into package

Insert *medium shredding disc.* Lay celery horizontally in feed tube and use light pressure to process.

Heat oil in 12-inch (30cm) skillet over medium heat. Add garlic, onion, and celery and cook 1 to 2 minutes.

Insert *2mm slicing disc* and use medium pressure to process cabbage. Add to vegetables in skillet and cook until cabbage is just tender, about 3 minutes.

Transfer vegetable mixture to colander and let stand until cool, pressing down on vegetables occasionally to remove excess moisture. Place vegetables in large mixing bowl.

Insert *medium shredding disc* and use firm pressure to process jicama. If jicama is very moist, squeeze shreds to remove excess moisture. Add jicama, bean sprouts, and rice mixture to vegetables in bowl. Add sesame oil and watercress and mix well.

Beat egg and water in small bowl until they are well combined. Place one egg-roll wrapper on work surface so a corner points toward you. (Keep remaining wrappers covered so they don't dry out.) Measure ⅓ cup of filling (75g) and place it on egg-roll wrapper, slightly below center. Shape filling into firm cylinder, 4 to 5 inches (10 to 13cm) long. Fold nearest corner up over filling, then fold in two side corners. Brush top flap lightly with egg mixture, then push egg roll away from you, shaping it into a neat, tight package.

Brush seams with egg mixture and set roll on lightly oiled baking sheet. Repeat with remaining filling and wrappers.

Heat ½ inch (12mm) of oil to 375°F. (190°C.) in 12-inch (30cm) skillet. Fry 4 to 6 egg rolls at a time until golden brown, about 2 minutes on each side. Drain well on paper towels and keep in warm oven while frying remaining egg rolls. Serve as soon as possible with Lime Dipping Sauce.

Egg rolls may be made ahead, wrapped air-tight when cool, and frozen. To reheat, place frozen rolls on baking sheet and set in preheated 400°F. (205°C.) oven for 15 minutes.

Makes 14 to 15 egg rolls.

LIME DIPPING SAUCE

This sauce may be made several hours ahead. At table, each diner takes some carrots and turnips, then spoons sauce into an individual bowl for dipping egg rolls.

2 large fresh limes (8 ounces total, 225g), peeled and cut into 1-inch (2.5cm) pieces
1 cup (240ml) water
2 tablespoons soy sauce
¼ cup (60ml) cider vinegar
⅓ to ½ cup firmly packed light-brown sugar
1 medium carrot (4 ounces, 115g), scrubbed and cut into lengths to fit feed tube
1 medium turnip, peeled and cut to fit feed tube

Insert *metal blade*, put limes in work bowl, and process until puréed, about 1 minute. Add water, soy sauce, vinegar, and ⅓ cup brown sugar. Process 10 seconds to blend. Taste and add additional brown sugar if necessary. Strain mixture into serving bowl, discarding residue.

Insert *2x2mm square julienne disc.* Lay carrot pieces horizontally in feed tube and use firm pressure to process. Process turnip in same way. Add vegetables to lime sauce.

Makes 1½ cups (360ml).

VEGETARIAN CHILI

A spicy chili with a rich tomato flavor. You will have some leftover cooked beans. Use them in a salad, or turn them into refried beans, a perfect side dish for a Mexican meal.

Beans

1 pound (455g) pinto beans
4 quarts (4L) water
1 teaspoon salt, if desired
4 parsley sprigs
½ teaspoon dried thyme leaves
1 bay leaf
1 medium onion (4 ounces, 115g), peeled and halved

Chili

2 garlic cloves, peeled
2 medium green bell peppers (10 ounces total, 285g), cored, seeded, and cut into 1-inch (2.5cm) squares
1 large onion (8 ounces, 225g), peeled and cut in half vertically
2 tablespoons oil
1 tablespoon chili powder
1½ teaspoons ground cumin
½ teaspoon dried oregano
½ teaspoon ground coriander
½ teaspoon sweet paprika
½ teaspoon freshly ground black pepper
2 1-pound (455g) cans whole plum tomatoes, undrained
1 8-ounce (225g) can tomato sauce
1 12-ounce (360ml) can beer
4 cups cooked drained pinto beans
¾ teaspoon salt, if desired
Saltine crackers or cooked brown rice, if desired

Put beans and half the water in 5-quart (5L) saucepan. Cover and bring to boil over high heat. Uncover and boil for exactly 2 minutes. Cover, remove from heat, and let stand for 1 hour. Drain beans and return to pan. Add remaining water and salt. Tie parsley, thyme and bay leaf together in washed cheesecloth and add to beans, along with onion. Bring to boil over high heat, uncovered. Reduce heat to low and cook at very slow simmer until beans are just tender but not soft or mushy, about 1 hour. Test frequently to avoid overcooking; beans will cook more later. Remove onion and herb bouquet and drain beans well. Set aside until needed. (Beans may be prepared to this point up to 3 days ahead and refrigerated.)

Insert *metal blade*, turn on machine and drop garlic through feed tube. Process until minced, about 10 seconds. Scrape work bowl, add peppers and pulse 3 times. Scrape work bowl and pulse 2 or 3 more times; peppers should be chopped medium-fine. Leave in work bowl and remove metal blade.

Insert *French-fry disc*, put onion halves vertically in feed tube and use medium pressure to process.

Heat oil in 5-quart (5L) saucepan over medium-high heat. Add garlic, peppers and onion. Cook, stirring frequently, until vegetables are tender but not browned, about 3 to 4 minutes. Add chili powder, cumin, oregano, coriander, paprika and pepper. Cook, stirring, for 1 minute.

Insert *metal blade*, put tomatoes and their juice in work bowl and pulse rapidly 4 times to chop coarsely. Add to saucepan with tomato sauce and beer. Stir well and bring to boil over high heat. Reduce heat to low, partially cover and let simmer, stirring occasionally, until slightly thickened. Cook about 1 hour; you should have about 6 cups (1.5L).

Add beans and simmer slowly for another 15 minutes, until beans are tender. Taste, add salt if desired, and serve plain, with saltine crackers, or over rice.

Makes about 10 cups (2.5kg), or 6 servings.

CHICKEN STROGANOFF

This variation of Beef Stroganoff is nicely comple-mented by noodles, either those made with white flour or those made with a mixture of white and whole-wheat flours.

1 pound (455g) boneless, skinless chicken breast halves

¼ cup parsley leaves, washed and patted dry (see NOTE)

2 garlic cloves, peeled

2 medium onions (about 10 ounces, 285g total), peeled and quartered

4 tablespoons butter

2 tablespoons unbleached all-purpose flour

2 cups (480ml) chicken stock

1 teaspoon Dijon mustard

2 teaspoons tomato paste

½ pound (225g) mushrooms, cleaned and trimmed flat at opposite ends

2 teaspoons lemon juice

½ cup (120ml) sour cream

1 teaspoon salt, if desired

¼ teaspoon freshly ground black pepper

Place each piece of chicken on sheet of plastic wrap, with original skin side down. Fold about 1 inch (2.5cm) of each end toward center and roll breast to form cylinder. Wrap securely in plastic to maintain cylindrical shape. Freeze on baking sheet until flesh resists when squeezed but can easily be pierced with tip of sharp knife, about 60 minutes. (If chicken is frozen solid, let it sit at room temperature for 15 to 20 minutes before testing with knife.) Remove plastic wrap and cut breasts in half crosswise.

Insert *6mm or 4mm slicing disc*, put chicken pieces in feed tube cut sides down, and use firm pressure to process. Remove and set aside. Carefully wipe work bowl with paper towels; be sure it is dry.

Insert *metal blade*, put parsley in work bowl and process until finely chopped, about 20 seconds. Remove and set aside.

With *metal blade* in place, turn machine on and drop garlic through feed tube. Process until minced, about 10 seconds. Add onions and pulse 3 times. Scrape inside of work bowl and pulse 3 or 4 more times, until onions are finely chopped.

Melt 2 tablespoons of butter in 3-quart (3L) saucepan over medium heat. Add flour, whisk until blended and cook for 1 or 2 minutes. Add 1½ cups (360ml) of chicken stock and bring to boil. Whisk constantly until sauce is thick and smooth. Stir in mustard and tomato paste. Keep sauce warm over low heat.

Pour remaining ½ cup (120ml) of chicken stock into 12-inch (30cm) skillet over medium heat. Stir in garlic and onions. Reduce heat to medium-low, cover skillet and cook, stirring occasionally, until onions are tender, 6 to 8 minutes. Uncover, raise heat to medium-high, and cook, tossing frequently, until liquid is absorbed. Do not let onions brown.

Meanwhile, insert *2mm slicing disc*. Wedge mushrooms into feed tube, flat sides down, and use light pressure to process. Add mushrooms to onions and cook until mushrooms are heated through. Stir this mixture into sauce and add lemon juice.

Melt remaining 2 tablespoons of butter in skillet over medium-high heat. When foam subsides, add chicken strips. Toss and cook quickly until chicken is opaque, then add chicken to sauce. Stir in sour cream and adjust seasoning, if necessary, with salt, pepper, and more lemon juice. Just before serving, bring sauce slowly to simmer. (Do not let it boil, as sour cream may curdle.) Serve with buttered noodles and garnish with chopped parsley.

Makes 6 to 8 servings.

NOTE: You may substitute 3 tablespoons of chopped fresh dill for the parsley, and garnish the dish with additional sprigs of dill.

PHYLLO STROGANOFF ROLLS

This delicious chopped beef filling, seasoned like a classic Beef Stroganoff, is wrapped in phyllo pastry and served with a sour-cream sauce. If fresh dill is available, use 3 tablespoons of it, chopped fine, instead of the parsley, and omit the dill weed.

- 2 pounds (910g) lean chuck or round steak, trimmed and cut into 1-inch (2.5cm) pieces
- ¼ cup parsley leaves, washed and patted dry
- 2 tablespoons oil
- 1 large onion (8 ounces, 225g), peeled and cut into eighths
- ½ pound (225g) medium mushrooms, cleaned
- 1½ sticks unsalted butter (6 ounces, 170g), melted
- 1½ teaspoons salt, if desired
- ¼ teaspoon freshly ground black pepper
- 2 cups (480ml) sour cream
- 2 teaspoons dry mustard
- 2 teaspoons dry dill weed
- ½ teaspoon sugar
- 2 tablespoons lemon juice
- 32 sheets phyllo pastry (about 1 pound, 455g), at room temperature
- ½ teaspoon prepared horseradish

Set pieces of meat on foil-lined baking sheet and freeze until meat is well chilled, about 30 minutes.

Insert *metal blade*, put parsley in work bowl and process until finely chopped. Remove and set aside.

Divide meat into 3 batches. With *metal blade* in place, add 1 batch to work bowl, pulse 5 times, then process continuously just until meat is chopped fine, about 10 seconds. Do not overprocess. Remove from work bowl and process remaining batches in same way. Wipe out work bowl with paper towels.

Heat oil in 12-inch (30cm) skillet over medium heat. Add meat and cook, stirring frequently, until it loses its pink color. Transfer to colander to drain off excess fat. Do not wash skillet.

With *metal blade* in place, put onion in work bowl. Pulse 3 times, scrape work bowl, and pulse 2 or 3 more times, until onion is finely chopped. Remove and set aside.

Insert *French-fry disc.* Place mushrooms on their sides in feed tube and use light pressure to process. Remove and set aside.

Put 1 tablespoon of melted butter in same skillet used to cook meat. Set pan over medium heat, add onions, and cook, stirring occasionally, until onions are tender but not browned, about 5 minutes. Add mushrooms and cook until they begin to release their juices, 3 to 4 minutes. Stir in cooked beef, salt, and pepper. Remove pan from heat and set aside.

With *metal blade* in place, put 1 cup sour cream, mustard, dill, sugar, and 1 tablespoon lemon juice in work bowl. Pulse 4 or 5 times, just to mix well. Remove and add to beef mixture in skillet, along with parsley. Stir to combine well, taste, and adjust seasoning if necessary. Set aside to cool slightly; mixture must be barely warm when used.

Keep phyllo sheets covered; use dry towel with damp towel over it. Remove 2 phyllo sheets, one directly on top of other, and place them on work surface so a short side is nearest you. Brush top

Arranging filling in log shape   *Folding long sides of dough*

sheet lightly with melted butter. Measure ⅓ cup of beef mixture and arrange it in a neat log shape, 3 to 4 inches long (8 to 10cm), along short side of phyllo, keeping mixture about 3 inches (8cm) from edge nearest you. Fold long sides of phyllo over filling and brush lightly with melted butter. Lift end of pastry nearest you over filling, and roll pastry to opposite end, enclosing filling completely. Brush lightly all over with melted butter and set on ungreased baking sheet.

Repeat with remaining phyllo, filling, and butter, making 16 pastries in all. Set pastries about 1 inch (2.5cm) apart on baking sheet, using more than 1 baking sheet if necessary. Pastries may be prepared to this point up to 12 hours before serving, and refrigerated. For longer storage, see NOTE below.

Bake 1 sheet at a time on center rack of pre-heated 375°F. (190°C.) oven until pastries are golden brown, about 25 to 30 minutes.

To prepare sour-cream sauce, insert *metal blade*, put 1 cup (240ml) sour cream in work bowl with 1 tablespoon lemon juice and horseradish, and process for 5 seconds. Serve pastries hot with sour-cream sauce.

Serves 8.

NOTE: To reheat frozen baked pastries, bake as directed for fresh pastries, but only until they are hot and crisp, about 20 minutes. The pastry may crack and flake a bit on reheating.

To freeze unbaked pastries, arrange them on baking sheets lined with waxed paper, freeze until firm, transfer to airtight plastic bags and store in freezer for no more than 1 week. (The filling tends to become dry if they are stored longer.) Bake as directed for fresh pastries, but extend baking time to about 45 minutes.

Lifting end of pastry

Rolling pastry

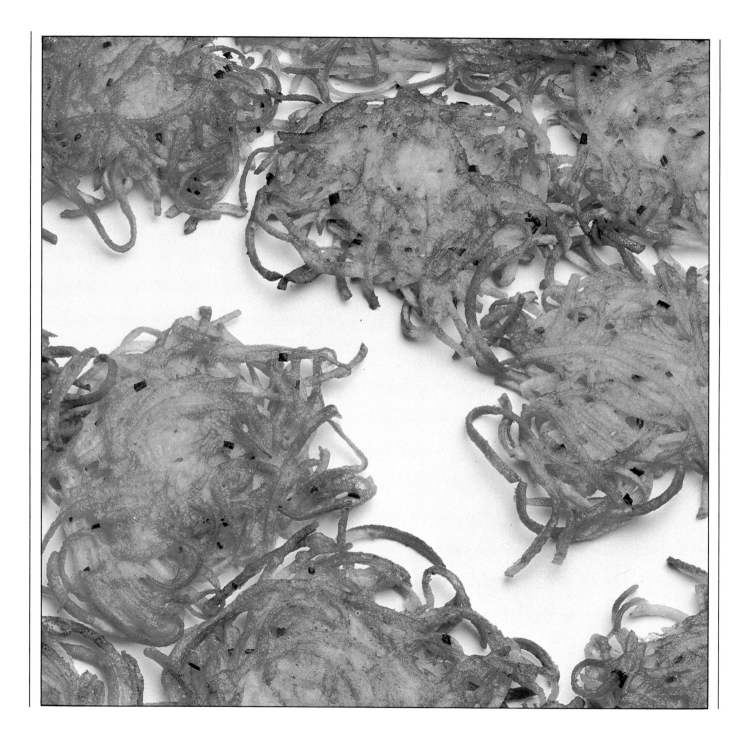

POTATOES
and
RICE

With this collection of recipes, I hope to chip away at the common notion that potatoes and rice are fattening. In fact, they are surprisingly low in calories when cooked in a small amount of fat and served without gobs of butter or ladles of creamy sauce. They are also important sources of the starch and complex carbohydrates needed in a balanced diet. So let's not banish these wonderfully nutritious foods from our tables; let's enjoy them in new ways.

All the recipes in this chapter are low in fat and easy to prepare. Many can be prepared entirely in advance and reheated before serving. They are all made easier and faster with the food processor. It ensures success with Mexican-Style Potatoes and Scalloped Potatoes, in which the potato slices must be thin and even. It makes long shreds of starchy baking potatoes, the essential ingredient for potato pancakes. And for Mushroom Pilaf, it slices mushrooms so thin that they are cooked by the heat of the rice, eliminating the task of cooking them *and* the calories in the fat needed to cook them.

The chapter includes a recipe for Spanish Rice. I'm aware that this has long been out of fashion and I'd like to lead its revival!

Potato Pancakes

SCALLOPED POTATOES

You may use boiling or baking potatoes in this version of a perennial cold-weather favorite. The amount of liquid is nicely calculated to make the potatoes tender, but not so soft that they lose their shape and become difficult to serve.

- 5 medium potatoes (2 pounds, 910g total)
- 1 garlic clove, peeled and split
- 3 tablespoons butter, melted
- ½ teaspoon salt, if desired
- 1½ cups (360ml) milk
- 2 tablespoons heavy cream *or* sour cream
- 1 large egg plus 1 yolk
- ⅛ teaspoon freshly grated nutmeg

Adjust oven rack to upper third position and preheat oven to 425°F. (220°C.).

Peel potatoes and wipe them with paper towels; do not rinse them.

Insert *2mm slicing disc,* lay potatoes horizontally in feed tube, and use firm pressure to process.

Rub garlic over bottom and sides of 12 by 8 by 2-inch (30 by 20 by 5cm) baking dish and brush pan lightly with melted butter. Arrange layer of potatoes in pan, overlapping slices slightly; brush with butter and sprinkle lightly with salt. Repeat with remaining potatoes, butter, and salt, making about 4 layers.

Insert *metal blade,* put remaining ingredients into work bowl and process for 5 seconds. Pour liquid over potatoes; it should just reach top layer.

Bake until top is golden brown, 40 to 45 minutes. Halfway through baking, use wide metal spatula to press down potatoes, ensuring that top layer receives enough liquid. Cool slightly before serving.

Makes 6 servings.

POTATO PANCAKES

The natural starch in the potatoes helps to hold these pancakes together. Use baking potatoes, which have more starch than other varieties. As you peel them, drop them into a bowl of cold water, where they can stay until you're ready to shred them. Just before shredding them, pat them dry. Do not rinse them after you shred them; that washes away some of the essential starch.

- 5 medium baking potatoes (2 pounds, 910g total)
- 2 large eggs
- 2 tablespoons unbleached all-purpose flour
- ¼ teaspoon baking powder
- 1 teaspoon salt, if desired
- 2 tablespoons fresh snipped chives *or* 1 tablespoon freeze-dried chopped chives
- 2 tablespoons butter
- 2 tablespoons oil

Peel potatoes and put them into bowl of cold water.

Insert *medium shredding disc* or *fine shredding disc.* Pat potatoes dry, put them horizontally in feed tube, and use firm pressure to process. Transfer to large mixing bowl.

Insert *metal blade.* Put eggs, flour, baking powder, salt, and chives into work bowl and process for 5 seconds. Stir egg mixture into potatoes.

Heat half the butter and half the oil in 12-inch (30cm) skillet over medium heat. Divide half the potato mixture into 4 rounds, place them in skillet and flatten them to make pancakes about 4 inches (10cm) in diameter. Cook until undersides are brown and crispy, about 5 minutes. Turn and cook for 5 minutes longer. Repeat with remaining butter, oil, and potatoes. Serve as soon as possible.

Makes 8 servings.

MEXICAN-STYLE POTATOES AND CHEESE

Green chiles and cheese are combined with thinly sliced potatoes in this piquant side dish, which is a perfect complement to roast chicken or grilled hamburgers. Use mild or hot chiles, according to your taste.

1½ ounces (45g) Parmesan cheese, in 2 pieces
6 ounces (170g) sharp Cheddar cheese, chilled (see NOTE)
4 medium boiling potatoes (1½ pounds, 680g total), peeled
1 medium onion (5 ounces, 140g), peeled
1 4-ounce (115g) can diced green chiles, drained
¼ teaspoon salt, if desired
¼ teaspoon freshly ground black pepper
2 tablespoons butter, chilled and cut into small pieces
½ cup (120ml) heavy cream

Adjust oven rack to center position and preheat oven to 375°F. (190°C.). Lightly butter 12 by 8 by 2-inch (30 by 20 by 5cm) baking dish or 10-inch (25cm) glass pie plate.

Insert *metal blade.* With machine running, drop Parmesan cheese through feed tube and process until it is finely chopped, about 20 seconds. Remove and set aside.

Insert *medium shredding disc,* put Cheddar cheese in feed tube and use light pressure to process. Remove and set aside.

Insert *2mm slicing disc,* put potatoes in feed tube, and use firm pressure to process. Remove and set aside.

With *2mm slicing disc* in place, put onion in feed tube, and use medium pressure to process. Transfer to bowl and add chiles; mix to combine them well.

Arrange ⅓ of potato slices in baking dish, overlapping them slightly. Sprinkle with ½ the salt and pepper, spread with ½ the onion and chile mixture, and sprinkle with ½ the Cheddar cheese. Arrange ½ the remaining potatoes on top, sprinkle with remaining salt and pepper, spread with remaining onion and chile mixture, and sprinkle with remaining Cheddar cheese. Arrange remaining potatoes on top and sprinkle with Parmesan cheese. Dot top with butter and pour cream evenly over all.

Bake until potatoes are tender and top begins to brown, about 40 minutes. Check after 30 minutes; if top is brown enough, cover with foil for last 10 minutes of cooking. Let stand for 5 to 10 minutes before serving.

Makes 6 to 8 servings.

NOTE: For Cheddar, you may substitute Swiss, Fontina, Monterey Jack, or a mixture of Cheddar and Monterey Jack.

POTATOES STUFFED WITH HAM AND CHEESE

These potatoes, with their creamy stuffing, are hearty enough to serve as a main course, accompanied by a salad. They are also good as a side dish with a light main course.

3	large baking potatoes (1½ pounds, 680g total)
	Oil
2	scallions, trimmed and cut into 1-inch (2.5cm) lengths
4	ounces (115g) cooked ham, cut into 1-inch (2.5cm) pieces
4	ounces (115g) sharp or extra-sharp Cheddar cheese, chilled
1	tablespoon Dijon mustard
⅓	cup (80ml) sour cream
¼	teaspoon salt, if desired
	Pinch of cayenne

Adjust oven rack to center position and preheat oven to 400°F. (205°C.).

Wash potatoes, dry them, and cut them in half lengthwise. With sharp knife, score cross-hatched pattern on cut surfaces, cutting to depth of ⅛ inch (3mm). Rub cut surfaces lightly with oil and place potatoes on oiled baking sheet, cut sides down. Bake until potatoes are cooked through, about 30 minutes. Test with tip of sharp knife.

Remove potatoes from oven, invert them on baking sheet, and let them stand until they are cool enough to handle. Carefully spoon out flesh, leaving ¼- to ½-inch (6 to 12mm) shell. Set flesh aside and replace shells on baking sheet.

Insert *metal blade*. With machine running, drop scallions and ham through feed tube and process until both are finely chopped, about 10 to 15 seconds. Carefully remove metal blade, leaving scallions and ham in bowl. Scrape work bowl with spatula.

Insert *medium shredding disc*, put cheese in feed tube and use light pressure to process; leave in work bowl. Put potato flesh in feed tube and use very light pressure to process. Remove shredding disc, leaving mixture in work bowl.

Insert *metal blade*, pushing it down firmly to bottom of bowl. Add mustard, sour cream, salt, and cayenne, and pulse quickly 3 times. (Do not overprocess or potatoes may become gluey.) Scrape work bowl and stir with spatula to complete mixing. Mixture will be thick.

Spoon mixture into potato shells, dividing it equally among them and mounding it slightly in center.

Bake until hot, about 20 minutes. Potatoes may be stuffed hours ahead, covered loosely with plastic wrap and refrigerated. To serve, bake in preheated 400°F. (205°C.) oven until hot, 20 to 25 minutes. Or you may freeze stuffed potatoes on baking sheet, then wrap them airtight in foil and store them in freezer. To serve, unwrap and place on baking sheet in preheated 325°F. (160°C.) oven and bake until hot, about 45 minutes.

Makes 6 servings.

FRIED BROWN RICE

Brown rice, with its nutty flavor, makes the difference in this variation of a classic from Chinese cooking. It is chewier in texture than white rice, and more nutritious.

1	large egg
1	tablespoon water
2½	tablespoons oil
6	large scallions (4 ounces, 115g total), trimmed and cut into 1-inch (2.5cm) lengths

Fried Brown Rice

4 **ounces (115g) fresh mushrooms, cleaned and trimmed flat on opposite ends**
2 **tablespoons dry sherry**
3 **cups cooked brown rice, chilled**
1 **cup cooked peas**
3 **tablespoons soy sauce**
Freshly ground black pepper

Combine egg and water and beat lightly with fork. Heat ½ tablespoon oil in 10-inch (25cm) skillet over medium-high heat. When hot, pour in egg mixture and swirl in pan rapidly to make thin egg crêpe; cook only until egg is set, a few seconds. Turn crêpe out onto work surface, and roll like jelly roll, then use sharp knife to cut roll into fine shreds. Set aside.

Insert *metal blade*, put scallions into work bowl, and pulse until finely chopped. Leave scallions in work bowl.

Insert *4mm slicing disc*, put mushrooms in feed tube, and use light pressure to process.

Put remaining oil in same skillet used to cook egg and set pan over medium heat. Add scallions and mushrooms, toss, and cook about 1 minute. Add sherry and continue to cook, stirring, until liquid is absorbed. Add rice and cook, stirring constantly, until heated through. Add peas, soy sauce, and pepper to taste, mix well and cook for 30 seconds. Add egg, mix in gently, and turn into serving dish.

Makes about 4½ cups.

SPANISH RICE

An updated version of an old favorite, this is perfect for those occasions when you want something more elaborate than boiled rice, but don't have a lot of time to prepare it.

> **4 slices bacon (4 ounces, 115g total), cut crosswise into ¼-inch (6mm) strips**
>
> **3 ounces (85g) Parmesan cheese, cut into 1-inch (2.5cm) pieces**
>
> **1 large onion (8 ounces, 225g), peeled and cut into eighths**
>
> **1 medium green bell pepper (5 ounces, 140g), cored, seeded, and cut into 1-inch (2.5cm) pieces**
>
> **1 8-inch (20cm) celery stalk, cut into 1-inch (2.5cm) pieces**
>
> **2 tablespoons butter**
>
> **¾ cup long-grain rice**
>
> **1 1-pound (455g) can whole plum tomatoes, undrained**
>
> **½ cup (120ml) chicken stock**
>
> **½ teaspoon salt, if desired**
>
> **¼ teaspoon freshly ground black pepper**
>
> **¼ teaspoon dried thyme leaves**

Cook bacon in 3-quart (3L) saucepan over medium heat, stirring occasionally, until it is browned and crisp. Set aside on paper towels and discard fat; do not wash pan.

Insert *metal blade* and turn on machine. Drop cheese through feed tube and process until finely chopped, about 45 seconds. Remove and set aside.

With *metal blade* in place, put onion, green pepper, and celery into work bowl. Pulse 3 times, scrape work bowl, and pulse 3 more times, or until vegetables are chopped medium-fine.

Melt butter over medium heat in saucepan used to cook bacon. Add rice and stir well. Cook, stirring frequently, until rice becomes opaque and just begins to color slightly, 2 or 3 minutes. (Watch it carefully to prevent burning.) Add chopped vegetables, stir well, and cook for 5 minutes, stirring occasionally.

With *metal blade* in place, put tomatoes into work bowl with their juices and pulse 4 times to chop them coarsely. Add them to saucepan with bacon, stock, salt, pepper, and thyme. Stir and bring mixture to boil over medium heat. Cover and reduce heat to low. Cook, without stirring, until liquid is absorbed and rice is tender, 30 to 40 minutes. Pass cheese separately for sprinkling over rice.

Makes 6 servings.

MUSHROOM PILAF

Thinly sliced mushrooms, added to hot pilaf just before it is served, are cooked by the heat of the rice. This dish is good with grilled meat or poultry.

> **¼ cup parsley leaves, washed and patted dry**
>
> **1 medium onion (4 ounces, 115g), peeled and quartered**
>
> **2 tablespoons butter**
>
> **1 cup converted rice (7 ounces, 200g)**
>
> **1⅔ cups (400ml) chicken broth**
>
> **¼ teaspoon dried thyme**
>
> **Salt (see NOTE)**
>
> **⅛ teaspoon freshly ground black pepper**
>
> **¼ pound (115g) fresh mushrooms, cleaned and trimmed flat on 2 opposite sides**

Insert *metal blade*, put parsley into work bowl, and process until minced, about 25 seconds. Remove and set aside.

With *metal blade* in place, put onion into work bowl and pulse 3 times, just to chop onion coarsely.

Put butter in 3-quart (3L) saucepan and heat until melted. Add onion and cook, stirring occasionally, until onion is tender and just beginning to brown, about 10 minutes. Add rice and stir well, then add chicken broth, thyme, salt, and pepper. Stir once or twice to mix, then bring mixture to rolling boil over high heat without stirring further. Reduce heat to very low, cover pan, and cook until liquid is absorbed and rice is tender, about 20 minutes.

Insert *1mm slicing disc*, wedge mushrooms into feed tube 1 layer at a time, flat side down, and use light pressure to process.

Add mushrooms and parsley to hot pilaf and toss gently. Mushrooms will be cooked by heat of rice. Serve immediately.

Makes 6 servings.

NOTE: If using homemade unsalted chicken broth, add 1 teaspoon of salt; if using canned chicken broth, add only ¼ teaspoon of salt.

RICE AND ONION CASSEROLE

This creamy mixture of braised rice and onions is similar to the sauce of puréed onions that the French named Sauce Soubise, after the Prince de Soubise, a general of King Louis XV. There are two secrets to success: the onions must be sliced very thin, and the dish must be cooked very slowly. No liquid is added during cooking because the onions provide sufficient moisture. There are many versions of this recipe; mine is based on one in Mastering the Art of French Cooking *by Simone Beck, Louisette Bertholle and Julia Child.*

2 quarts (2L) water
½ cup long-grain rice (3½ ounces, 100g)
2 ounces (55g) Swiss cheese, cut into 1-inch (2.5cm) pieces
2 tablespoons parsley, washed and dried
6 medium onions (2 pounds, 910g total), peeled and halved lengthwise
2 tablespoons butter
½ teaspoon sugar
1 teaspoon salt, if desired
⅛ teaspoon freshly ground black pepper
⅛ teaspoon freshly grated nutmeg
¼ cup (60ml) heavy cream

Adjust oven rack to lower third position and preheat oven to 300°F. (150°C.).

Bring water to rolling boil in 4-quart (4L) pot over high heat. Drop in rice and cook for 5 minutes, then drain and set aside. Do not rinse rice.

Insert *metal blade*. With machine running, drop cheese through feed tube and process until very finely chopped, about 45 seconds. Remove and set aside.

With *metal blade* in place, turn on machine, drop parsley through feed tube, and process until finely chopped, about 20 seconds. Remove and set aside, covered.

Insert *2mm slicing disc*. Stand onions vertically in feed tube and use medium pressure to process.

Melt butter in 4-quart (4L) ovenproof casserole over medium heat. When butter is hot, add onions and stir to coat them well. Add rice, sugar, salt, pepper, and nutmeg. Stir well, cover pan tightly, and let mixture heat thoroughly, stirring it once or twice.

Place casserole in oven and cook, stirring every 15 minutes, until onions are very tender and have begun to turn light golden, about 1 hour or longer. (The onions should be so tender that they are almost melted.) Dish may be cooked ahead to this point; remove from oven and set aside. Reheat slowly over medium-low heat.

Before serving, stir cheese and cream into hot rice and onions; mixture will be very creamy.

Taste and adjust seasoning if necessary. Turn into warm serving dish and sprinkle lightly with parsley.

Makes 6 servings.

RICE AND ZUCCHINI CASSEROLE

You may prepare much of this savory dish well before baking it. It goes well with all meats or with fish. Or it can be served on its own as a first course. This is based on a recipe by Simone Beck and Julia Child in Mastering the Art of French Cooking, Volume II.

3 ounces (85g) Parmesan cheese, cut into 1-inch (2.5cm) pieces
5 or 6 medium zucchini (2 pounds, 910g total), trimmed amd cut into 3-inch (8cm) lengths
1 teaspoon salt (see NOTE)
2 quarts (2L) water
½ cup long-grain rice
Milk
2 garlic cloves, peeled
1 medium onion (5 ounces, 140g), peeled and quartered
2 tablespoons olive oil
2 tablespoons unbleached all-purpose flour

Insert *metal blade.* With machine running, drop cheese through feed tube and process until finely chopped, about 45 seconds. Remove and set aside.

Insert *medium shredding disc.* Lay zucchini horizontally in feed tube and use medium pressure to process. Transfer to large bowl and toss with salt. Let stand for about 1 hour, to draw out moisture.

Meanwhile, bring water to rolling boil in 4-quart (4L) pot over high heat. Add rice and cook for 5 minutes, then drain and set aside; do not rinse. This preliminary cooking tenderizes the rice.

Firmly squeeze handfuls of zucchini to remove excess liquid. Save all liquid; it should measure 1½ to 2 cups (360 to 480ml). Add milk to measure 2½ cups (600ml) total. Put liquid in 1-quart (1L) sauce-

Rice and Zucchini Casserole

pan and bring to boil over high heat, watching closely to prevent overflowing. Remove and set aside.

With *metal blade* in place, turn on machine and drop garlic and onion through feed tube. Process until finely chopped, about 10 seconds.

Heat oil in 12-inch (30cm) skillet over medium-low heat. Add garlic and onion and cook slowly, stirring occasionally, until onion is tender but not browned, about 10 minutes. Add zucchini and increase heat to medium-high. Toss and cook until zucchini is tender, about 5 minutes. Stir in flour, cook another 2 minutes, and remove from heat. Gradually add hot milk mixture, stirring well. Return pan to medium heat and boil briefly, stirring frequently. (The technique is similar to that of making a white sauce.)

Add rice and ½ cup of cheese (2 ounces, 55g). Stir well, remove from heat, and taste for seasoning. Casserole may be prepared ahead to this point.

About 45 minutes before serving, adjust oven rack to center position and preheat oven to 425°F. (220°C.). Bring zucchini mixture to boil over medium heat, stirring occasionally. Turn it into lightly buttered 2-quart (2L) casserole or soufflé dish and sprinkle remaining cheese evenly over top.

Bake, uncovered, until casserole is bubbly and top is nicely browned, about 25 minutes. Let stand for 10 minutes before serving. (Leftovers may be served cold, at room temperature, or reheated.)

Makes 6 to 8 servings.

NOTE: To reduce salt, prepare zucchini as directed, but discard juices. Rinse zucchini thoroughly in cold water and squeeze dry again. Use 2½ cups milk for cooking liquid.

VEGETABLES

Whether a vegetable is chopped, sliced, shredded or julienned, the food processor accomplishes it in seconds, with a minimum of waste. Perhaps more important, it gives you uniform pieces that cook evenly. This is particularly critical for dishes in which the vegetables are arranged in layers, like the Baked Vegetable Strata.

Other dishes, like the Julienne of Gingered Carrots and Zucchini and the Zucchini and Red-Pepper Stir-Fry illustrate use of julienne and French-fry discs to cut vegetables into thin, even strips that cook quickly, retaining all their fresh crispness.

Savory Butter-Crumb Tomatoes

JULIENNE OF GINGERED CARROTS AND ZUCCHINI

This colorful dish, characterized by contrasting textures, may be served hot or at room temperature. If you can find the carrots called "juice carrots," use them here. They are less fibrous than ordinary carrots, and easier to process with the julienne disc.

2 teaspoons cornstarch
1 teaspoon sugar
¼ cup (60ml) chicken broth *or* water
2 tablespoons red wine vinegar
¼ teaspoon salt, if desired
⅛ teaspoon freshly ground black pepper
1 teaspoon Oriental sesame oil
1 slice peeled ginger, 1 inch (2.5cm) in diameter and ¼ inch (6mm) thick
4 large carrots (1¼ pounds, 570g total), peeled and cut into 3-inch (8cm) lengths
2 medium zucchini (¾ pound, 340g total), trimmed and cut into 3-inch (8cm) lengths
2 tablespoons oil

Combine cornstarch, sugar, broth, vinegar, salt, pepper, and sesame oil in small bowl and set aside.

Insert *metal blade*, turn on machine, and drop ginger through feed tube. Process until finely chopped, about 20 seconds. Remove and set aside.

Insert *3mm slicing disc* or *3mm julienne disc* to process carrots.

If using *slicing disc*, lay carrots horizontally in feed tube and use firm pressure to process. Remove slices, reassemble them, and wedge them horizontally in feed tube, positioned at right angle to first cut. Use medium pressure to process. This double-slicing will yield matchstick strips 3mm in cross-section. Remove them and set them aside.

If using *julienne disc*, lay carrots horizontally in feed tube and use firm pressure to process. Remove

julienne strips and set them aside.

Process zucchini in same way as carrots, using medium pressure.

Heat 2 tablespoons of oil in 12-inch (30cm) skillet over medium-high heat. Add ginger and carrots and cook, tossing frequently, until carrots are partially cooked but still crisp, about 3 to 4 minutes. Add zucchini and cook, tossing, for 1 to 2 minutes. Stir sauce mixture and add it to skillet. Toss until sauce thickens and is absorbed by vegetables, about 30 seconds. Serve hot, or at room temperature.

Makes 6 servings.

Julienne of Carrots and Zucchini

SAUTEED MUSHROOMS WITH BASIL

Use only fresh mushrooms for this low-calorie dish. When buying mushrooms, squeeze them gently to make sure they're firm, and inspect the undersides to make sure that they are closed and show no gills.

1 pound (455g) large mushrooms, cleaned and cut flat on opposite sides
½ cup (120ml) chicken broth
¼ cup (60ml) dry white vermouth
2 teaspoons lemon juice
1 teaspoon dried basil leaves
¼ teaspoon salt, if desired
⅛ teaspoon freshly ground black pepper
1 tablespoon olive oil
Parsley sprigs, for garnish

Insert *8mm or 6mm slicing disc.* Wedge mushrooms into feed tube in single layer, flat sides down, and use light pressure to process. Repeat until all mushrooms are sliced.

Put broth, vermouth, lemon juice, basil, salt, and pepper into 12-inch (30cm) skillet, bring to boil over high heat, and cook for 2 minutes, stirring occasionally. Add mushrooms and toss well, then reduce heat to medium-high and cook, uncovered, tossing occasionally, until liquid is syrupy and nearly absorbed. Add oil and cook, tossing, just until mushrooms begin to brown, 1 to 2 minutes. Transfer to serving dish and garnish with parsley. Serve hot or warm.

Makes 4 to 6 servings.

SAVORY BUTTER-CRUMB TOMATOES

Use firm, ripe tomatoes for this quick and easy dish, which provides a perfect complement in color and flavor to most meats and fish.

3 large tomatoes (1½ pounds, 680g total)
1 ounce (30g) Parmesan cheese
2 tablespoons parsley leaves, washed and patted dry
¼ cup fine dry unseasoned bread crumbs
¼ teaspoon ground savory
¼ teaspoon salt, if desired
⅛ teaspoon freshly ground black pepper
3 tablespoons melted butter

Remove stems from tomatoes, cut them in half crosswise, and squeeze gently to remove seeds and juice. Set aside.

Adjust oven rack to center position and preheat oven to 375°F. (190°C.). Lightly brush shallow baking dish with olive oil.

Insert *metal blade,* turn on machine, and drop cheese through feed tube. Process until finely chopped, about 35 to 40 seconds. Add parsley and process for 20 seconds. Add remaining ingredients and process for 5 seconds.

Spread equal portions of mixture onto tomato halves. Arrange tomatoes on baking sheet, separating them slightly. (May be prepared to this point hours ahead, covered and set aside.)

Bake until tops of tomatoes are lightly browned, about 15 minutes.

Makes 6 servings.

ZUCCHINI AND RED PEPPER STIR-FRY

An attractive dish with good nutritional value: it is low in calories, high in fiber, and it contains no cholesterol.

⅓ **cup parsley leaves, washed and patted dry**

1 **small garlic clove, peeled**

1 **large onion (8 ounces, 225g), peeled and halved vertically**

1 **tablespoon olive oil**

4 **medium zucchini (1½ pounds, 680g total), trimmed and halved crosswise**

1 **medium red bell pepper (4 ounces, 115g)**

¾ **teaspoon salt, if desired**

⅛ **teaspoon freshly ground black pepper**

¼ **teaspoon dried oregano leaves**

Insert *metal blade*, put parsley in work bowl, and process until finely chopped, about 20 seconds. Remove and set aside.

With *metal blade* in place, turn on machine, drop garlic through feed tube and process until finely chopped, about 10 seconds. Carefully remove metal blade, leaving garlic in work bowl.

Insert *French-fry disc*, stand onion halves vertically in feed tube and use medium pressure to process.

Heat oil in 12-inch (30cm) skillet over medium heat. Add onion and garlic and stir well, then cover and cook over medium-low heat, stirring occasionally, until onion is tender and just beginning to brown, 5 to 8 minutes.

With *French-fry disc* in place, stand zucchini sections vertically in feed tube and use medium pressure to process.

Stand pepper upright on cutting board. Use sharp knife to cut 3 or 4 vertical slices, leaving core and seeds. Halve each section lengthwise.

Insert *6mm slicing disc*. Wedge pepper slices vertically in feed tube and use light pressure to process, producing pepper strips of same size as zucchini strips.

Add zucchini to skillet, increase heat to medium-high, and cook, uncovered, tossing frequently, until zucchini is tender but still has some bite, about 5 minutes. Add salt, pepper, oregano, red pepper, and parsley and cook, tossing frequently, until red pepper is cooked but still crisp, about 2 minutes. Serve at once.

May also be made ahead, chilled, and tossed with vinaigrette to serve as cold side dish or salad.

Makes 6 servings.

VARIATIONS: For an appropriate accompaniment to roast lamb, substitute ¼ teaspoon ground cumin for oregano and ¼ cup (¼ ounce, 7g) fresh cilantro leaves for parsley.

For a very simple variation, add 1 ounce (30g) of freshly grated Parmesan cheese to skillet at very end of cooking. Toss well and serve at once.

JERUSALEM ARTICHOKE SAUTE

Cooked Jerusalem artichokes are tender but crunchy; they have a delicate flavor that is faintly reminiscent of globe artichokes. To preserve their color, the artichokes are first cooked in a mixture called a blanc — a combination of flour, water, and lemon juice. They are then sautéed in olive oil and seasoned with herbs.

⅓	cup parsley leaves, washed and patted dry
2	small garlic cloves, peeled
3	tablespoons olive oil
2	pounds (910g) Jerusalem artichokes
1	quart (1L) water mixed with 2 tablespoons lemon juice
⅓	cup unbleached all-purpose flour (1⅔ ounces, 50g)
5	cups (1.2L) water
3	tablespoons lemon juice
½	teaspoon salt, if desired
¼	teaspoon freshly ground black pepper
½	teaspoon dried oregano leaves

Insert *metal blade*, put parsley in work bowl, and process until finely chopped, about 20 seconds. Remove, cover, and set aside.

With *metal blade* in place, turn on machine, drop garlic through feed tube and process until finely chopped, about 10 seconds. Remove to small cup, add olive oil, and set aside.

Use sharp paring knife to peel artichokes. Drop them promptly into large bowl containing water and lemon-juice mixture. (They discolor quickly in air.) There should be about 1½ pounds (680g).

Put flour in 5-quart (5L) saucepan and add 1 cup (240ml) of water, whisking until smooth. Add remaining 4 cups (1L) of water and 3 tablespoons of lemon juice and whisk to combine.

Insert *French-fry disc*, drain artichokes, and use firm pressure to process them. Add them to saucepan containing flour and water mixture.

Set saucepan over medium-high heat and bring mixture to boil, stirring occasionally. Reduce heat and cook at medium-slow boil, stirring almost constantly during first few minutes to prevent sticking. Continue cooking until artichokes are tender but still slightly firm, 25 to 30 minutes. Test occasionally; do not overcook. (May be prepared to this point 2 or 3 days in advance. Cool, then refrigerate, uncovered, in cooking liquid.) Drain artichokes thoroughly in colander.

Heat garlic and oil mixture in 12-inch (30cm) skillet over medium-high heat. Add artichokes and toss frequently just until they are heated through and begin to brown, about 10 minutes. (They will not brown much because of the preliminary cooking. Also, they tend to stick; if you have a non-stick skillet, use it.) Add salt, pepper, and oregano during final cooking. When cooked, add parsley off heat, toss well, and let dish cool a few minutes before serving.

Makes 6 servings.

JERUSALEM ARTICHOKE CHIPS

Crisp, chewy, and slightly sweet, these make an unusual and surprising vegetable course. Jerusalem artichokes, also known as sunchokes, are increasingly easy to find in supermarkets. Try to select chokes that are not too knobby; they will be easier to clean and they will yield more uniform chips.

> **2 pounds (910g) Jerusalem artichokes, well scrubbed and patted dry**
> **Oil, for deep-frying**
> **Salt, if desired**

Heat 1 inch (2.5cm) of oil to 375°F. (190°C.) in large skillet or deep fryer.

Insert *3mm slicing disc* and use firm pressure to process artichokes. (Process only as many as can cook at one time; this vegetable discolors quickly when exposed to air.)

Put about ¼ of slices into hot oil and cook, stirring once or twice, until they are golden brown and crisp, 2 to 3 minutes. Remove with slotted spoon and drain on paper towels. Keep slices warm in 200°F. (95°C.) oven until all artichokes are processed and cooked. Bring oil back to 375°F. (190°C.) before frying subsequent batches.

Chips may be made a few hours before serving and set aside at room temperature. To reheat, adjust oven rack to center position and preheat oven to 450°F. (230°C.). Place chips on ungreased baking sheet and bake until crisp and heated through, about 5 minutes.

Serve hot, sprinkled lightly with salt, if desired. Makes 6 servings.

CAULIFLOWER AND BACON CASSEROLE

Especially good with roast chicken or turkey and a cooked green vegetable.

> **1 large head cauliflower (about 2 pounds, 910g)**
> **5 slices bacon (5 ounces, 140g total), halved crosswise**
> **¼ cup parsley leaves, washed and dried**
> **14 medium pitted black olives**
> **12 saltine crackers (1⅓ ounces, 40g total)**
> **1 ounce (30g) Parmesan cheese**
> **4 tablespoons butter, chilled**
> **2 ounces (55g) Swiss cheese, chilled**
> **1 medium onion (5 ounces, 140g), peeled and quartered**
> **2 cups (480ml) milk**
> **3 tablespoons unbleached all-purpose flour**
> **¼ teaspoon white pepper**
> **⅛ teaspoon freshly grated nutmeg**
> **¾ teaspoon salt, if desired**

Bring 4 quarts (4L) of unsalted water to rapid boil over high heat. Cut cauliflowerets from head in large clusters that will fit into feed tube.

Insert *8mm or 6mm slicing disc* and use medium pressure to process cauliflower. Drop into boiling water and cook, uncovered, just until tender, 5 to 8 minutes. Drain immediately, plunge into large basin of cold water, and let stand until completely cool. Drain well and set on paper towels; there should be about 5 cups. (May be prepared to this point a day ahead; wrap in paper towels and plastic wrap and refrigerate.) Wipe out work bowl.

Cook bacon in 3-quart (3L) heavy-bottomed saucepan over medium-low heat, stirring occasionally, until all fat has been rendered and bacon is crisp and brown, 10 to 15 minutes. Drain on paper towels and discard fat. Do not wash saucepan.

Insert *metal blade*, put parsley into work bowl, and process until finely chopped, about 20 seconds. Remove and set aside. Put olives into work bowl and process until finely chopped, about 5 seconds. Remove and set aside.

Break saltines into work bowl and process for 20 seconds. With machine running, drop Parmesan cheese through feed tube and process until finely chopped, about 30 seconds. Add half of butter, in 2 pieces, and process until butter is cut into small pieces, about 10 seconds. Remove mixture and set it aside.

Insert *medium shredding disc* and use light pressure to process Swiss cheese. Remove and set aside.

Insert *metal blade*, put onion into work bowl and pulse 3 times. Add onion to milk in 1-quart (1L) saucepan, and bring almost to boil over medium heat. Keep hot until needed, but do not allow to boil.

With *metal blade* in place, put bacon into work bowl and process until finely chopped, about 5 seconds.

Adjust oven rack to upper third position and pre-heat oven to 375°F. (190°C.).

Melt remaining 2 tablespoons of butter over medium heat in saucepan used to cook bacon. Add flour and cook for 2 minutes, whisking constantly. (Mixture will bubble and foam. Flour will turn light brown from bacon, but do not allow it to burn.) Remove pan from heat and pour hot milk mixture through strainer into saucepan. Discard onion. Whisk briskly until smooth. Return pan to medium heat and bring sauce to boil, whisking constantly. Boil until sauce is consistency of medium-thick cream, about 1 minute. Remove from heat.

Add Swiss cheese, pepper, nutmeg, salt, parsley, bacon, and olives to sauce and stir well. Add cauliflower and stir to coat with sauce.

Lightly butter 12 by 8 by 2-inch (30 by 20 by 5cm) shallow baking dish. Spread cauliflower mixture in pan and sprinkle top evenly with cracker mixture. (Cassserole may be prepared to this point a day ahead; cover it loosely with plastic wrap and refrigerate it.)

Bake until casserole is lightly browned on top, about 30 minutes (slightly longer if dish was refrigerated.) For a darker top, place dish under broiler for a few seconds, watching it constantly to prevent burning.

Makes 8 servings.

ZUCCHINI STUFFED WITH ONION

These hearty zucchini boats can be a meal in themselves or can be served as an accompaniment to grilled meats.

3 **large zucchini (1½ pounds, 680g total)**
5 **slices bacon (5 ounces, 140g total), cut crosswise into ¼-inch (6mm) strips**
2 **slices (3 ounces, 85g total) firm white or whole-wheat bread, torn into pieces**
3 **ounces (85g) Swiss cheese, chilled**
1 **small garlic clove, peeled**
1 **medium onion (5 ounces, 140g), peeled and cut into quarters**
1 **medium green bell pepper (6 ounces, 170g), cored, seeded, and cut into 1-inch (2.5cm) pieces**
1 **tablespoon olive oil**
½ **teaspoon dried marjoram leaves *or* ¼ teaspoon dried oregano leaves**
¼ **teaspoon salt, if desired**
⅛ **to ¼ teaspoon freshly ground black pepper**
Tomato sauce (recipe follows)

Wash zucchini, trim off ends, and cut in half lengthwise. Use grapefruit spoon to scoop out pulp, leaving shell about ¼ inch (6mm) thick. Reserve pulp; there should be about 2 cups.

Drop zucchini halves into large pot of rapidly boiling water and cook uncovered for exactly 3 minutes. Drain zucchini well, plunge into basin of cold water, and let stand until completely cool. Drain again, then set on paper towels to drain completely. (Zucchini may be prepared to this point hours ahead; wrap in dry paper towels and plastic wrap and refrigerate.)

Cook bacon slowly in 10-inch (25cm) skillet over medium-low heat, stirring occasionally, until bacon is browned and crisp. Set on paper towels to drain; discard bacon fat but do not wash skillet.

Insert *metal blade*, put bread into work bowl, and process for 10 to 15 seconds to make crumbs. Add bacon and process until finely chopped, 3 to 5 seconds. Remove and set aside.

Insert *medium shredding disc* or *fine shredding disc* and use light pressure to process cheese. Remove and set aside.

Insert *metal blade.* Turn on machine, drop garlic through feed tube, and process for 10 seconds. Add onion and green pepper to work bowl, pulse 3 times, and scrape bowl. (Vegetables should be coarsely chopped; if necessary, pulse once or twice more.) Carefully remove metal blade, leaving vegetables in work bowl.

Insert *medium shredding disc* and use light pressure to process zucchini pulp.

Adjust oven rack to upper third position and preheat oven to 425°F. (220°C.).

Heat oil over medium heat in same skillet used to cook bacon. Add garlic, onion, green pepper, zucchini pulp, marjoram, salt, and pepper to skillet and cook, stirring occasionally, until vegetables are tender and liquid is absorbed, 10 to 15 minutes. Remove from heat and stir in bacon mixture and two-thirds of cheese. Mix well, then stuff filling into zucchini shells and sprinkle with remaining cheese.

Lightly butter small, shallow baking dish and arrange zucchini in it. (Zucchini may be prepared to this point several hours ahead; cover loosely with plastic wrap and refrigerate.)

Bake zucchini until filling is lightly browned on top, about 15 minutes (5 to 10 minutes longer if zucchini were refrigerated). Pass sauce separately.

Makes 6 servings.

TOMATO SAUCE

3 medium tomatoes (1 pound, 455g total)
¼ teaspoon crumbled dried marjoram *or* crumbled dry oregano leaves
¼ cup (60ml) dry white wine *or* chicken broth
Pinch of freshly ground black pepper
¼ teaspoon salt, if desired
¼ teaspoon sugar, if desired

Drop tomatoes into pot of rapidly boiling water and cook for 20 seconds. Drain tomatoes and place them in large pan of cold water. When cool, use sharp paring knife to peel tomatoes. Remove stems, cut tomatoes in half crosswise, and gently squeeze halves to remove seeds.

Insert *medium shredding disc* and use light pressure to process tomatoes. Place in 2-quart (2L) saucepan. Add marjoram, wine, and pepper and cook over medium heat, covered, until mixture boils, about 5 minutes. Uncover pan and increase heat to medium high; continue cooking at medium-fast boil for 5 minutes longer, stirring occasionally.

Insert *metal blade* and pour mixture into work bowl. Process until tomatoes are puréed, about 1 minute. Return mixture to saucepan and bring to boil over medium-high heat. (Sauce should be consistency of thick cream; if necessary, cook uncovered, stirring frequently, until sauce thickens to desired consistency.) Taste and adjust seasoning, adding salt and sugar if needed.

Makes about 1 cup (240ml).

Zucchini Stuffed with Onion

SWEET AND SOUR RED CABBAGE

The vinegar not only provides the sour flavor in this quick and easy dish. It also provides acid, which prevents the cabbage from losing its rich color.

> 2 garlic cloves, peeled
>
> 1 large onion (8 ounces, 225g), peeled and halved lengthwise
>
> 2 tablespoons oil
>
> 1 pound (455g) red cabbage, cut into wedges to fit feed tube
>
> ¼ teaspoon freshly ground black pepper
>
> 1 tablespoon plus 1 teaspoon firmly packed light brown sugar
>
> 5 tablespoons cider vinegar
>
> ½ cup (120ml) chicken broth *or* water
>
> ¼ teaspoon salt, if desired

Insert *metal blade,* turn on machine, and drop garlic through feed tube. Process until minced, about 10 seconds. Leave in work bowl.

Insert *2mm slicing disc,* stand onion halves in feed tube, and use medium pressure to process.

Heat oil in 12-inch (30cm) skillet over medium heat. Add garlic and onion and cook, stirring occasionally, until onion is tender but not browned, about 5 minutes.

Meanwhile, with *2mm slicing disc* in place, wedge cabbage sections into feed tube and use medium pressure to process. Add cabbage to skillet with remaining ingredients and cook over high heat, tossing, until mixture comes to fast boil. Cover, reduce heat to medium-high, and cook for 5 minutes, tossing cabbage often. Mixture should boil vigorously during cooking. Uncover and cook, tossing cabbage frequently, until almost all liquid is absorbed and cabbage is tender but still crisp, about

5 minutes. Taste for seasoning and add more vinegar or sugar if necessary. Serve hot, cold, or at room temperature.

Makes 6 servings.

BAKED VEGETABLE STRATA

This combination of layered vegetables is seasoned with herbs, bound with a light cream and egg mixture, and covered with a cheese and bread-crumb topping. Although it takes a while to prepare, it can be done entirely in advance. Reheating actually improves the flavor.

> 2 slices firm white or whole-wheat bread (2 ounces, 85g total), torn into pieces
>
> 2 tablespoons melted butter
>
> 4 ounces (115g) Fontina cheese, chilled
>
> 1 medium onion (6 ounces, 170g), halved lengthwise
>
> 2 medium potatoes (10 ounces, 285g total), peeled
>
> 1 large green bell pepper (8 ounces, 225g)
>
> 3 medium firm, ripe tomatoes (1 pound, 455g total), with stem ends removed
>
> 1 teaspoon salt, if desired
>
> ¼ teaspoon freshly ground black pepper
>
> ½ teaspoon dried oregano leaves, crumbled
>
> ½ teaspoon dried thyme leaves, crumbled
>
> ¼ cup (60ml) melted butter
>
> ⅓ cup long-grain white rice
>
> ¼ cup (60ml) water
>
> ¾ cup (180ml) light cream
>
> 1 large egg
>
> ⅛ teaspoon freshly grated nutmeg

Adjust oven rack to center position and preheat oven to 350°F. (175°C.). Butter 9 by 9 by 2-inch (22 by 22 by 5cm) baking dish.

Insert *metal blade,* put bread into work bowl, and process for 30 seconds. Add 2 tablespoons melted butter and process for 5 seconds. Remove and set aside.

Insert *medium shredding disc* and use light pressure to process cheese. Remove, cover, and set aside.

Insert *3mm slicing disc,* put onion vertically in feed tube and use medium pressure to process. Remove and set aside.

Lay potatoes horizontally in feed tube and use firm pressure to process. Remove and set aside.

Stand pepper vertically on cutting board. Use sharp knife to cut 3 or 4 vertical slices, leaving core and seeds. Wedge pepper slices horizontally in feed tube and use light pressure to process. Remove and set aside.

Insert *6mm slicing disc* and use light pressure to process tomatoes.

Combine salt, pepper, oregano, and thyme in small bowl and set aside.

Arrange half of tomato slices in bottom of baking dish, drizzle 1 tablespoon of melted butter over them, and sprinkle evenly with about ¼ teaspoon of herb mixture. Arrange half of onions on top and sprinkle with ¼ teaspoon of herb mixture. Arrange half of potato slices over onions, drizzle 1 tablespoon of melted butter over top, and sprinkle with ¼ teaspoon of herb mixture. Arrange half of peppers on top and sprinkle with ¼ teaspoon of herb mixture. Distribute rice evenly over peppers.

Continue making layers with remaining vegetables in this order: onions, potatoes, peppers, and tomatoes. Sprinkle ¼ teaspoon of herb mixture over each layer and drizzle butter over potato and tomato layers only. Pour water evenly over vegetables, cover dish tightly with foil, and bake for 90 minutes.

Rinse work bowl and shake out excess water. Insert *metal blade* and process cream, egg, and nutmeg for 5 seconds. Pour mixture over vegetables, return dish to oven and bake, uncovered, for 20 minutes.

Sprinkle top evenly with cheese, then with bread crumbs. Bake, uncovered, until top is golden brown, about 10 minutes. Let stand for 10 minutes before serving. To serve, cut into squares with sharp knife.

(May be reheated next day in a preheated 325°F. (160°C.) oven until heated through, 20 to 25 minutes.)

Makes 4 to 6 main-course servings, or 8 servings as side dish.

BREAD

In bread-making, the food processor truly excels. It mixes and kneads yeast doughs in minutes, with consistently good results. It's best to weigh the flour for bread. If you don't have a scale, use the method described on page 174.

To adapt yeast-bread recipes for the food processor: 1) Use ⅓ cup (80ml) of liquid for each cup of flour (5 ounces, 140g). 2) Proof yeast in small amount of warm liquid, then add remaining liquid, which should be cold; dough warms when kneaded and cold liquid prevents overheating that can kill yeast cells. 3) Put dry ingredients in work bowl first. With motor running, add liquid in slow, steady stream only as fast as flour absorbs it. 4) When dough gathers into ball that cleans work bowl, knead it for 60 to 90 seconds (breads that use rye or 100% whole-wheat flour tend to stick as they're kneaded.)

In a recipe that calls for 3½ or more cups of flour, (about 15 ounces or 425g) use the dough blade. The dough blade kneads better, doing a more thorough job of activating gluten, the ingredient that gives bread its elasticity.

From top: Challah with Sesame Seeds; 43% Whole-Wheat Bread Slices; Russian Black Bread; 43% Whole-Wheat Loaf; Whole-Grain Muffins; Challah with Poppy Seeds; Whole-Wheat Pita Pockets

WHITE BREAD WITH WHEAT GERM

Buttermilk and wheat germ add flavor and nutritional value to this light all-purpose bread.

1 tablespoon active dry yeast
½ teaspoon sugar
¼ cup (60ml) warm water (105 to 115°F., 40 to 46°C.)
1 large egg
¾ cup (180ml) cold buttermilk
3 cups bread flour (15 ounces, 425g)
3 tablespoons butter, chilled and cut into 3 pieces
1 teaspoon salt, if desired
½ cup untoasted wheat germ (2 ounces, 55g)
1½ tablespoons sugar

Sprinkle yeast and ½ teaspoon of sugar over water in 2-cup (480ml) measure. Stir well and let stand until yeast is dissolved and mixture is very foamy, about 10 minutes. Use fork to blend egg lightly into yeast mixture and stir in buttermilk.

Insert *dough blade* or *metal blade,* put remaining ingredients into work bowl, and process for 30 seconds. With machine running, pour liquid through feed tube in slow, steady stream, taking 20 to 30 seconds to do so. Once dough forms ball, process for 1 minute to knead. Dough should clean sides of work bowl. If dough is wet and sticks to side of bowl, add flour by tablespoons, with machine running; if dough is too dry, add water by teaspoons. Dough should be soft, smooth, elastic, and slightly sticky when kneading is complete.

Transfer dough to oiled 3-quart (3L) bowl and turn to coat all over with oil. Cover tightly with plastic wrap and let rise at room temperature until almost tripled in volume, about 1½ hours.

Grease standard loaf pan (8½ by 4½ by 2¾ inches, 21 by 11 by 7cm). Punch down risen dough to deflate it and shape into loaf. Place in pan and cover loosely with lightly oiled plastic wrap. Let rise at room temperature until center of loaf has risen 1½ to 2 inches (4 to 5cm) above rim, about 1½ hours.

Adjust oven rack to lower third position and preheat oven to 375°F. (190°C.). Uncover loaf and bake until bread is well browned and sounds hollow when rapped on bottom, 35 to 40 minutes. Turn loaf out onto rack to cool.

Makes one 1½-pound (680g) loaf.

WHITE CORNELL BREAD

Cornell Bread, developed many years ago at Cornell University by nutrition researcher Dr. Clive McCay, has inspired many variations. A true Cornell Bread must include these three ingredients, which boost the nutritive value of refined flour: wheat germ, soy flour, and non-fat dry milk. The bread has a fine, soft texture and pale golden crumb; it toasts well and is excellent for sandwiches.

1 tablespoon active dry yeast
½ teaspoon sugar
⅓ cup (80ml) warm water (105 to 115°F., 40 to 46°C.)
2 tablespoons honey
1 large egg
⅓ cup (80ml) cold milk
2½ cups bread flour (12½ ounces, 355g)
3 tablespoons soy flour
¼ cup untoasted wheat germ (1 ounce, 30g)
⅓ cup instant nonfat dry milk
1 teaspoon salt, if desired
2 tablespoons butter, chilled and cut into 2 pieces

Sprinkle yeast and sugar over water in 2-cup (480ml)

measure. Stir well and let stand until yeast is dissolved and mixture is very foamy, about 10 minutes. Stir honey into yeast mixture until dissolved, then add egg; use fork to mix until combined. Stir in milk.

Insert *dough blade* or *metal blade*, put remaining ingredients into work bowl, and process for 30 seconds. With machine running, pour liquid mixture through feed tube in slow, steady stream, taking about 20 to 30 seconds to do so. Once dough forms ball, process for 1½ minutes to knead. Dough should clean sides of work bowl. If dough is wet and sticks to sides, add bread flour by tablespoons, with machine running; if dough is too dry, add milk by teaspoons. Dough should be soft, smooth, and elastic when kneading is complete.

Transfer dough to oiled 3-quart (3L) bowl and turn it to coat all over with oil. Cover tightly with plastic wrap and let rise at room temperature until almost tripled in volume, about 1½ hours.

Grease standard loaf pan (8½ by 4½ by 2¾ inches, 21 by 11 by 7cm). Punch down risen dough to deflate it and shape into loaf. Place into pan and cover loosely with lightly oiled plastic wrap. Let rise at room temperature until center of loaf has risen almost 2 inches (5cm) above rim, about 1½ hours.

Adjust oven rack to lower third position and preheat oven to 375°F. (190°C.). Uncover loaf and bake until bread is well browned and sounds hollow when rapped on bottom, 35 to 40 minutes. If loaf seems to be browning too much, cover loosely with foil during last 10 minutes of baking. Turn loaf out onto rack to cool.

Makes one 1½-pound (680g) loaf.

43% WHOLE-WHEAT BREAD

This is one of the best and easiest all-purpose breads. If your food processor is larger than the standard size, you can make two loaves at once. Just double all the ingredients except the yeast and granulated sugar. (First, check the instruction manual for your processor to be sure you don't exceed the recommended amount of flour.)

> **1 tablespoon active dry yeast**
> ½ **teaspoon sugar**
> **3 tablespoons warm water (105 to 115°F., 40 to 46°C.)**
> **2 cups bread flour (10 ounces, 285g)**
> 1½ **cups whole-wheat flour (7½ ounces, 215g)**
> 1½ **teaspoons salt**
> **2 tablespoons firmly packed light-brown sugar**
> **2 tablespoons butter, chilled and cut into 2 pieces**
> **1 cup (240ml) cold water**

Sprinkle yeast and sugar over warm water in 1-cup (240ml) glass measure. Stir and let stand until yeast is dissolved and mixture is foamy, about 10 minutes.

Insert *dough blade* or *metal blade,* put flours, salt, brown sugar, and butter into work bowl, and process for 20 seconds. Add yeast mixture, start machine, and add water through feed tube in steady stream only as fast as flour absorbs it. When dough forms ball, process for 1½ minutes to knead. Dough should clean sides and bottom of work bowl. If dough is too dry, add water by teaspoons, with machine running; if it is too wet, add bread flour by tablespoons. Dough should be slightly sticky and very elastic when kneading is complete. Pull and stretch dough between your hands to test consistency; if necessary, return dough to work bowl to process a few seconds more.

Transfer dough to lightly floured 1-gallon (4L) plastic bag. Squeeze out air and seal bag tightly, allowing room for dough to rise. Set aside to rise at room temperature until dough has almost tripled in volume, 1½ to 2 hours. (Alternatively, place dough in refrigerator for several hours or overnight; it will rise slowly in the cold.) Punch down risen dough and shape into loaf. Place in greased 9 by 5 by 3-inch (23 by 13 by 8cm) loaf pan, cover loosely with lightly oiled plastic wrap and towel, and let rise in warm place until dough is light and almost tripled in size, 1 to 1½ hours. Center of loaf should be about 2 inches (5cm) above rim.

Adjust oven rack to lower third position and preheat oven to 375°F. (190°C.). Uncover loaf and bake until it sounds hollow when tapped on bottom, about 35 minutes. Turn loaf out onto rack to cool.

Makes one 1½-pound (680g) loaf.

WHOLE-WHEAT SUNFLOWER BREAD

Ground sunflower kernels give special flavor to this firm but not dense bread. They also slow the action of yeast. To get around this problem, I made a "sponge", which is a mixture of flour, yeast, and water that is allowed to rise before the addition of the sunflower kernels and other ingredients.

1 tablespoon active dry yeast
½ teaspoon sugar
½ cup (120ml) warm water (105 to 115°F., 40 to 46°C.)
½ cup raw, unsalted sunflower kernels
1 cup whole-wheat flour (5 ounces, 140g)
2 cups bread flour (10 ounces, 285g)
¼ cup untoasted wheat germ (1 ounce, 30g)
1 teaspoon salt, if desired
2 tablespoons butter, cut into 4 pieces
¼ cup (60ml) honey
1 large egg
⅓ cup cold mashed potatoes, packed into dry measure

Sprinkle yeast and sugar over water in small bowl or 1-cup (240ml) glass measure. Stir and let stand until yeast is dissolved and mixture is very foamy, about 10 minutes.

Meanwhile, insert *metal blade*, put sunflower kernels into work bowl, and process until finely chopped, about 2 minutes. Remove and set aside. Put whole-wheat flour into work bowl, pour in yeast mixture, and process for 1 minute. A ball of dough will form; it will clean sides of work bowl at first but dough will begin to stick to sides of bowl during last few seconds of processing. Scrape dough into 1-quart (1L) glass measure or bowl; it will be soft and slightly sticky. Cover dough tightly with plastic wrap and let rise at room temperature for 1 hour or longer; it will reach almost to top of bowl.

With *dough blade* or *metal blade* in place, put bread flour, sunflower kernels, wheat germ, salt, butter, and honey into work bowl and pulse 5 times in pulses lasting 1 second each. Scrape work bowl well and pulse 3 more times.

Stir down risen dough to deflate it and use fork to mix in egg and mashed potatoes. Batter will be very thick. Scrape it onto dry ingredients in work bowl.

Start machine. Dough should form ball within 30 seconds and clean sides of work bowl. If dough is too dry, add tablespoon of water through feed tube; if it is too wet, add bread flour by tablespoons. Once dough forms ball, process for 1½ to 2 minutes. Dough will be elastic and slightly sticky at end of kneading.

Transfer dough to oiled 3-quart (3L) bowl and turn it to coat all over with oil. Cover bowl tightly with plastic wrap and let dough rise at room temperature until almost tripled in volume, about 1½ hours.

Use solid shortening to grease 8½ by 4½ by 2¾-inch (21 by 11 by 7cm) loaf pan. Turn dough out onto unfloured surface and pat it into rectangle about 9 by 12 inches (22 by 30cm). Roll dough up tightly, starting at short side, and pinch seam to seal it. Turn roll seam side down, pinch ends and tuck them under. Place loaf in pan, cover loosely with lightly oiled plastic wrap, and let rise at room temperature until center of loaf has risen 1½ to 2 inches (4 to 5cm) above rim, 1½ to 2 hours. Tears may develop on top or sides of dough; this is all right.

Adjust oven rack to lower third position and preheat oven to 375°F. (190°C.). Uncover loaf and bake until it is well browned and sounds hollow when rapped on bottom, 35 to 40 minutes. (This bread will not rise much in oven.) Turn loaf out onto rack to cool.

Makes one 1½-pound (680g) loaf.

WHOLE-WHEAT PITA POCKETS

These flat breads from the Near East enjoy great popularity throughout the United States, where they are often sliced crosswise and stuffed with sandwich filling. No special equipment is necessary to make pita bread, but it does take time.

1 tablespoon active dry yeast
½ teaspoon sugar
⅔ cup (160ml) warm water (105 to 115°F., 40 to 46°C.)
¾ cup (180ml) cold water
1 tablespoon olive oil
1¾ cups whole-wheat flour (8¾ ounces, 250g)
2 cups bread flour (10 ounces, 285g)
1 teaspoon salt, if desired

Sprinkle yeast and sugar over warm water in 2-cup (480ml) measure. Stir well and let stand until yeast is dissolved and mixture is very foamy, about 10 minutes. Stir in cold water and olive oil.

Insert *dough blade* or *metal blade* and put flours and salt into work bowl. With machine running, pour liquid through feed tube in slow, steady stream, taking about 20 to 30 seconds to do so. Once dough forms ball, process for 1 minute to knead. Dough should clean sides of work bowl during kneading. If dough is too wet, add bread flour by tablespoons, with machine running; if it is too dry, add water by teaspoons. Dough should be fairly firm, smooth, elastic, and only very slightly sticky when kneading is complete.

Transfer dough to ungreased 3- to 4-quart (3 to 4L) bowl, cover tightly with plastic wrap, and let rise at room temperature until it is slightly more than doubled in volume, about 1½ hours. Punch down dough to deflate it, reshape into ball, and replace in bowl. Cover tightly with plastic wrap and let rise again at room temperature until doubled in volume,

about 1 hour.

Turn dough out onto floured surface and pat out air bubbles. Divide dough into 12 equal pieces and shape each piece into a ball, pinching together at bottom. Place balls seam sides down on floured surface, cover loosely with cloth, and let rest for 10 minutes.

Roll each ball on floured surface into 5-inch (13cm) circle. Place circles on floured board, cover with cloth, and let rest for 20 to 25 minutes.

Meanwhile, adjust oven rack to lower third position and place ungreased, large heavy baking sheet on rack. Preheat oven to 500 or 550°F. (260 or

Shaping dough into ball　　　*Pinching edges together*

290°C.). This will take about 20 minutes.

Remove hot baking sheet from oven and quickly arrange 4 to 6 circles of dough on sheet, leaving about ½ inch (12mm) between them. Quickly return sheet to oven and bake until pitas are puffed up and very slightly browned, 3 to 5 minutes. Use wide metal spatula to transfer pitas to racks; cover loosely with dry towel.

Repeat with remaining circles of dough. When pitas are cool enough to handle, collapse them gently between your palms. When they are completely cool, wrap pitas airtight.

(Pitas may be frozen. To refresh, wrap several

together loosely in foil and set on baking sheet. Place in center of preheated 325°F. (160°C.) oven until they are thoroughly warmed, 10 to 15 minutes.)

Makes 12 pitas.

CRACKED-WHEAT BREAD

Apple juice is used to soften the cracked wheat (bulgur); it adds a pleasant hint of sweetness to this healthful all-purpose bread. This is my adaptation of a recipe that appeared in the Detroit Free Press.

⅓ **cup coarse bulgur**
⅔ **cup (160ml) unsweetened apple juice**
1 **tablespoon active dry yeast**
½ **teaspoon sugar**
¼ **cup (60ml) warm water (105 to 115°F., 40 to 46°C.)**
2 **tablespoons honey**
⅓ **cup (80ml) cold water**
2 **cups bread flour (10 ounces, 285g)**
½ **cup whole-wheat flour (2½ ounces, 70g)**
1 **teaspoon salt, if desired**
2 **tablespoons butter, at room temperature, cut into 2 pieces**

Put bulgur and apple juice into 1-quart (1L) saucepan and bring mixture to boil over medium-high heat. Reduce heat to low and cook, uncovered, at slow boil, stirring occasionally, until bulgur is tender and juice is absorbed, about 10 minutes. Set aside and cool until mixture is barely warm. (Bulgur may be prepared 3 days ahead and refrigerated.)

Sprinkle yeast and sugar over warm water in 1-cup (240ml) glass measure. Stir and let stand until yeast is dissolved and mixture is very foamy, about 10 minutes. Add honey and stir until dissolved, then mix in cold water.

Insert *dough blade* or *metal blade*, put flours, salt, and butter into work bowl, and process for 15 seconds. Add cooled bulgur and process just to mix, 5 seconds. With machine running, gradually pour yeast mixture through feed tube as fast as flour absorbs it; this will take about 20 seconds. Dough will soon form ball that cleans sides of work bowl. If dough is too moist, add bread flour by tablespoons, with machine running; if dough is too dry, add water by teaspoons. Once dough forms ball, process for 1½ minutes. Dough should be soft, very elastic, and slightly sticky.

Place dough in lightly oiled bowl, cover with plastic wrap, and let rise at room temperature until doubled in size, about 1 hour. Punch down risen dough to deflate it and shape into loaf. Place in greased 8½ by 4½ by 2¾-inch (21 by 11 by 7cm) loaf pan, cover loosely with lightly oiled plastic wrap, and let rise at room temperature until center of loaf is 1½ to 2 inches (4 to 5cm) above rim, about 1½ hours.

Adjust oven rack to lower third position and preheat oven to 375°F. (190°C.). Uncover loaf and bake until bread is golden brown and sounds hollow when tapped on bottom, 35 to 40 minutes. Turn out onto rack to cool.

Makes one 1½-pound (680g) loaf.

RUSSIAN BLACK BREAD

This is a dense and chewy loaf. Dark rye flour (called pumpernickel in some regions) gives the bread its wonderful texture. The flour is usually available in health-food stores; if you are unable to find it, substitute medium rye flour.

1 tablespoon butter
1 cup (240ml) water
2 tablespoons light molasses
1 tablespoon cider vinegar
1 tablespoon active dry yeast
1½ cups bread flour (7½ ounces, 215g)
1 cup medium rye flour (5 ounces, 140g)
½ cup dark rye flour (2½ ounces, 70g)
½ cup All-Bran or Bran Buds cereal
2 tablespoons unsweetened cocoa
1 teaspoon powdered instant coffee
½ teaspoon salt, if desired
¼ teaspoon fennel seed, crushed
Cornmeal, for baking sheet
½ teaspoon cornstarch combined with 2 tablespoons water

Melt butter in 1-quart (1L) saucepan over low heat. Stir in water, molasses, and vinegar and heat until warm (105 to 115°F., 40 to 46°C.). Remove from heat, stir in yeast, and set aside until yeast is dissolved, about 10 minutes.

Insert *dough blade* or *metal blade.* Put flours, cereal, cocoa, coffee powder, salt, and fennel seed into work bowl and process for about 20 seconds.

With machine running, pour yeast mixture through feed tube in slow, steady stream, taking 20 to 30 seconds to do so. After dough forms ball and cleans sides of work bowl, process for 45 seconds more to knead. If dough is too sticky, add additional bread flour by tablespoons, with machine running; if it is too dry, add water by teaspoons.

Transfer dough to lightly floured 1-gallon (4L) plastic bag and seal tightly, leaving space for dough to rise. Set aside in a warm place (75 to 80°F., 24 to 27°C.) and allow it to rise until doubled in volume, about 1½ hours.

Sprinkle baking sheet lightly with cornmeal and set aside.

Punch down dough in bag, then remove and knead between your hands for about 30 seconds. Shape into ball about 5 inches (13cm) in diameter and place on baking sheet. Cover with oiled plastic wrap and set aside in warm place to rise until almost doubled in volume, about 1 hour.

Adjust oven rack to lower third position and pre-heat oven to 400°F. (205°C.).

Brush top of dough lightly with a little cornstarch and water mixture. Use sharp knife to make 3 parallel slashes across top.

Bake for 10 minutes at 400°F. (205°C.). Brush again with cornstarch mixture, reduce temperature to 375°F. (190°C.), and bake until loaf sounds hollow when rapped on bottom, 20 to 25 minutes. Remove to wire rack to cool.

Makes one 1-pound (455g) loaf.

CHALLAH

The traditional bread of the Jewish Sabbath is a perfect egg bread for any occasion. The texture and flavor of the dough is developed by two preliminary rises. This bread makes sensational French toast.

Rolling dough into strands   *Braiding three strands*

1 tablespoon active dry yeast
½ teaspoon sugar
¼ cup (60ml) warm water (105 to 115°F., 40 to 46°C.)
¼ cup (60ml) oil, preferably safflower, sunflower, or peanut
1 large egg
½ cup (120ml) cold water
3 cups unbleached all-purpose flour (15 ounces, 425g)
1½ teaspoons salt, if desired
1 egg yolk beaten with 2 teaspoons water
Poppy seeds or sesame seeds

Sprinkle yeast and sugar over warm water in 2-cup (480ml) measure. Stir well and let stand until yeast is dissolved and mixture is very foamy, about 10 minutes. Use fork to blend oil, egg, and cold water lightly into yeast mixture.

Insert *dough blade* or *metal blade* and put flour and salt into work bowl. Start machine and pour liquid through feed tube in slow, steady stream, taking 20 to 30 seconds to do so. Once dough forms ball, process for 1 minute to knead. Dough should clean sides of work bowl. If dough is too wet, add flour by tablespoons, with machine running; if it is too dry, add water by teaspoons. Dough should be soft, smooth, elastic, and not sticky when kneading is complete.

Transfer dough to ungreased 3-quart (3L) bowl, cover tightly with plastic wrap, and let rise at room temperature until double in volume, about 1 hour. Turn dough out onto lightly floured surface and pat

out air bubbles. Then gently reshape dough into ball and replace in bowl. Cover tightly with plastic wrap and let dough rise at room temperature a second time until it is doubled in volume, 1 to 1½ hours.

Grease baking sheet and set aside.

To shape dough, turn it out onto lightly floured surface and pat out air bubbles. Divide dough into thirds and roll each piece into strand 15 inches long (38cm). (If dough resists handling, cover and let rest at room temperature another 10 minutes to relax gluten.) Braid three strands of dough, pinching ends and tucking them under braid. Braid will be about 12 inches (30cm) long.

Transfer to baking sheet, cover loosely with lightly oiled plastic wrap, and let rise at room temperature until dough is light and doubled in size, 1 to 1½ hours.

Adjust oven rack to lower third position and preheat oven to 375°F. (190°C.). Brush braid with egg glaze and sprinkle with poppy or sesame seeds.

Bake until bread is rich golden-brown and sounds hollow when rapped on bottom, about 35 minutes. Remove from cookie sheet and cool on rack.

Makes one 1½ pound (680g) braid.

CINNAMON ROLLS

These light rolls have an intense cinnamon flavor and are best when very fresh. They are the result of years of experimentation in developing the ultimate cinnamon roll.

Dough

- 1 tablespoon active dry yeast
- ½ teaspoon sugar
- ¼ cup (60ml) warm water (105 to 115°F., 40 to 46°C.)
- 1 large egg
- 1 teaspoon vanilla
- ½ cup (120ml) cold milk
- 3 cups unbleached all-purpose flour (15 ounces, 425g)
- ⅓ cup sugar (2½ ounces, 70g)
- ¾ teaspoon salt, if desired
- 4 tablespoons unsalted butter (2 ounces, 55g), chilled and cut into 4 pieces

Filling

- ½ cup pecan halves or large pieces (4 ounces, 115g)
- ¾ cup raisins (3⅓ ounces, 95g)
- ⅔ cup firmly packed light-brown sugar (5½ ounces, 155g)
- 2 teaspoons cinnamon
- 6 tablespoons unsalted butter (3 ounces, 85g), at room temperature, cut into 4 pieces
- 1 teaspoon vanilla

Glaze

- 1 large egg yolk
- 2 teaspoons heavy cream or milk

Sprinkle yeast and ½ teaspoon of sugar over warm water in 2-cup (480ml) measure. Stir well and let

stand until yeast is dissolved and mixture is very foamy, about 10 minutes. Use fork to blend egg lightly into yeast mixture; then stir in vanilla and milk.

Insert *dough blade* or *metal blade,* put remaining ingredients into work bowl, and process for 30 seconds. With machine running, pour liquid mixture through feed tube in slow, steady stream, taking 20 to 30 seconds to do so. Once dough forms ball, process for 45 seconds to knead. Dough should clean sides of work bowl. If dough is too wet, add flour by tablespoons, with machine running; if it is too dry, add milk by teaspoons. Dough should be soft, smooth, elastic, and slightly sticky when kneading is complete.

Transfer dough to oiled 3-quart (3L) bowl and turn to coat all over with oil. Cover bowl tightly with plastic wrap and let dough rise at room temperature until it has doubled in volume, about 1½ hours. Wipe out work bowl.

Rolling up filled dough   *Pinching seam to seal*

To make filling, insert *metal blade,* put pecans into work bowl, and process until nuts are coarsely chopped, about 5 seconds. Remove and set aside.

With *metal blade* in place, put raisins, brown sugar, and cinnamon into work bowl and process just to chop raisins coarsely, about 10 seconds. Add butter and vanilla and process for 10 seconds. Then add chopppped pecans and pulse 5 times to combine mixture. Set filling aside, covered.

Butter 15½ by 10½ by 1-inch (40 by 25 by 2.5cm) jelly-roll pan and set aside. Deflate risen dough and put it back in bowl; cover tightly and refrigerate for 1 to 2 hours or longer. (Dough is soft and easier to handle when chilled.) Turn chilled dough out onto lightly floured surface. Roll into rectangle approximately 10 by 15 inches (25 by 38cm), with one of long sides near you. Use narrow metal spatula to distribute filling mixture evenly over dough, covering all but ½ inch (12mm) along long edge farthest from you.

Cutting roll into slices

Roll dough up tightly, starting with long side nearest you, and pinch seam securely to seal it. Turn roll seam side down and use very sharp knife to cut roll into 1-inch (2.5cm) slices. Place slices on prepared pan, cut sides up, leaving ½ to 1 inch (12 to 25mm) between them. Cover loosely with towel and let rise in warm place (80 to 90°F., 27 to 32°C.) until rolls are light and doubled in size, about 1 hour. Rolls should be touching one another.

Adjust oven rack to center position and preheat oven to 350°F. (175°C.).

To make glaze, use fork to beat ingredients together in small bowl. Brush mixture evenly over risen rolls. Place pan in oven and bake until rolls are golden brown and toothpick inserted into thickest part comes out clean and dry, 20 to 25 minutes. Let rolls cool slightly in baking pan, then use 2 forks to separate them. Serve very warm.

(To freeze rolls, cool completely and wrap airtight in foil. To reheat, place wrapped frozen rolls on baking sheet in preheated 350°F. (175°C.) oven until they are thoroughly warmed, about 15 minutes.)

Makes 15 rolls.

VARIATION: For more traditional cinnamon rolls, brush 2 tablespoons melted unsalted butter over rolled-out dough to within ½ inch (12mm) of farthest side. Sprinkle evenly with mixture of 2 tablespoons sugar and 2 teaspoons cinnamon. Continue with above instructions, through baking. A few minutes before rolls are done, prepare powdered-sugar glaze. Insert *metal blade* and put 1¼ cups confectioners' sugar (5 ounces, 140g), ¾ teaspoon vanilla, and 2 tablespoons hot water into work bowl. Process until mixture is smooth, about 5 seconds. Glaze should be fairly thick; adjust consistency if necessary with more confectioners' sugar or hot water. When rolls come out of oven, brush tops with glaze. Serve warm. Rolls may also be frozen and reheated as described above.

FRENCH-BREAD ROLLS

Two long, slow rises before shaping give these rolls the characteristic chewiness and flavor of authentic French bread.

> 1 tablespoon active dry yeast
> ½ teaspoon sugar
> ¼ cup (60ml) warm water (105 to 115°F., 40 to 46°C.)
> 1¼ cups (300ml) cold water
> 2 cups unbleached all-purpose flour (10 ounces, 280g)
> 1½ cups bread flour (7½ ounces, 210g)
> 1½ teaspoons salt

Sprinkle yeast and sugar over warm water in 2-cup (480ml) glass measure. Stir well and set aside at room temperature until yeast is dissolved and mixture is very foamy and bubbly, about 10 minutes. Stir in cold water.

Insert *dough blade* or *metal blade.* Put both flours and salt in work bowl and process for 3 seconds. With machine running, add yeast mixture through feed tube in steady stream as fast as flour absorbs it. This will take 20 to 30 seconds. When dough gathers into ball, process for 60 seconds to knead. Dough should clean sides of work bowl as it is kneaded. Adjust consistency of dough with a bit more flour or water, if necessary. After processing, dough will be smooth and elastic but sticky; this is as it should be. Some stickiness will disappear after you work dough between your hands for a few seconds.

Transfer dough to clean, ungreased 3-quart (3L) glass bowl. Cover securely with plastic wrap and set aside at room temperature until dough has tripled in bulk and reaches top of bowl; this might take about 3 hours. Dislodge dough from bowl with plastic scraper and turn out onto lightly floured surface. Pat dough to remove air bubbles, reshape dough into ball, and replace in bowl. Cover tightly with plastic wrap and let dough rise again at room temperature until it is slightly more than double in bulk, about 2 hours. (Dough can rise in refrigerator both times, if necessary.)

Turn dough out onto lightly floured surface and divide into 12 equal pieces. Shape each into round or oval roll and place, seam side down, onto lightly greased 14 by 17-inch (36 by 43cm) baking sheet, leaving about 1 to 2 inches (2.5 to 5cm) of space between rolls. Cover loosely with lightly oiled plastic wrap and kitchen towel and set pan in warm place (80 to 85°F., 26 to 30°C.) until rolls are light and doubled in size, about 45 minutes.

Adjust oven rack to center position and preheat oven to 450°F. (230°C.).

If desired, slash tops of risen rolls at angle with sharp blade in one or two places. Use spray mister to spray rolls lightly with water and place pan into oven immediately. In three minutes, quickly open oven door and spray again. Repeat spraying after another 5 minutes. Bake about 15 to 18 minutes total, until rolls are crusty and rich golden brown. Bottoms should sound hollow when tapped. Turn off oven, prop oven door open a few inches and let rolls stand in oven another 5 minutes. Transfer rolls to cooling racks and let stand until completely cool.

Makes 12 large rolls.

NOTE: These rolls may be made ahead and frozen for up to 1 month. To reheat, place frozen rolls on baking sheet in 400°F. (205°C.) oven for 10 minutes. Let them cool a bit, then serve. Rolls seem even crustier and more flavorful when prepared this way.

WHOLE-GRAIN MUFFINS

These muffins, which are light and not too sweet, are made with whole-wheat flour, wheat germ, and rolled oats. The batter can be stored in the refrigerator for up to a month, so you can bake them whenever you like. If the batter separates, stir it thoroughly to combine the ingredients.

1 cup whole-wheat flour (5 ounces, 140g)
2 tablespoons wheat germ, toasted or untoasted
1½ teaspoons baking soda
½ teaspoon salt, if desired
¼ cup firmly packed light-brown sugar (2 ounces, 55g)
¼ cup granulated sugar (1¾ ounces, 50g)
½ cup raisins (2½ ounces, 70g)
4 tablespoons unsalted butter (2 ounces, 55g), chilled and cut into 4 pieces
1½ cups quick-cooking rolled oats (4½ ounces, 125g; not instant oatmeal)
½ cup (120ml) boiling orange juice
1 large egg
½ teaspoon vanilla
1 cup (240ml) buttermilk

Adjust oven rack to center position and preheat oven to 375°F. (190°C.). Generously butter 15 standard-size muffin cups (2¾ inches, 7cm across and 1⅛ inches, 3cm deep) and set aside.

Insert *metal blade.* Put flour, wheat germ, baking soda, salt, sugars, and raisins into work bowl and process until raisins are coarsely chopped, about 30 seconds. Add butter and process for 10 seconds. Transfer mixture to large sheet of waxed paper and set aside.

With *metal blade* in place, put oats into work bowl and process until finely chopped, about 30 seconds. Pour orange juice in circle over oatmeal and pulse rapidly 3 times, just to combine; do not over-process. Add egg, vanilla, and buttermilk and pulse rapidly 4 or 5 times. Scrape work bowl. Pour half of flour mixture in circle over oatmeal mixture and pulse twice only. Scrape work bowl, add remaining flour mixture, and pulse twice, using plastic spatula to complete mixing if necessary.

Fill prepared muffin cups about ¾ full and place in oven. (Allowing them to stand for 20 minutes before baking will produce lighter muffins.) Bake until tops are rich brown and muffins spring back when lightly pressed, 20 to 25 minutes. Turn muffins out onto racks to cool. Serve warm.

Makes 15 muffins.

PUMPKIN DATE-NUT LOAF

This is a large, dark and very moist quick bread, with a variety of well blended flavors.

8 ounces (225g) pitted dates
1 cup sifted rye flour (4 ounces, 115g)
1½ cups sifted unbleached all-purpose flour (6 ounces, 170g)
2 teaspoons baking soda
2 teaspoons cinnamon
½ teaspoon allspice
½ teaspoon ground ginger
½ teaspoon powdered instant coffee
½ teaspoon salt, if desired
1 cup firmly packed light or dark-brown sugar (8 ounces, 225g)
½ cup granulated sugar (3¾ ounces, 105g)
Zest of 1 large orange
2 large eggs
1 teaspoon vanilla
½ cup (120ml) oil, preferably safflower, sunflower, or corn
1 1-pound (455g) can solid-pack pumpkin
¾ cup walnuts (3 ounces, 90g)

Adjust oven rack to lower third position and preheat oven to 350°F. (175°C.). Generously grease 10-cup (2.4L) loaf pan (11 by 4½ by 2¾ inches, 28 by 11 by 7cm) and dust it lightly with flour; tap out excess.

Pick through dates to be sure there are no pits. Place dates in single layer on small shallow pan and freeze for 15 minutes only.

Insert *metal blade.* Put flours, baking soda, cinnamon, allspice, ginger, instant coffee, and salt into work bowl and process for 5 seconds. Transfer to medium mixing bowl. Return 1 cup to work bowl along with dates. Pulse 5 times, then process continuously to chop dates coarsely, about 10 seconds. Transfer date mixture to bowl with remaining dry ingredients. Mix together well and set aside.

With *metal blade* in place, put sugars and orange zest into work bowl and process until zest is finely chopped, 1 to 2 minutes. Add eggs and vanilla and process until mixture is fluffy, about 1 minute. With machine running, add oil through feed tube in thin stream, taking about 30 seconds to do so. Process another 30 seconds.

Add pumpkin by spoonfuls in ring over egg mixture and process for 10 seconds. Scrape work bowl, then add walnuts and date mixture. Pulse 3 times, scrape work bowl well, and pulse 1 more time if necessary to incorporate dry ingredients. Do not overprocess.

Turn batter into prepared pan. Shake pan to level batter; use spatula to smooth top.

Bake until cake tester inserted in center comes out clean and barely dry, 70 to 75 minutes. Loaf will be rich brown and may have developed crack on top. Cool in pan on rack for 15 minutes, then turn out onto rack. When completely cool, wrap loaf airtight and let stand overnight before serving.

Makes 1 loaf.

BANANA BRAN BREAD

This moist bread is flecked with pieces of dried apricots. Wrapped airtight, it keeps well at room temperature for several days. I find it especially good spread with cream cheese.

1½ cups sifted unbleached all-purpose flour (6 ounces, 170g)
½ teaspoon salt, if desired
1 teaspoon baking powder
½ teaspoon baking soda
½ cup dried apricots (3 ounces, 85g)
¾ cup sugar (5½ ounces, 155g)
2 large eggs
2 teaspoons vanilla
1 stick unsalted butter (4 ounces, 115g), at room temperature, cut into 6 pieces
4 small, very ripe bananas (1 pound, 455g total), peeled and cut into 1-inch (2.5cm) chunks
1 cup All-Bran cereal
¾ cup pecans (2½ ounces, 70g)

Adjust oven rack to lower third position and preheat oven to 350°F. (175°C.). Generously butter 9 by 5 by 3-inch (23 by 13 by 8cm) loaf pan or 8½ by 4½ by 2¾-inch (21 by 11 by 7cm) loaf pan. (Larger pan will yield flat, wide loaf; smaller pan will produce narrow, tall loaf.)

Insert *metal blade* and put flour, salt, baking powder, baking soda, and apricots into work bowl. Pulse 6 to 8 times, in pulses lasting 1 second each, just until apricots are very coarsely chopped. Remove and set aside.

With *metal blade* in place, put sugar, eggs, and vanilla into work bowl and process for 30 seconds. Add butter and process for another 30 seconds, stopping once to scrape work bowl. Mixture may look curdled; this is all right. Add bananas and process for 10 seconds. Mixture will not be completely smooth; some small pieces of banana should remain. Add cereal and process for 5 seconds only. Finally, add pecans and dry ingredients to work bowl. Pulse rapidly 3 times, scrape bowl well, and pulse 1 more time. Do not overprocess.

Turn batter into prepared pan. Bang pan on countertop to level batter; use spatula to smooth top.

Bake until loaf is very well browned and cake tester inserted into center comes out clean, about 60 minutes for larger pan, 70 minutes for smaller pan. A few cracks may develop on top of loaf. Cool bread in pan for 15 minutes, then turn out onto rack to cool completely.

Makes 1 loaf.

YOGURT COFFEE CAKE

Yogurt and a delicious cinnamon and nut filling combine to make this beautiful coffee cake moist and flavorful.

Filling

- ½ cup firmly packed light brown sugar (4 ounces, 115g)
- Zest of 1 large orange
- 2 teaspoons cinnamon
- ⅔ cup walnuts (2⅔ ounces, 80g)
- ¼ cup currants (1¼ ounces, 35g)

Batter

- 2¾ cups sifted unbleached all-purpose flour (11 ounces, 310g)
- 1½ teaspoons baking powder
- 1 teaspoon baking soda
- 1 cup sugar (7½ ounces, 215g)
- 3 large eggs
- 1 tablespoon vanilla
- 1½ sticks unsalted butter (6 ounces, 170g), at room temperature, cut into 8 pieces
- 1½ cups (360ml) plain yogurt

Glaze

- 1 cup confectioners' sugar (4 ounces, 115g)
- ½ teaspoon vanilla
- 4 teaspoons milk

Adjust oven rack to lower third position and preheat oven to 375°F. (190°C.). Use solid shortening to grease 10-inch (25cm) Bundt pan (12-cup, 2.8L capacity). Dust lightly with fine, dry unseasoned bread crumbs and tap out excess.

Insert *metal blade,* put sugar and zest into work bowl, and process until zest is finely minced, 1 to 2 minutes. Add cinnamon and walnuts and pulse 8 to 10 times until walnuts are finely chopped. Transfer to small bowl and stir in currants; set aside.

To make batter, resift flour with baking powder and baking soda; set aside.

With *metal blade* in place, put sugar, eggs, and vanilla into work bowl and process for 1 minute. Add butter and process 45 seconds more, stopping once to scrape work bowl. Mixture will look curdled; this is all right. Add yogurt in circle on top of egg mixture and process for 3 seconds. Scrape work bowl. Add dry ingredients and pulse 3 times, then scrape work bowl again and pulse 3 more times, just to incorporate dry ingredients. Do not overprocess; stir gently with plastic spatula to complete mixing if necessary.

Spoon one-third (scant 2 cups, 480ml) of batter into prepared pan and spread evenly over bottom. Sprinkle evenly with half of nut filling. Place another third of batter by small spoonfuls over nut layer and spread carefully to cover the nuts. Sprinkle with remaining nut mixture and then cover with remaining batter. Smooth top.

Bake until cake tester comes out dry and top of cake is well browned and springs back when pressed with fingertip, 50 to 60 minutes. Cool cake in pan for 10 minutes, then turn out onto rack to cool completely. (Cake may be made to this point, wrapped airtight, and frozen. To serve, thaw cake in its wrapping, then unwrap and ice.)

With *metal blade* in place, put all glaze ingredients into work bowl and process until smooth, about 5 seconds. Mixture should be consistency of very thick cream sauce. Adjust as necessary with more sugar or milk.

Set cake on rack over large piece of waxed paper. Pour icing over top, letting it dribble down sides. When icing has set, transfer cake to cake plate. Store, covered, at room temperature.

Makes 1 Bundt cake, about 12 to 16 servings.

YOGURT AND JALAPENO CORN BREAD

Yogurt gives moisture to this corn bread and the chile gives it just a hint of bite.

> 4 ounces (115g) Monterey Jack cheese, chilled
>
> 1 jalapeño chile, halved and seeded (see NOTE)
>
> 1 small (walnut-size) piece of onion
>
> 1 cup unbleached all-purpose flour (5 ounces, 140g)
>
> 2/3 cup yellow cornmeal (4 ounces, 115g)
>
> 2 tablespoons sugar
>
> 2 teaspoons baking powder
>
> 1/2 teaspoon baking soda
>
> 3/4 teaspoon salt, if desired
>
> 4 tablespoons unsalted butter (2 ounces, 55g), chilled and cut into 4 pieces
>
> 1 cup (240ml) plain yogurt
>
> 3 large eggs

Adjust oven rack to center position and preheat oven to 350°F. (175°C.). Butter 9 by 9 by 2-inch (22 by 22 by 5cm) baking pan and set aside.

Insert *medium shredding disc*, place cheese in feed tube, and use light pressure to process. Remove and set aside.

Insert *metal blade.* With machine running, drop chile and onion through feed tube and process until finely chopped, about 10 seconds. Scrape work bowl.

Add flour, cornmeal, sugar, baking powder, baking soda, salt, butter, and half the cheese and process for 10 seconds. Scrape work bowl.

Add yogurt in circle on top of dry ingredients, then add eggs. Pulse rapidly 3 times, scrape work bowl, and pulse rapidly 1 more time. Do not overprocess; if necessary, complete mixing in work bowl with plastic spatula.

Turn batter into prepared pan. (To get all of batter out, replace bowl and blade and pulse once to spin blade clean.) Spread batter level and sprinkle top with remaining cheese.

Bake until top is flecked with golden brown and toothpick inserted into center comes out clean, about 30 minutes. Serve hot or warm.

Makes 8 or 9 servings.

NOTE: Jalapeño chiles are hot and can irritate the skin and eyes. Always handle them with rubber gloves.

DESSERTS

You'll find many familiar faces here: Cream Puffs, Strawberry Shortcake, Chocolate-Chip Cookies, and Chocolate Layer Cake. But making them has never been easier.

The procedures are slightly different with the food processor. The biggest difference is in cake making. Instead of creaming butter and sugar before adding eggs, you process the eggs with the sugar and then add the butter — a change that gives superior results. Remember this point when adapting recipes for the food processor.

Another important difference is that all the liquid goes in first, then dry ingredients are added and quickly incorporated. You must be careful not to overprocess the batter, or the cake will be tough. I give very specific instructions in each recipe; please follow them carefully.

Finally, always measure the flour precisely. If you cannot weigh it, follow the procedure described on page 174. I always use cake flour, which is made of soft wheat that develops less gluten than all-purpose flour.

In addition to making cakes, the food processor mixes stiff cookie batters, purées fruit for smooth sherbets, chops fruit for bar cookies, and slices fruit for tarts and pies.

Strawberry Shortcake

OLD-FASHIONED CHOCOLATE LAYER CAKE

This moist and fudgy layer cake is filled and frosted with a sour-cream chocolate icing.

Cake

- 2 cups sifted cake flour (8 ounces, 225g)
- ½ cup unsweetened cocoa (1¾ ounces, 50g)
- 1 teaspoon baking soda
- 1 teaspoon baking powder
- ½ teaspoon salt, if desired
- 3 large eggs
- ¾ cup granulated sugar (5½ ounces, 160g)
- ¾ cup firmly packed dark brown sugar (6 ounces, 170g)
- 2 teaspoons vanilla
- 1½ sticks unsalted butter (6 ounces, 170g), at room temperature, cut into 9 pieces
- 1¼ cups (300ml) milk

Chocolate Sour-Cream Frosting

- 1 pound (455g) confectioners' sugar
- ½ cup plus 2 tablespoons unsweetened cocoa (2 ounces, 55g)
- ⅛ teaspoon salt, if desired
- 1 stick unsalted butter (4 ounces, 115g), at room temperature, cut into 6 pieces
- ½ cup (120ml) sour cream
- 1 teaspoon vanilla

Adjust oven rack to center position and preheat oven to 350°F. (175°C.). Grease two 9-inch (23cm) layer-cake pans and dust lightly with flour; tap out excess.

Insert *metal blade*, put flour, cocoa, baking soda, baking powder, and salt into work bowl, and process for 10 seconds. Transfer to large sheet of waxed paper and set aside.

With *metal blade* in place, put eggs, sugars, and vanilla into work bowl and process for 1 minute, stopping once to scrape bowl. Add butter and process for 1 minute, stopping twice to scrape bowl and blade. Mixture should be smooth and creamy; process a few seconds more if necessary. Add milk and process for 5 seconds; mixture will be very thin.

Add dry ingredients to batter in work bowl. In standard-size food processor, dry ingredients will come almost to top of work bowl. Pulse 8 times, very rapidly, allowing blade to come to rest between pulses. Each pulse should last only as long as it takes to say ON/OFF. Dry ingredients may not be completely incorporated. Scrape work bowl very thoroughly with plastic spatula, then pulse 1 or 2 more times, very rapidly, to make batter quite smooth, creamy, and slightly thick.

Divide batter evenly between prepared pans and tilt pans gently to level batter. Bake until tops barely spring back when pressed with fingertip and layers just begin to come away from sides, 25 to 30 minutes.

Cool in pans for 5 minutes, then turn out onto racks to cool completely. Use small, sharp knife to trim away any rough edges.

Insert *metal blade,* put all frosting ingredients into work bowl and process, stopping once to scrape work bowl, until thick, creamy, and very smooth, about 1 minute. If too thick, add a little more sour cream and process a few seconds longer.

Line edges of cake plate with 4 strips of waxed paper, each about 12 inches (30cm) long and 3 inches (8cm) wide. Place cooled cake layer upside down on plate, making sure waxed-paper strips are just under edges of cake. Spread layer with about ¾ cup (180ml) of frosting. Place second layer on top, right side up. Spread remaining frosting over top and sides of cake, smoothing it or making swirls. Gently pull out strips of waxed paper; cake platter should be clean.

Makes one 9-inch (23cm) layer cake, about 12 to 16 servings.

GRAND MARNIER SPICE CAKE

A generous amount of Grand Marnier brushed over this light and tender cake makes it quite different from the usual carrot cake. And the whole-wheat flour gives it a rich flavor.

- 2 medium carrots (7 ounces, 200g total), trimmed, peeled, and cut into 1-inch (2.5cm) pieces
- Zest from ½ lemon
- Zest from ½ orange
- 1 cup sugar (7½ ounces, 215g)
- ½ cup firmly packed light-brown sugar (4 ounces, 115g)
- 3 large eggs
- 1½ teaspoons vanilla
- 1½ sticks unsalted butter (6 ounces, 170g), at room temperature, cut into 6 pieces
- ¼ cup (60ml) plain yogurt
- ⅔ cup walnuts or pecans
- 1 cup sifted whole-wheat flour (4½ ounces, 130g)
- 1 teaspoon baking powder
- 1 teaspoon baking soda (see NOTE)
- 2 teaspoons cinnamon
- ¼ teaspoon freshly grated nutmeg
- ¼ teaspoon mace
- ¾ teaspoon ground ginger
- 1 cup sifted unbleached all-purpose flour (4 ounces, 115g)
- ½ cup (120ml) Grand Marnier liqueur
- Confectioners' sugar

Adjust oven rack to lower third position and preheat oven to 350°F. (175°C.). Butter 8½-inch (21cm) Bundt or fluted tube pan and dust lightly with fine dry bread crumbs; tap out excess.

Insert *metal blade,* put carrots into work bowl, and pulse 4 or 5 times, then process continuously until carrots are finely chopped, about 20 seconds. Remove and set aside. Put zests and sugars into work bowl and process until zests are finely minced, 1 to 2 minutes. Add eggs and vanilla and process for 30 seconds. Add butter and process until mixture is fluffy, 30 seconds to 1 minute. Scrape work bowl, add carrots, yogurt, and nuts and process for 3 seconds *only.*

Sprinkle whole-wheat flour evenly over batter in work bowl. Add baking powder, baking soda, and spices, and sprinkle all-purpose flour evenly over all.

Pulse quickly 3 or 4 times, scrape work bowl, and pulse 1 or 2 more times, just until dry ingredients are incorporated. Do not overprocess; if necessary, complete mixing with plastic spatula.

Transfer batter to prepared pan, spreading it level. Bake until cake tester comes out clean and dry and top is well browned and springs back when pressed lightly with fingertip, 55 to 60 minutes.

As soon as cake comes out of oven, spoon ¼ cup (60ml) of Grand Marnier over top of cake. Let cake cool in pan for 10 minutes, then turn out onto rack and brush all over with remaining Grand Marnier. Let stand until completely cool.

Dust cake with confectioners' sugar and serve.

Makes 12 servings.

NOTE: At elevations of 3,000 feet (915m) or more, decrease baking soda to ½ teaspoon.

KENTUCKY CHOCOLATE CAKE

I got the basic recipe for this cake years ago from a friend who came from Kentucky, hence my name for it! The cake is very rich and chocolaty; the frosting is wonderfully smooth and creamy.

Cake

2 cups sifted cake flour (8 ounces, 225g)
1 teaspoon baking soda
¼ teaspoon salt, if desired
4 ounces (115g) unsweetened chocolate, broken into pieces
½ cup (120ml) boiling water
½ cup (120ml) ice water
½ cup (120ml) buttermilk
2 cups (15 ounces, 425g) sugar
2 large eggs
1 teaspoon vanilla
1 stick unsalted butter (4 ounces, 115g), at room temperature, cut into 6 pieces

Chocolate Frosting

3 ounces (85g) unsweetened chocolate
⅔ cup sugar (5 ounces, 140g)
6 tablespoons (3 ounces, 85g) unsalted butter, at room temperature, cut into 4 pieces
1 teaspoon vanilla
2 large eggs

Adjust oven rack to center position and preheat oven to 350°F. (175°C.). Grease 13 by 9 by 2-inch (33 by 23 by 5cm) baking dish and dust it lightly with fine, dry bread crumbs; tap out excess.

Resift flour with baking soda and salt; set aside.

Insert *metal blade.* Put chocolate into work bowl, pulse 3 times, then process continuously until chocolate is finely chopped, about 1 minute. With machine running, pour boiling water through feed tube and process for 30 seconds, stopping once to scrape work bowl. Mixture should be smooth and chocolate should be completely dissolved; if necessary, process a few seconds longer. With machine running, add ice water through feed tube and process for 5 seconds. Add buttermilk and process for 3 seconds. Transfer mixture to 2-cup (480ml) measure and set aside. Let stand until completely cool.

With *metal blade* in place, put sugar, eggs, and vanilla into work bowl and process for 1 minute. Add butter and process until smooth, about 1 minute. Add chocolate mixture and process for 10 seconds; batter will be very thin. Scrape work bowl well and add dry ingredients on top. Pulse 4 times, very rapidly, allowing blade to come to rest between pulses. Each pulse should last only as long as it takes to say ON/OFF. Scrape work bowl well and pulse rapidly 2 more times. If dry ingredients are not incorporated, use plastic spatula to complete mixing. Batter may not appear completely smooth; it will be slightly thicker than heavy cream.

Turn batter into prepared pan and let stand at room temperature for 5 minutes. Bake until top springs back when lightly pressed with fingertip and edges pull away slightly from sides, 30 to 35 minutes; do not overcook. Cool in pan on rack for 10 minutes. Run small sharp knife around sides of cake to release it and invert it onto rack. Cover with a second rack and invert again. Let cool right side up.

To make frosting, put chocolate in small saucepan set over pan of hot water and melt over medium heat. Set aside to cool slightly.

Insert *metal blade*, put sugar, butter, vanilla, and 1 egg into work bowl and process for 2 minutes, stopping machine every 30 seconds to scrape work bowl. Add remaining egg and process for 30 seconds. Add melted chocolate and process for another 30 seconds. Scrape work bowl and process a few seconds more; frosting should be very smooth and creamy and sugar should be completely dissolved. Process a few seconds more if necessary. Use as soon as frosting is of spreading consistency.

Line serving platter with 4 strips of waxed paper, each about 15 inches (38cm) long and 3 inches (8cm) wide. Place cake upside down on plate, making sure waxed-paper strips are under edges of cake. Spread frosting over top and sides of cake, making it thicker on top. Carefully remove waxed-paper strips.

Makes 1 cake, about 12 to 16 servings.

BLUE MOUNTAIN SPICE CAKE

This is a mildly spiced cake, fairly plain, and ideal for light snacks.

1¾ cups sifted cake flour (7 ounces, 200g)
1 teaspoon baking soda
¼ teaspoon salt, if desired
1 teaspoon cinnamon
½ teaspoon nutmeg
⅛ teaspoon ground cloves
Zest of 1 large orange
1 cup firmly packed light-brown sugar (8 ounces, 225g)
1 large egg
1 teaspoon vanilla
1 stick unsalted butter (4 ounces, 115g), at room temperature, cut into 6 pieces
1 cup (240ml) buttermilk
Confectioners' sugar, if desired

Adjust oven rack to center position and preheat oven to 350°F. (175°C.). Butter 9 by 9 by 2-inch (23 by 23 by 5cm) baking pan and dust lightly with flour; tap out excess.

Insert *metal blade.* Put flour, baking soda, salt, cinnamon, nutmeg, and cloves into work bowl and process for 5 seconds. Transfer to large piece of waxed paper and set aside.

With *metal blade* in place, put zest and brown sugar into work bowl and process, stopping twice to scrape bowl, until zest is finely chopped, about 2 minutes.

Add egg and vanilla to work bowl and process for 1 minute, stopping once to scrape work bowl. Add butter and process for about 1 minute, stopping once or twice to scrape work bowl; mixture should be smooth and fluffy. With machine running, add buttermilk through feed tube and process for 10 seconds.

Add dry ingredients in circle on top of batter. Pulse rapidly 4 times, scrape work bowl gently, and pulse once more, just until dry ingredients are incorporated. Do not overprocess; if necessary, stir with plastic spatula to complete mixing. Batter may not be completely smooth.

Turn batter into pan and tilt gently to level it. Bake until top is well browned and springs back when gently pressed with fingertip, and cake pulls slightly away from sides of pan, about 30 minutes. Cool in pan for 5 minutes, then turn out onto rack. Remove pan, cover with another rack, and invert again to let cake cool completely right side up. Before serving, sprinkle top lightly with confectioners' sugar, if desired.

Makes one 9-inch (23cm) cake, 8 or 9 servings.

STRAWBERRY SHORTCAKE

This version of the All-American classic is especially good because the shortcake itself is tender and delicate, quite unlike a typical biscuit dough. Lavish amounts of strawberries and whipped cream make this a glorious dessert.

Shortcake

2 cups sifted cake flour (8 ounces, 225g)

3 tablespoons sugar

2 teaspoons baking powder

¼ teaspoon salt, if desired

1 stick unsalted butter (4 ounces, 115g), chilled and cut into 8 pieces

1 large egg

1 teaspoon vanilla extract

Milk

Strawberries and Cream

3 pints strawberries (2¼ pounds, 1kg), cleaned and hulled

3 tablespoons sugar, or to taste

2 cups (480ml) whipping cream

¼ cup confectioners' sugar (1 ounce, 30g)

¼ cup instant nonfat dry milk

2 large egg whites

1 teaspoon vanilla extract

Adjust oven rack to center position and preheat oven to 425°F. (220°C.). Lightly butter 8- or 9-inch (20 or 23cm) round metal cake pan; set aside.

Insert *metal blade* and put flour, sugar, baking powder, salt, and butter into work bowl. Pulse 5 or 6 times, then process continuously until butter particles are size of small peas, about 5 seconds.

Crack egg into 1-cup (240ml) glass measure and beat lightly with fork. Add 1 teaspoon of vanilla and enough milk to make ⅔ cup (160ml). Pour mixture in ring over dry ingredients. Pulse quickly 6 to 8 times, just until dough begins to hold together. Mixture will be thick and will not look smooth.

Turn batter into prepared pan and pat firmly into place. Bang pan on counter 2 or 3 times to settle batter.

Bake until top is well browned and toothpick inserted in center comes out dry, about 20 minutes for 8-inch (20cm) pan, 18 minutes for 9-inch (23cm) pan. Turn cake onto rack and let cool completely.

Reserve 8 perfect berries for garnish.

Insert *2mm slicing disc*, place berries in feed tube, and use light pressure to process. Transfer to 2-quart (2L) bowl and add sugar. Mix well and set aside. Do not wash work bowl.

With *metal blade* in place, put about 1 cup (240ml) of whipping cream, sugar, dry milk, egg whites, and vanilla into work bowl. Start machine and pour remaining cream through feed tube. Process until cream is thick and holds shape, about 2 minutes. Do not overprocess. (Ultrapasteurized cream may take 3 to 4 minutes to whip.)

To assemble dessert, use serrated knife to slice shortcake into 2 layers. Place one layer on serving platter, cut side up. Cover with half the sliced strawberries and juice, and spread with half the whipped cream. Top with second cake layer, cut side up, and cover with remaining strawberries. Spread remaining cream evenly over berries and garnish with the reserved whole strawberries. Serve at once.

Makes one 8- or 9-inch (20 or 23cm) shortcake, about 8 servings.

CAROLYN'S CHEESECAKE

The inspiration for this cheesecake was a recipe given to me many years ago by a friend, Carolyn Smoller. The cake is dense and creamy, but also light. The sequence of preparation is carefully planned so you can whip the egg whites, make the crumb crust, prepare the filling, and make the topping without having to wash the work bowl.

3 large egg whites, at room temperature
1 tablespoon lemon juice
4 ounces (115g) graham crackers (8 double crackers, 16 squares)
4 tablespoons unsalted butter (2 ounces, 55g), at room temperature, cut into 4 pieces
Zest of 1 lemon
½ cup sugar (3¾ ounces, 105g)
1 pound (455g) cream cheese, at room temperature, cut into 1-inch (2.5cm) pieces
⅛ teaspoon cinnamon
⅛ teaspoon freshly grated nutmeg
½ teaspoon vanilla
3 large egg yolks
1 cup (240ml) sour cream
1 tablespoon sugar
1 teaspoon vanilla

Adjust oven rack to center position and preheat oven to 300°F. (150°C.). Lightly butter sides only of 8-inch (20cm) springform pan; set aside.

Insert *metal blade*, put egg whites into work bowl, and process for 10 seconds. With machine running, pour in lemon juice and process until whites are thick and hold definite shape, about 1 minute. Transfer whites to 1-quart (1L) bowl. (Pulse once to spin any remaining whites off blade, then scrape work bowl.) Set whites aside and proceed promptly. Do not wash work bowl or blade.

With *metal blade* in place, break up graham crackers into work bowl. Pulse once or twice, then process continuously for 30 seconds. Add butter and pulse 4 times, then process for 15 seconds. Turn crumb mixture into prepared pan and set aside. Wipe out work bowl.

With *metal blade* in place, put zest and ½ cup of sugar into work bowl and process until zest is finely chopped, 1 to 2 minutes. Meanwhile, press crumbs firmly into bottom of pan.

Add cream cheese, cinnamon, nutmeg, ½ teaspoon of vanilla, and egg yolks to work bowl and process for 1 minute, stopping once to scrape bowl. Mixture will be very thick at first, but will thin out to consistency of heavy cream.

Add egg whites in ring on top of cream-cheese mixture. Pulse twice, scrape work bowl well, and pulse once more. Do not overprocess; a few streaks of egg white may still remain. Turn mixture into pan, scraping work bowl thoroughly. Tilt pan to level batter. Do not wash work bowl or metal blade.

Bake for 45 minutes. Do not turn oven off.

With *metal blade* in place, put sour cream, 1 tablespoon of sugar, and 1 teaspoon of vanilla into work bowl. Pulse 5 times, scrape work bowl, and pulse twice more. Spread topping over hot cheesecake and return to oven for 10 minutes. Cool completely, then cover pan with plastic wrap or foil and refrigerate for several hours or overnight.

To serve, run small sharp knife around cheesecake to loosen sides from pan. Remove side of pan. Either set cheesecake (still resting on pan bottom) onto dessert platter or use two wide metal spatulas to lift cheesecake carefully off pan and onto platter.

Makes one 8-inch (20cm) cake, 8 to 10 servings.

BAKLAVA

Baklava is surely one of the sweetest and tastiest of all sinful treats. It is made of layers of phyllo pastry, lavishly brushed with melted butter, interspersed with finely chopped walnuts, and saturated with a honey syrup.

Phyllo dough is now widely available in supermarkets and specialty-food shops. Work with only one sheet at a time, keeping the remainder under wraps until needed. Cover the unwrapped leaves, first with a dry towel, then with a damp one. The towels provide just enough moisture to keep the dough pliable.

Brushing dough with butter   Folding edges into pan

1 pound (455g) phyllo dough, thawed
4½ cups walnuts (1 pound, 455g)
¼ cup sugar (1¾ ounces, 50g)
3 sticks unsalted butter (12 ounces, 340g)
½ cup (120ml) oil, preferably safflower, sunflower, or corn
1 cup (240ml) honey
½ cup (120ml) water
1 tablespoon lemon juice
2 thin slices lemon
1 cinnamon stick, about 3 inches (8cm) long

Follow package instructions for thawing phyllo. Remove thawed phyllo from refrigerator at least 2 hours before using.

Adjust oven rack to center position and preheat oven to 350°F. (175°C.).

Insert *metal blade.* Put half the walnuts and half the sugar into work bowl and pulse rapidly 10 to 15 times, just until nuts are chopped medium-fine. Transfer to large mixing bowl. Repeat with remaining walnuts and sugar and add to mixture in bowl.

Put butter in 1-quart (1L) saucepan and melt slowly over low heat; do not stir it or shake pan. When melted, carefully skim foam off top. Then very

carefully pour off clear liquid into medium bowl, leaving milky residue in pan. The clear liquid is clarified butter; stir oil into it and set aside.

Unwrap and unroll phyllo sheets and cover them with dry towel, then damp towel.

Lightly brush bottom and sides of 13 by 9 by 2-inch (33 by 23 by 5cm) baking pan with butter and oil mixture. Place one phyllo sheet in pan and brush lightly with butter mixture; fold overhanging edges into pan. Repeat with 3 more phyllo sheets, brushing

Sprinkling evenly with nuts *Scoring top in diamond shapes*

each one with butter mixture. Sprinkle evenly with one-fourth of walnut mixture (about 1 cup).

Repeat procedure with remaining pastry and nuts. You will make a total of 5 layers of pastry, each composed of 4 phyllo sheets brushed with butter, and 4 layers of nuts. End with phyllo, using more than 4 sheets for top layer if you like.

Use small, sharp knife to score top of pastry into diamond shapes, dividing it into 5 lengthwise strips, then dividing it on bias into sixths. Pour any remain-ing butter mixture over top and spread it evenly with pastry brush.

Bake at 350°F. (175°C.) for 30 minutes, then reduce temperature to 300°F. (150°C.) and bake until baklava is golden brown and crisp, another 45 to 60 minutes. Do not underbake.

Meanwhile, as soon as baklava goes into oven, prepare honey syrup.

Put honey and remaining ingredients into 2- to 3-quart (2 to 3L) saucepan. Bring carefully to boil over medium-high heat, stirring frequently, then reduce heat to low and simmer for 5 minutes. Remove from heat and set syrup aside to cool. When syrup is slightly cooled, discard lemon slices and cinnamon.

As soon as baklava comes out of oven, pour syrup (it may be slightly warm) over top and down sides of pastry. Baklava will sizzle and crackle. Set aside for at least several hours until completely cool. Cut through scored top to make individual pieces. (Baklava may be wrapped in plastic wrap and foil and frozen for 2 to 3 weeks. Thaw in wrapper, then unwrap.)

Makes about 30 pastries.

CREAM PUFFS

Puff-shell dough is the pastry miracle responsible for these crisp and delicate puffs. When split and filled with whipped cream, they make a splendid dessert.

Pastry

1 cup (240ml) water
1 stick unsalted butter (4 ounces, 115g), cut into a few pieces
¼ teaspoon salt, if desired
1 cup unbleached all-purpose flour (5 ounces, 140g)
4 large eggs

Filling

3 cups (720ml) whipping cream
½ cup confectioners' sugar (2 ounces, 55g)
¼ cup instant nonfat dry milk
1½ teaspoons vanilla

Adjust oven rack to center position and preheat oven to 425°F. (220°C.). Line large baking sheet (14 by 17 inches, 35 by 43cm) or 2 standard cookie sheets (12 by 15 inches, 30 by 38cm) with aluminum foil.

Put water, butter, and salt into 3-quart (3L) saucepan. Set over moderately high heat and cook until butter is melted, stirring occasionally. Bring mixture to rolling boil, then remove from heat and immediately add flour. Blend thoroughly with wooden spoon and return to moderately high heat. Cook, stirring constantly, until dough gathers into smooth, compact mass and begins to film bottom of pan, 1 to 2 minutes.

Insert *metal blade* and transfer hot flour mixture to work bowl. Process for 15 seconds, then add eggs all at once and process for 30 seconds, stopping once to scrape work bowl. Eggs should be completely incorporated and mixture should be very thick and smooth. Shape puffs right away or cover mixture and let it cool completely.

Measure ¼ cup of dough for each puff. On large baking sheet, make 10 mounds of dough, spacing them 2 to 3 inches (5 to 8cm) apart. (On each of 2 standard-size cookie sheets, make 5 mounds of dough, spacing them well apart; reserve 1 cookie sheet at room temperature, covered loosely with lightly oiled plastic wrap, while first batch bakes.) Set baking or cookie sheet with puff batter on top of another baking or cookie sheet, to protect bottoms of puffs.

Bake for 15 minutes at 425°F. (220°C.), then reduce heat to 350°F. (175°C.) and bake for 35 minutes more. Do not open oven for at least first 30 minutes of baking or puffs may collapse. Five minutes before puffs are due to be done, open oven door and pull out oven rack slightly. Use small, sharp knife to pierce sides and top of each puff quickly in 2 or 3 places, to allow steam to escape. Close oven and continue baking until puffs are done. They should be a rich, even, golden-brown color all over. If in doubt, let them bake a few minutes longer.

Use wide metal spatula to remove puffs to cooling racks. Let cool completely. (Puffs may be prepared to this point, wrapped airtight, and frozen for up to 2 months. Thaw them in their wrapping, then unwrap and place on baking sheet. Heat in preheated 325°F. (160°C.) oven for 5 to 7 minutes, and cool before using.)

Use sharp knife to slice off tops of cooled puffs about one-third of way down from top. Remove any soft dough from inside.

Prepare filling no more than 1 hour before serving. With *metal blade* in place, put 1 cup of cream, sugar, dry milk, and vanilla into work bowl. Start machine and pour remaining cream through feed tube. Process until cream is thick and holds shape, about 2 minutes. (Ultrapasteurized cream will take about 3 minutes.)

Fill puffs with cream mixture and replace tops. Dust with additional confectioners' sugar and serve. (If necessary, these can be refrigerated for up to 1 hour.)

Makes 10 cream puffs.

QUICK MOCHA MOUSSE

One of the smoothest and lightest of all mousses, and also one of the easiest. Be sure your work bowl and metal blade are absolutely clean and free of grease, otherwise the egg whites will not increase in volume as much as they should.

Mousse

8 large egg whites, at room temperature
1 tablespoon distilled white vinegar
1 tablespoon water
8 ounces (225g) semisweet chocolate, broken into pieces, or 1⅓ cups semisweet chocolate morsels (8 ounces, 225g)
2 teaspoons instant-coffee powder (preferably espresso)
⅓ cup (80ml) boiling water
6 large egg yolks
2 tablespoons coffee liqueur
1 teaspoon vanilla

Coffee Whipped Cream

1½ cups (360ml) whipping cream
1 large or extra-large egg white
1½ teaspoons instant-coffee powder (preferably espresso)
⅓ cup confectioners' sugar (1⅓ ounces, 40g)
¼ cup instant nonfat dry milk
1½ teaspoons vanilla
Grated semisweet chocolate, if desired

Insert *metal blade* and put egg whites into work bowl. Combine vinegar and 1 tablespoon of water in small cup. Start machine and process whites for 10 seconds. With machine running, pour vinegar mixture through feed tube and process until whites hold definite shape, about 45 seconds. Use rubber spatula to transfer whites to 1-quart (1L) bowl and set aside. (Pulse once to spin any remaining whites off blade, then scrape work bowl thoroughly.) Do not wash bowl or blade.

With *metal blade* in place, put chocolate and coffee into work bowl. Pulse 4 or 5 times, then process continuously until chocolate is finely chopped, about 1 minute. With machine running, pour boiling water through feed tube and process for 30 seconds. Then scrape work bowl, add remaining ingredients, and process for 20 seconds.

Scrape work bowl and add about half of egg whites in ring on top of chocolate. (Whites may have released a bit of liquid; add it.) Pulse quickly 2 times, to incorporate whites only partially. Add remaining whites and pulse 2 more times. Scrape work bowl gently but thoroughly. Pulse 1 or 2 more times, just until whites are thoroughly incorporated. Mixture will be very fluid.

Transfer mousse to 1-quart (1L) glass measure and divide it among 6 8-ounce (240ml) stemmed glasses or dessert bowls. (Do not quite fill them.) Cover with plastic wrap and refrigerate for at least 2 hours. (Mousse may be made to this point 1 or 2 days ahead.)

Prepare coffee whipped cream when ready to serve or up to 2 hours before. With *metal blade* in place, put all ingredients except grated chocolate into work bowl and process until cream is only slightly thickened (not stiff), about 1 minute. Spoon or pour cream over each dessert and sprinkle with grated chocolate. Serve very cold.

Makes 6 servings.

ALMOST SUGARLESS APPLE PIE

I use apple-juice concentrate as the major sweet-ener in this pie. Apple juice is not entirely without sugar, of course, but its sugar is unrefined and accompanied by valuable vitamins and minerals. The best apples for this pie are Granny Smith, Rome Beauty, or Golden Delicious. If you prefer a really sweet apple pie, add the optional sugar to the filling. The pastry for this pie is flaky, slightly crunchy, and foolproof.

Pastry

⅓	cup sifted unbleached all-purpose flour (1⅓ ounces, 40g)
¼	cup (60ml) water
1⅔	cups sifted unbleached all-purpose flour (6½ ounces, 185g)
¼	teaspoon salt, if desired
6	tablespoons unsalted butter (3 ounces, 85g), chilled and cut into 6 pieces
6	tablespoons lard or vegetable shortening (3 ounces, 85g), chilled and cut into 6 pieces

Filling

1	12-ounce (340g) can frozen concentrated unsweetened apple juice, thawed
8 or 9	firm cooking apples (2½ to 3 pounds, 1.1 to 1.4kg total)
1	quart (1L) water mixed with 3 tablespoons lemon juice
2	tablespoons lemon juice
¼	cup sugar (2 ounces, 55g), if desired
3	tablespoons cornstarch
½	teaspoon freshly grated nutmeg
¼	teaspoon ground ginger
1½	teaspoons cinnamon
2	teaspoons vanilla

Almost Sugarless Apple Pie

Combine ⅓ cup flour and water in small bowl, stirring with fork to make mixture consistency of thick cream. (It need not be smooth.) Set aside.

Insert *metal blade* and put remaining Pastry ingredients into work bowl. Pulse 4 or 5 times, just until fat particles are size of large peas. Pour flour and water mixture evenly over dry ingredients in work bowl. Pulse very rapidly about 30 times, just until dough looks as though it will gather into ball with a few more pulses. (There should be small pieces of fat visible in dough.) Turn pastry out onto large sheet of waxed paper and divide in two, making 1 piece slightly larger than the other. Shape each into ball (dusting with flour if necessary) and flatten slightly into disc. Wrap in plastic wrap and refrigerate until filling is prepared. Wipe out work bowl.

To make filling, reserve 2 teaspoons of apple-juice concentrate and set aside. Put remaining juice in heavy-bottomed 3-quart (3L) saucepan and boil over medium-high heat, swirling pan occasionally, until juice is reduced to ¾ cup (180ml) and appears syrupy, about 10 minutes. Watch carefully; it burns easily. Set aside to cool.

Peel, quarter, and core apples and drop them promptly into water and lemon juice. When all apples are prepared, remove from water and shake off excess moisture.

Insert *3mm slicing disc*, place apples in feed tube, and use medium pressure to process. Transfer apples to large mixing bowl, add lemon juice, and toss to mix well. For a very sweet pie, add sugar.

Insert *metal blade*. Put cooled apple juice and remaining ingredients into work bowl and process for 15 seconds. Scrape work bowl, then process for 1 or 2 seconds more. Mixture should be smooth. Pour over apples and mix well.

Adjust oven rack to center position and preheat oven to 450°F. (230°C.).

Roll out larger piece of pastry on lightly floured surface into 13-inch (33cm) circle. Brush excess flour from dough and place in 9-inch (23cm) pie pan. Let excess pastry hang over edge.

Roll out second piece of dough on lightly floured surface to 12-inch (30cm) circle.

Turn filling into pie crust, mounding it slightly in center. Pat apples down gently to eliminate air spaces. Brush edges of pastry lightly with water and carefully place second piece of dough on top. Press edges firmly together to seal. Trim pastry to leave ½-inch (12mm) overhang, then form standing rim and flute. Use sharp knife to make 4 slits in top of pie, to allow steam to escape. Brush reserved apple juice over top crust.

Bake at 450°F. (230°C.) for 10 minutes, then reduce heat to 350°F. (175°C.) and continue baking until crust is browned and apples are tender, another 45 to 60 minutes. Use sharp knife to test apples. If they were very firm, pie may need to bake for more than 1 hour at 350°F. (175°C.). If crust is getting too brown, cover loosely with aluminum foil.

Cool pie on rack and serve warm or at room temperature.

Makes one 9-inch (23cm) pie, about 8 servings.

APPLE-GINGER CRISP

Pieces of crystallized ginger melt during baking to give this dessert a spicy sharpness. Use McIntosh, Jonathan, or Rome Beauty apples. Serve small portions.

- ½ **cup unbleached all-purpose flour (2½ ounces, 70g)**
- ½ **cup whole-wheat flour (2½ ounces, 70g)**
- 1 **teaspoon cinnamon**
- ¼ **teaspoon salt, if desired**
- ½ **cup light-brown sugar (4 ounces, 115g), firmly packed**
- 1½ **sticks unsalted butter (6 ounces, 170g), chilled and cut into 8 pieces**
- ½ **cup old-fashioned or quick-cooking rolled oats (not instant oatmeal)**
- ½ **cup granulated sugar (3¾ ounces, 105g)**
- **Zest of 1 lemon**
- 1 to 1½ **ounces (30 to 45g) crystallized ginger**
- 6 **firm medium cooking apples (2 pounds, 910g total), peeled, halved vertically, and cored**
- 1 **tablespoon lemon juice**

Adjust oven rack to center position and preheat oven to 350°F. (175°C.).

Insert *metal blade*, put flours, cinnamon, salt, and brown sugar into work bowl, and pulse 10 to 12 times to combine dry ingredients. Add butter and pulse 8 to 10 times until butter is cut into very small pieces. Add oats and pulse twice to combine. Remove mixture and set it aside on large sheet of waxed paper.

With *metal blade* in place, put sugar and zest into work bowl and process until zest is as fine as sugar, about 2 minutes. Add ginger, pulse 3 times, then process continuously until ginger is very finely chopped, 20 to 30 seconds. Transfer to large mixing bowl.

Insert *3mm or 4mm slicing disc*. Wedge apples upright in feed tube and use medium pressure to process. Add apples and lemon juice to ginger mixture and fold together gently with rubber spatula.

Measure 1½ cups of crumb mixture and press it firmly and evenly into ungreased 9 by 9 by 2-inch (23 by 23 by 5cm) baking pan. (Mixture will be dry but will hold together when pressed.) Spread apple mixture over crust, pressing it into pan with rubber spatula. Top with remaining crumb mixture, patting it evenly into place; do not pack it down.

Bake until top is lightly browned and apples are tender, 65 to 70 minutes. Crumb topping may develop a few cracks. Serve warm. (Apple-ginger crisp will keep well at room temperature for 3 or 4 days. To reheat, place in center of preheated 325°F. (160°C.) oven just to heat through and recrisp topping, 10 to 15 minutes.)

Makes one 9-inch (23cm) square apple crisp, 8 to 10 servings.

GLAZED CHOCOLATE-FUDGE COOKIES

These are a chocolate lover's dream: fudge cookies topped with a thick chocolate glaze.

Cookies

- 1½ **cups unbleached all-purpose flour (7½ ounces, 215g)**
- 1 **teaspoon baking soda**
- ½ **cup unsweetened cocoa (2⅓ ounces, 65g)**
- 1 **cup sugar (7½ ounces, 215g)**
- 2 **large eggs**
- 1½ **teaspoons vanilla**
- 1 **stick unsalted butter (4 ounces, 115g), at room temperature, cut into 6 pieces**

Glaze

> 3 ounces (85g) unsweetened chocolate, coarsely broken
>
> 1½ cups confectioners' sugar (6 ounces, 170g)
>
> ¼ cup (60ml) boiling water
>
> 3 tablespoons unsalted butter, at room temperature, cut into 3 pieces
>
> ½ teaspoon vanilla
>
> Pinch of salt

Insert *metal blade*, put flour, baking soda, and cocoa into work bowl, and process for 10 seconds. Transfer to sheet of waxed paper and set aside.

With *metal blade* in place, put sugar, eggs, and vanilla into work bowl and process for 1 minute. Add butter and process for 30 seconds, stopping once to scrape work bowl. Add half the dry ingredients in ring over butter mixture and pulse quickly 3 times. Dry ingredients will not be completely incorporated. Add remaining dry ingredients and pulse 3 or 4 times, just until they are incorporated. Mixture will be very stiff. If necessary, complete mixing with plastic spatula.

Turn mixture out onto large sheet of waxed paper. Moisten hands slightly and pat dough into rectangle measuring about 5 by 6 inches (13 by 15cm). Wrap dough and refrigerate until firm, about 2 hours. (Dough may be refrigerated several hours or overnight.)

Adjust oven rack to center position and preheat oven to 350°F. (175°C.). Tear off several sheets of aluminum foil to fit cookie sheet.

Remove dough from refrigerator and use sharp knife to cut it into 30 1-inch (2.5cm) pieces. Roll each piece into a ball (wet hands lightly if dough sticks) and place on foil 2 to 3 inches (5 to 8cm) apart. Slide cookie sheet under foil and place in oven.

Bake about 10 minutes. Cookies will be puffy-looking with cracks on top, and cracks will appear moist—that is, cookies will not seem done. Nevertheless, do not overbake them or they'll lose their fudginess.

Remove cookies from oven and slide foil off sheet. Let cookies stand a minute or two to firm up, then use wide metal spatula to transfer cookies to cooling racks.

Repeat with remaining dough. Cool cookies completely.

To make glaze, insert *metal blade* and put chocolate and sugar into work bowl. Pulse 5 times, then process continuously until chocolate is finely chopped, about 1 minute. With machine running, add water through feed tube and process for 30 seconds. Add remaining ingredients and process for 30 seconds, scrape work bowl well, and process a few seconds more. Glaze should be semifluid but not runny; adjust consistency if necessary with additional boiling water (added a few drops at a time) or sugar. Transfer glaze to small saucepan. If it becomes too firm, set it over very low heat and stir well.

Drizzle generous spoonful of glaze over each cookie, spreading it to edges. Set cookies on large sheet of waxed paper until glaze is set, then serve. (Cookies may be wrapped airtight and stored at room temperature for 2 or 3 days. They may also be frozen.)

Makes 30 cookies.

VARIATION: At Halloween, these cookies can be made to resemble witches' hats. Use scissors to snip ends off 30 marshallows. Bake cookies for 9 minutes, then quickly place marshmallow in center of each, cut side down. Return cookies to oven and bake exactly 1 minute longer. Proceed with instructions, spooning glaze over marshmallow "hat."

WHOLE-WHEAT PEANUT-BUTTER COOKIES

Lovers of peanut-butter cookies will wholeheartedly approve of these chewy, but crunchy versions.

⅔	cup whole-wheat flour (3⅓ ounces, 95g)
⅔	cup unbleached all-purpose flour (3⅓ ounces, 95g)
½	teaspoon baking soda
½	cup dry roasted peanuts (2 ounces, 55g)
½	cup creamy peanut butter, at room temperature
1	stick unsalted butter (4 ounces, 115g), at room temperature, cut into 6 pieces
⅓	cup granulated sugar (2½ ounces, 70g)
⅓	cup firmly packed light brown sugar (2½ ounces, 70g)
¼	cup (60ml) honey
1	teaspoon vanilla
1	large egg

Adjust oven rack to center position and preheat oven to 375°F. (190°C.). Tear off sheets of aluminum foil to fit cookie sheet.

Insert *metal blade,* put flours, baking soda, and peanuts into work bowl, and process for 5 seconds. Transfer to sheet of waxed paper and set aside.

With *metal blade* in place, put peanut butter, butter, sugars, honey, and vanilla into work bowl and process for 40 seconds, stopping once to scrape bowl. Mixture will look curdled; this is all right. Add egg, process for 15 seconds, scrape work bowl, and process for 15 seconds more. Mixture may not be entirely smooth.

Add dry ingredients and pulse rapidly 6 times. Scrape work bowl well and pulse 6 more times. If necessary, complete mixing with plastic spatula.

Shape dough into balls, using heaping teaspoonful for each one. Place balls 2 to 3 inches (5 to 8cm)

apart on foil and slide cookie sheet under foil.

Bake just until cookies are very pale golden brown, 10 to 11 minutes. Let cookies cool on sheet for 1 minute, then use wide metal spatula to transfer them to racks. Cookies will be soft and fragile, so handle them carefully. Repeat with remaining dough. (Cookies may be wrapped airtight and stored at room temperature for several days. They may also be frozen.)

Makes 24 cookies.

OATMEAL RAISIN-NUT COOKIES

These semisoft drop cookies are not too sweet and they are loaded with raisins.

¾	cup unbleached all-purpose flour (3¾ ounces, 105g)
½	teaspoon baking powder
½	teaspoon baking soda
½	teaspoon cinnamon
½	teaspoon freshly grated nutmeg
¼	teaspoon salt, if desired
½	cup sugar (3¾ ounces, 105g)
1	stick unsalted butter (4 ounces, 115g), at room temperature, cut into 6 pieces
1	large egg
1	teaspoon vanilla
3	tablespoons milk
¾	cup quick-cooking rolled oats, not instant oatmeal (2¼ ounces, 65g)
¾	cup raisins (3¾ ounces, 105g)
½	cup walnut or pecan halves (2 ounces, 55g)

Adjust two oven racks to divide oven into thirds and preheat oven to 350°F. (175°C.). Line 2 cookie sheets with aluminum foil.

Insert *metal blade.* Put flour, baking powder,

soda, cinnamon, nutmeg, and salt into work bowl and process for 5 seconds. Transfer to large sheet of waxed paper and set aside.

With *metal blade* in place, put sugar and butter into work bowl and process for 1 minute, stopping once to scrape work bowl. Add egg and vanilla and process for 30 seconds, stopping once to scrape work bowl. Add milk and process for 5 seconds.

Add flour mixture in ring over butter mixture, then pour oats in ring over flour and add raisins and nuts. Pulse twice, scrape work bowl, and pulse twice more. Use plastic spatula to distribute raisins evenly.

Scoop up batter with teaspoon and push it off onto foil with another teaspoon, shaping cookies as evenly as possible and spacing them about 2 inches (5cm) apart.

Bake until cookies are browned all over and tops spring back lightly when pressed with fingertip, 17 to 20 minutes. Rotate pans top to bottom and front to back as necessary during baking to ensure that cooking is even.

Use wide metal spatula to transfer cookies to racks. When completely cool, store airtight.

Makes 24 cookies.

CRUNCHY RAISIN-OATMEAL COOKIES

These chewy, crunchy drop cookies are made with whole-wheat flour, rolled oats, and raisins.

| ½ cup sifted whole-wheat flour (2 ounces, 55g) |
| 1¼ cups old-fashioned or quick-cooking rolled oats, not instant oatmeal (4 ounces, 115g) |
| ¼ teaspoon baking soda |
| ½ cup firmly packed light-brown sugar (4 ounces, 115g) |
| ¼ cup (60ml) honey |
| 3 tablespoons unsalted butter, at room temperature, cut into 3 pieces |
| 1 large egg |
| 2 tablespoons milk |
| 1 cup raisins (5 ounces, 140g) |

Adjust two oven racks to divide oven into thirds and preheat oven to 350°F. (175°C.). Tear off 3 sheets of aluminum foil to fit cookie sheets and set aside.

Insert *metal blade*, put flour, oats, and baking soda into work bowl, and process for 15 seconds. Transfer to sheet of waxed paper and set aside.

With *metal blade* in place, put brown sugar, honey, and butter into work bowl and process for 1 minute. Add egg and milk and process for 1 minute, stopping once to scrape work bowl. Batter may look curdled; this is all right. Add dry ingredients to work bowl and distribute raisins over them. Pulse rapidly 8 times, just to incorporate ingredients. (Raisins will remain whole.) Do not overprocess; if necessary, complete mixing with plastic spatula.

Scoop up well-rounded teaspoonfuls of batter and use second teaspoon to push them off onto foil, spacing them 3 inches (8cm) apart. Place 8 cookies on each sheet of foil. Slide cookie sheets under foil.

Place 1 sheet on each oven rack (let third sheet wait at room temperature) and bake until cookies are lightly browned all over and tops barely spring back when pressed lightly with fingertip, 17 to 20 minutes. Rotate sheets top to bottom and front to back 2 or 3 times during baking to ensure even browning. When baking only 1 sheet, use upper rack.

Slide foil off cookie sheets and let cookies stand for 1 to 2 minutes. Then use wide metal spatula to transfer cookies to racks to cool completely. Store cookies airtight; they are best when very fresh. (They may also be frozen for up to 2 months.)

Makes 24 cookies.

CHOCOLATE-CHIP COOKIES

This is my favorite version of the American classic. The small amount of corn syrup ensures that cookies will be chewy even when well browned.

- 1 **cup unbleached all-purpose flour (5 ounces, 140g)**
- ½ **teaspoon baking soda**
- ½ **teaspoon salt, if desired**
- 2 **tablespoons untoasted wheat germ**
- 1 **stick unsalted butter (4 ounces, 115g), at room temperature, cut into 4 pieces**
- ⅓ **cup granulated sugar (2½ ounces, 70g)**
- ⅓ **cup light-brown sugar (2½ ounces, 70g), firmly packed**
- 1 **tablespoon light corn syrup**
- 1 **teaspoon vanilla**
- 1 **large egg**
- ½ **cup pecans**
- 1 **cup semisweet chocolate morsels (6 ounces, 170g)**

Insert *metal blade,* put flour, baking soda, salt, and wheat germ into work bowl, and process for 5 seconds. Transfer to waxed paper and set aside.

With *metal blade* in place, put butter, sugars, corn syrup, and vanilla into work bowl and process for 1

minute, stopping once to scrape work bowl. Add egg and process for 1 minute, stopping once to scrape work bowl. After processing, scrape again.

Add pecans and dry ingredients in ring on top of batter and pulse quickly 3 times. (Flour mixture may not be all incorporated.) Scrape work bowl well. Add chocolate morsels and use plastic spatula to stir them into batter.

Adjust two oven racks to divide oven into thirds. Preheat oven to 375°F. (190°C.). Line 2 cookie sheets with aluminum foil.

Use 2 teaspoons to shape cookies. Dip one spoon into batter to scoop up well rounded teaspoonful. Push batter off spoon and onto sheet with second teaspoon. Make cookies as round and neat as you can. Space cookies 2 to 3 inches (5 to 8cm) apart, making 12 cookies on each sheet.

Bake for 10 to 12 minutes, reversing sheets top to bottom and front to back once during baking. Cookies are done when evenly browned around edges, with centers just a bit lighter. (For chewier cookies, remove from oven before they are quite brown.)

Slide foil off sheets and let cookies stand for 1 to 2 minutes to firm up. Then use wide metal spatula to transfer cookies to racks. Let cool completely and store airtight. (They keep well at room temperature for a few days, or they may be frozen.)

Makes 2 dozen cookies.

EXTRAVAGANT BROWNIES

Extravagant is the right word for these rich brownies: they are made with ground pecans and ³/₄ pound (340g) of chocolate chips.

> **6 tablespoons unsalted butter (3 ounces, 85g)**
> **¹/₃ cup firmly packed dark-brown sugar (2¹/₂ ounces, 70g)**
> **¹/₄ cup granulated sugar (1³/₄ ounces, 50g)**
> **2 tablespoons honey**
> **2 tablespoons milk**
> **¹/₂ teaspoon powdered instant coffee *or* 1 teaspoon instant-coffee granules**
> **¹/₄ cup plus 2 tablespoons whole-wheat flour (1³/₄ ounces, 50g)**
> **¹/₄ cup plus 2 tablespoons unbleached all-purpose flour (1³/₄ ounces, 50g)**
> **¹/₄ cup pecans (1 ounce, 30g)**
> **¹/₄ teaspoon baking soda**
> **2 cups semisweet chocolate morsels (12 ounces, 340g)**
> **2 large eggs**
> **1¹/₂ teaspoons vanilla**

Adjust oven rack to lower third position and preheat oven to 325°F. (160°C.).

Melt butter in 1-quart (1L) saucepan over low heat. Add sugars, honey, milk, and instant coffee, increase heat to medium-high, and cook, stirring occasionally, until mixture comes to full rolling boil. Stop stirring and boil mixture for exactly 1 minute. Remove from heat and let cool for 10 minutes.

Meanwhile, line 9 by 9 by 2-inch (23 by 23 by 5cm) baking pan with foil. Butter foil with soft butter and dust it lightly with flour, tapping out excess. Set aside.

Insert *metal blade*, put flours, pecans, and baking soda into work bowl, and process for 20 seconds. Transfer to sheet of waxed paper.

With *metal blade* in place, put 1 cup of morsels (6 ounces, 170g) into work bowl. Pour in warm syrup and process for 30 seconds. Add eggs and vanilla and process for 15 seconds. Add nut mixture in circle over chocolate and pulse quickly 3 or 4 times. Do not overprocess. Scrape work bowl and add remaining morsels. Pulse only 1 or 2 times, then complete mixing with plastic spatula.

Turn mixture into prepared pan. To remove all chocolate from work bowl, pulse once to spin any remaining mixture off blade, then scrape bowl.

Bake brownies until toothpick inserted into center comes out barely clean, about 35 minutes. Do not overbake.

Let brownies cool in pan on rack for 15 minutes. Then gently tamp down edges with fingertips so mixture is level. Let stand another 15 minutes. Turn out onto rack, remove pan and foil, and let stand until completely cool. Refrigerate briefly to set chocolate morsels.

Use long sharp knife to cut into 16 brownies. Wrap each one individually in waxed paper. Store at room temperature or in refrigerator.

Makes 16 brownies.

ROCKY ROAD BROWNIE BARS

Brownies and Rocky Road are two American confections that beg to be combined. This recipe is based on one in Maida Heatter's Book of Great Cookies.

Brownies

- ½ cup granulated sugar (3¾ ounces, 105g)
- ⅓ cup firmly packed dark-brown sugar (2½ ounces, 70g)
- 1 ounce (30g) unsweetened chocolate, cut into 2 pieces
- 6 tablespoons unsalted butter (3 ounces, 85g), melted and bubbling hot
- 1 teaspoon vanilla
- 2 large eggs
- ½ cup pecan halves (2 ounces, 55g)
- ½ cup unbleached all-purpose flour (2½ ounces, 70g)
- ½ teaspoon baking powder
- ¼ teaspoon salt, if desired

Topping

- ⅔ cup pecan halves (2⅔ ounces, 75g)
- 1⅓ cups miniature marshmallows

Glaze

- ½ cup confectioners' sugar (2 ounces, 55g)
- 1 ounce (30g) unsweetened chocolate, cut into 2 pieces
- 2 tablespoons unsalted butter, at room temperature, cut into 2 pieces
- ½ teaspoon vanilla
- 2 tablespoons boiling water

Adjust oven rack to center position and preheat oven to 350°F. (175°C.). Butter 9 by 9 by 2-inch (23 by 23 by 5cm) metal baking pan and set aside.

Insert *metal blade* and put sugars and chocolate into work bowl. Pulse 3 or 4 times, then process continuously until chocolate is finely chopped, about 1 minute. With machine running, pour hot butter through feed tube in fast stream and process for 30 seconds.

Add vanilla and eggs and process for 30 seconds, stopping once to scrape work bowl. When processing is complete, scrape work bowl again. Add pecans and process for 3 seconds *only.* Sprinkle remaining ingredients in ring over batter, pulse 3 times, then scrape work bowl and pulse once more. Dry ingredients should be incorporated; complete mixing with plastic spatula if necessary.

Spread batter evenly in prepared pan. Bake just until toothpick inserted in center comes out barely dry, 20 to 22 minutes; do not overcook. Meanwhile, prepare topping and glaze.

With *metal blade* in place, put pecans into work bowl and process just to chop them coarsely, about 3 seconds.

As soon as brownie layer is done, remove from oven but do not turn oven off. Sprinkle marshmallows evenly over top and return pan to oven for 1 minute only, just to soften marshmallows. Remove from oven and sprinkle evenly with pecans. Set aside.

With *metal blade* in place, put confectioners' sugar and chocolate into work bowl. Pulse 4 times, then process continuously until chocolate is finely chopped, about 1 minute. Add remaining ingredients and process for 1 minute, stopping once or twice to scrape work bowl. Glaze should be thick but pourable; add few more drops of boiling water if needed.

Quickly drizzle glaze over marshmallows and pecans, leaving some spots visible. Let stand, uncovered, for at least 8 hours. Use small, sharp knife to release from pan. Then cut into 6 pieces, dipping knife into cold water before each cut. Use wide metal spatula to transfer pieces to cutting board. Cut each one into 4 bars, dipping knife into cold water before each cut. Transfer brownies to serving platter. Bars can be wrapped airtight and stored at room temperature for 2 or 3 days.

Makes 24 bars.

ROCKY MOUNTAIN MARATHON BARS

These sweet and tangy bars are filled with apricots and dates. In fact, they're practically all fruit, with just enough batter to hold them together. Measure the flour accurately; just a bit too much will make them dry. I call them marathon bars because I used to eat them when I trained for long-distance races!

8 ounces (225g) dried apricot halves
1 pound (455g) pitted dates, picked over carefully
1¼ cups sifted whole-wheat flour (4½ ounces, 130g)
1 teaspoon baking powder
½ teaspoon salt, if desired
3 large eggs
1 teaspoon vanilla
½ teaspoon freshly grated nutmeg
¾ cup (180ml) honey
32 large pecan halves
Confectioners' sugar, if desired

Adjust oven rack to center position and preheat oven to 350°F. (175°C.). Line 15½ by 10½ by 1-inch (39 by 25 by 2.5cm) jelly-roll pan with foil. Brush foil with melted butter and set pan aside.

Divide apricots, dates, flour, baking powder, and salt into 2 batches. Insert *metal blade* and put 1 batch into work bowl. Pulse 6 to 8 times, for about 1 second each, to chop fruit coarsely. Transfer to large sheet of waxed paper. Repeat with second batch and set aside with first.

With *metal blade* in place, put eggs, vanilla, nutmeg, and honey into work bowl and process for 1 minute. Add fruit and dry ingredients and pulse quickly 4 times, just until they are thoroughly moistened. If necessary, stir mixture with plastic spatula to complete mixing.

Turn batter into prepared pan and spread to make it level. Top with pecan halves, placing them round sides up and spacing them evenly. Bake for 25 to 30 minutes, turning the pan back to front once during baking. Cake should be golden brown and should spring back when lightly pressed with fingertip; do not overcook.

Cool in pan on rack for 5 minutes. Then turn out onto large rack and let cake cool completely.

Slide cake onto cutting board and use long, sharp, serrated knife to cut it into 32 bars. Dust with confectioners' sugar, if desired.

These bars dry out very quickly. Wrap each one in waxed paper and store in airtight container. (Bars may be wrapped and stored at room temperature for a week or more. They may also be frozen.)

Makes 32 bars.

APRICOT BARS

The original version of this recipe won a prize for me in an early Pillsbury Bake-Off. It is still one of my favorite desserts, and it's easier than ever to make with the food processor. The bars are delicious fresh but even better the day after they're baked.

Bars

- 1 pound (455g) dried apricots
- 2 cups (480ml) water
- 1 cup plus 2 tablespoons sugar (8 ounces, 225g)
- 2 cups sifted unbleached all-purpose flour (8 ounces, 225g)
- ½ teaspoon baking soda
- 1 cup sugar (7½ ounces, 215g)
- 1½ sticks unsalted butter (6 ounces, 170g), at room temperature, cut into 6 pieces
- 1 cup shredded coconut (3½ ounces, 100g)
- 1 cup walnuts (4 ounces, 115g)

Whipped Cream

- 2 cups (480ml) heavy cream, chilled
- ⅓ cup confectioners' sugar (1⅓ ounces, 40g)
- ¼ cup instant nonfat dry milk
- 2 large egg whites
- 1 teaspoon vanilla

Put apricots and water in heavy-bottomed 2- to 3-quart (2 to 3L) saucepan and bring to boil over medium-high heat. Reduce heat to low, cover pan, and cook at slow boil, stirring occasionally, until fruit is tender, about 40 minutes. Turn into large strainer set over bowl and let cool slightly. Reserve ¼ cup (60ml) of apricot juice.

Insert *metal blade.* Put apricots, reserved juice, and 1 cup plus 2 tablespoons of sugar into work bowl and process until smooth, about 30 seconds. Scrape purée into same saucepan; pulse once to spin any remaining apricot off blade, then scrape work bowl clean. Do not wash bowl or blade.

Bring apricot purée to boil over medium-high heat, stirring occasionally. Cook, stirring almost constantly, for 5 minutes. Set aside to cool to room temperature.

Adjust oven rack to center position and preheat oven to 400°F. (205°C.). Butter 13 by 9 by 2-inch (33 by 23 by 5cm) baking pan and set aside.

Resift flour with baking soda and set aside.

With *metal blade* in place, put 1 cup of sugar and butter into work bowl and process for 45 seconds. Add coconut and walnuts and pulse 4 times. Add dry ingredients and pulse 6 times. Scrape work bowl and pulse very quickly 6 to 8 more times, until mixture is crumbly and holds together only very slightly. Transfer to large sheet of waxed paper and break up any lumps with fingertips.

Press 2½ cups of crumb mixture over bottom and halfway up sides of pan. (It will be a thin layer.) Do not be concerned about making neat edges, but be sure there are no bare spots on bottom of pan.

Bake crust for 10 minutes; it will appear uneven and be lightly colored. Remove from oven but do not turn oven off. Spread apricot mixture into hot crust. Sprinkle remaining crumb mixture on top and pat crumbs gently into place.

Return to oven and bake until top is golden brown, another 20 to 25 minutes. Cool dessert in its pan on rack, then cut into 16 bars.

To make whipped cream topping, insert *metal blade,* put all ingredients into work bowl and process until mixture is thick and fluffy, 2 to 4 minutes. Refrigerate until serving time, then place generous spoonful on each bar.

Makes 16 bars.

NOTE: If you prefer smaller servings, let dessert stand overnight, cut into 48 1½-inch (4cm) squares and serve as apricot bar cookies.

FRENCH BUTTER TEA CAKES

These are sweet little cakes with a tender texture. Measure the flour by sifting it onto a sheet of waxed paper, spooning it into a dry-measure cup to overflowing, and sweeping across the top of the cup with a straight edge like a knife or chopstick.

1 stick unsalted butter (4 ounces, 115g)

½ cup sugar (3¾ ounces, 105g)

Zest of 1 large lemon

2 large eggs, at refrigerator temperature

½ teaspoon vanilla

1 cup minus 2 tablespoons sifted all-purpose flour (3¾ ounces, 105g) or 1 cup sifted cake flour (4 ounces, 115g) (see NOTE)

French Butter Tea Cakes

Adjust oven rack to center position and preheat oven to 375°F. (190°C.). Butter 2 dozen small muffin cups (1¾ to 1⅞ inches, 4 to 4.5cm top diameter and ¾ inch, 18mm deep) or 2 dozen madeleine molds.

Put butter in small saucepan and melt over very low heat. Set aside to cool; it must be no hotter than tepid when used.

Insert *metal blade.* Put sugar and zest into work bowl and process until zest is as fine as sugar, about 2 minutes. Scrape work bowl, add eggs and vanilla, and process for 1½ minutes.

Put flour in circle on top of egg mixture. Stir butter and pour it in circle over flour. Pulse quickly 3 or 4 times. If any flour is still visible, stir batter gently with plastic spatula. At first batter will be thin, but within a few minutes it will become firm and thick, almost like a buttercream. When it reaches this consistency, divide it into prepared molds, using rounded teaspoonful for each one. Do not spread batter.

Bake until cakes are golden on top and spring back when lightly pressed with fingertip, 12 to 15 minutes. Remove from pans immediately and let cool on racks. These are best when very fresh.

Makes 24 cakes.

NOTE: When made with unbleached flour, cakes retain light texture for 1 day, but become drier and denser after standing overnight, wrapped airtight. When made with cake flour, they are "cakier" in texture when fresh, but maintain their lightness after standing overnight, wrapped airtight.

PINEAPPLE SHERBET IN ALMOND COOKIE CUPS

A light and refreshing dessert that is easy to make and beautiful to look at.

Sherbet
- 1 large pineapple (3 to 4 pounds, 1.4 to 1.8kg)
- ¾ cup sugar (5½ ounces, 155g)
- 1 tablespoon lime juice
- 2 large egg whites

Cookie Cups
- 1 cup unbleached all-purpose flour (5 ounces, 140g)
- ⅓ cup whole blanched almonds (1⅔ ounces, 50g)
- 2 tablespoons sugar
- 1 stick unsalted butter (4 ounces, 115g), chilled and cut into 8 pieces
- 2 large egg yolks
- 2 teaspoons almond extract
- 1 tablespoon cold water
- 12 strawberry slices (for garnish)

Use sharp, heavy knife to cut crown and base off pineapple. Stand pineapple upright and cut away skin, removing it in thick strips. Use paring knife to remove any "eyes." Quarter pineapple lengthwise and remove core sections. Cut pineapple into 1-inch (2.5cm) chunks. Sherbet will require about 4 cups (1¼ pounds, 570 grams) of fruit.

Insert *metal blade* and put pineapple, sugar, and lime juice into work bowl. Process until pineapple is very smooth, about 2 minutes, stopping once to scrape work bowl. Add egg whites and process until mixture is very light and frothy and has increased in volume, another 2 minutes.

Transfer mixture to 8 by 8 by 2-inch (20 by 20 by 5cm) metal pan, cover with foil, and place in freezer until sherbet is partially frozen, 1½ to 2 hours. Mixture should be firm around edges and mushy in center. With *metal blade* in place, scrape sherbet back into work bowl and process again until mixture is very smooth, fluffy, and light in color, 1 to 2 minutes. Return to pan, then cover, refreeze, and process once again as before. (Work quickly so sherbet will not melt. However, if it has frozen too firm to work with, let it soften slightly at room temperature before processing.) Finally, return sherbet to pan, cover, and freeze until firm, several hours or overnight. If sherbet is too firm to serve, let it soften in refrigerator for 30 minutes.

To make cookie cups, insert *metal blade*, put flour, almonds, and sugar into work bowl, and process until almonds are very finely chopped, about 1 minute. Add butter, pulse 4 times, then process continuously until butter is in very fine pieces, 10 to 15 seconds. Scrape work bowl.

Mix egg yolks, almond extract, and water in small cup. Pour mixture through feed tube while pulsing rapidly. Pulse until dough begins to gather into ball.

Carefully remove dough, place on lightly floured surface, and shape into 8-inch (20cm) cylinder. Use heel of hand to "break" away 2-inch (5cm) pieces of

dough from cylinder, smearing them away from you rapidly. Gather dough and reform cylinder, then repeat procedure. Shape dough into ball and flatten it slightly to form cake. Wrap securely in plastic wrap and refrigerate for 1 hour. (If dough becomes too firm to work with, let it sit at room temperature until it can be rolled easily.)

Adjust oven rack to center position and preheat oven to 425°F. (220°C.).

Work with half of dough, keeping remainder chilled. Roll dough out on lightly floured surface to ⅛-inch (3mm) thickness, turning it over as necessary. Use 4- to 5-inch (10 to 13cm) round cookie cutter to make 6 circles.

Drape circles of dough over inverted muffin cups, pressing sides down gently to form pleats. Bake until cookie cups are golden brown with a few darker spots, 5 to 6 minutes. (Watch closely, as these burn easily.) Remove from oven and let cups cool in place, then carefully lift cups off pans. Repeat procedure with remaining dough.

Serve cookie cups filled with scoop of pineapple sherbet and slice of strawberry.

Makes about 1 quart (1L) of sherbet and 12 cookie cups.

STRAWBERRY SHERBET

This can be made with fresh strawberries or with frozen unsweetened berries. By slowing down the formation of ice crystals, the egg white and liqueur give the sherbet a smooth texture.

1 quart (1L) fresh strawberries, hulled, or 1 quart (1L) hulled unsweetened frozen strawberries, thawed (see NOTE)
½ cup sugar (3¾ ounces, 105g)
2 tablespoons strawberry liqueur or crème de cassis
1 tablespoon lemon juice
1 large egg white

Insert *metal blade.* Put strawberries, sugar, liqueur, and lemon juice into work bowl, pulse 4 or 5 times, then process continuously until mixture is very smooth, 1 to 2 minutes. With machine running, add egg white through feed tube. Process until mixture is fluffy, pale pink, and about the consistency of heavy cream, about 1½ minutes.

Transfer mixture to 9 by 9 by 2-inch (23 by 23 by 5cm) metal pan and freeze until sherbet is semifirm, 1½ to 2 hours. Cut sherbet into 1-inch (2.5cm) pieces and return to work bowl with *metal blade* in place. Pulse 4 or 5 times, then process continuously until sherbet is very smooth, about 1 minute. Return to pan, cover and freeze until firm. About 20 minutes before serving, place in refrigerator to soften.

Makes about 1 quart (1L).

NOTE: If using frozen strawberries, measure them while frozen, then thaw. Use any juices that are released.

NOTES ON ACCESSORIES

Accessories are available for most food procesors, making the machines more useful than ever. The following accessory discs are available for most Cuisinart food processors at this time. I suggest specific uses for each disc; you'll undoubtedly come up with others if you use your food processor often.

1mm SLICING DISC
The thinnest slicing disc available. I use it on vegeta-

bles, and sausages like pepperoni or salami to make canapés and pizza. For coleslaw almost as fine as angel's hair pasta, use this disc. It's also useful for cutting wafer-thin slices of cucumbers and super-thin potato chips. Thinly sliced mushrooms can be added raw to hot rice pilaf or pasta. I also use this disc to slice bell peppers for coleslaw, and cranberries for cranberry-apple crisp.

2mm SLICING DISC
The only disc for scalloped potatoes; the thickness is just right for a finished dish with perfect texture. Make carrot curls by processing carrots horizontally, rolling up each slice, securing it with a toothpick and refrigerating it in ice water. Remove the toothpicks before serving; the curls will hold their shape. I also use this disc to slice scallions and whole cored and seeded bell peppers to garnish salad.

3mm SLICING DISC
Slices apples for tarts and crisps; oranges and lemons for garnishes or punch bowls; onions for onion soup. Slices carrots and turnips to serve with dips for a healthful, low-calorie snack. Slices Jerusalem artichokes; pop them into

hot oil for delicious and unusual chips. This disc also does a marvelous job on all fruits and vegetables, especially those you plan to dehydrate.

5 or 6mm SLICING DISC
My choice for slicing tomatoes for salad, "shredding" lettuce and spinach for salads, preparing unpeeled oranges for a fruit platter, and slicing partially frozen meat for stir-frying. Pineapple, bananas, peeled oranges, kiwis, strawber-

ries and melons of this width are excellent for fresh fruit platters or desserts.

8mm SLICING DISC
The thickest slicing disc available. I use it in the same way as the 5 or 6mm disc when I want a slightly thicker cut. It "shreds" lettuce and spinach well for salads, and fruits sliced with this disc hold up a bit longer than those sliced with a thinner disc. I use it to slice whole, peeled grapefruit, to serve alone or in salads. This disc cuts hot pot roast beautifully as well as partially frozen beef for Beef Stroganoff. It's also good on vegetables for stews. Double slice pota-

toes with it to get straight French fries about ⅓ inch (8mm) thick. Slice the pota-

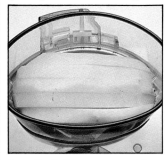

toes first, then reassemble the slices and insert them in the feed tube at right angles to the first cut.

2mm SQUARE JULIENNE DISC

Juliennes carrots for soups and celery root for salads. Mixtures of radishes, carrots and kohlrabi are quick to prepare, delicious to eat, and very attractive. Partially cooked beets, julienned and quickly heated in melted butter, make an excellent side

dish. And peeled julienned broccoli stems are especially good in soups or salads.

3mm SQUARE JULIENNE DISC

Makes strips a bit wider than the 2mm julienne disc.

Carrots and zucchini prepared with this disc hold their shape and retain some texture when sautéed. Julienned mushrooms make an attractive addition to salads, or an intriguing side dish when sautéed. This is the disc for shredded onions. You can also use it on partially cooked beets and broccoli stems. Whole peeled potatoes become perfect shoestring potatoes. Use the disc also to make fine dice. For diced

zucchini, for example, slice the zucchini vertically with the 3mm slicing disc, then process the slices horizontally with this disc. The technique works well for carrots, potatoes and other vegetables. Use this disc or the 2mm julienne disc to chop pecans or walnuts very fine.

FRENCH-FRY DISC

Probably the most versatile of all accessory discs. It's perfect for ¼-inch (6mm) French fries. For coarsely

chopped onions, process whole peeled onions. Whole tomatoes processed with this disc yield strips that are perfect for tacos,

guacamole, or as a garnish for gazpacho and other soups. It "dices" whole mushrooms and makes strips of zucchini sections, placed vertically in the feed tube. They're ideal for salads or stir fries. The same technique is useful with jicama and Jerusalem artichokes. I also use the French-fry disc on whole apples for crisps, tarts and Waldorf Salad. It makes beautiful strips of melon for fruit salad or dessert. In conjuction with the 6mm slicing disc, it makes coarse dice (¼-inch pieces) of many vegetables. Reassemble slices processed vertically, wedge them into the feed tube horizontally and process with the French-fry disc.

FINE SHREDDING DISC

A very useful disc with more functions than first meet the eye. Excellent for shredding carrots for car-

rot slaw or carrot cake; potatoes for potato pancakes; Cheddar and Monterey Jack cheeses for tacos; and Swiss cheese for quiches or salads. It also shreds Parmesan cheese beautifully. Use the metal blade after shredding for fluffy, powdery grated cheese. The disc also grates chocolate. A new use for the disc is to grate lemon peel. The lemon should be of a size that can move freely in the large feed tube without being wedged in place. Hold up the pusher with one hand and with the other, operate the pulse control frequently, with pulses lasting about 3 seconds each. The lemon will bounce around and the yellow peel will be stripped off. Check frequently to ensure that none of the bitter white part of the lemon is grated. For very

finely grated peel, remove the shredding disc, insert the metal blade, add some of the sugar called for in your recipe and process until the peel is as fine as the sugar, about 2 minutes.

NOTES ON INGREDIENTS

Because I've often been confounded by unfamiliar ingredients in a recipe, I include this section. It explains some ingredients that may be unfamiliar, and gives little-known facts about some familiar ingredients.

BULGUR
Also known as bulgar, burghul or cracked wheat. Whole wheat kernels that

have been steamed, dried and cracked open. Nutritious, with a nutty flavor. Available coarse or fine; either is good for Tabbouleh. Coarse form is better for Cracked Wheat Bread. Sold in supermarkets, healthfood stores and Middle Eastern specialty shops. Store airtight at room temperature or in the refrigerator for no more than a few weeks.

BUTTER
Salted
Salt helps to preserve butter and give reasonable shelf life. Each ¼-pound (115g) stick contains equivalent of about ½ teaspoon of salt. Be sure to wrap securely for storage; unwrapped, it picks up flavors from nearby foods. Can become rancid after prolonged refrigeration.

Unsalted
Also known as sweet butter. (But check package carefully; some butter labelled sweet may be lightly salted.) Because it lacks salt, it is highly perishable and should be frozen for storage. My choice for cooking because it tastes fresher than salted butter. Baking results are far more consistent because it has less water. In pastry making, liquid proportion can be critical.

CAPERS
Pickled buds of Mediterranean shrub called *Cappa-*

ris spinosa. Their piquant taste is delicious with fish, poultry, or in salads. Mix into tartar sauce for added zip. Store in their brine, tightly covered, at room temperature or in refrigerator. Drain well before using.

CHINESE CABBAGE
Also known as celery cabbage, comes in tightly

packed heads of broad, crinkled, pale-green leaves with white ribs. Can be used in addition to, or as a substitute for, lettuce. Wrapped in plastic and refrigerated, it keeps for 1 or 2 weeks.

CILANTRO
Also known as Chinese parsley or green coriander,

a staple herb in cuisines of the Orient, India and Mexico. Flat-leaved, sold in bunches like parsley. Use leaves only. Its pungent flavor is not for everybody. Adds wonderful richness to Guacamole. To store, wash, pat dry and seal airtight in glass jar. Keeps well refrigerated for about 1 week.

CREME DE CASSIS
Beautiful purple-red liqueur made from black currants. Mix with dry white wine to make popular aperitif called Kir. I use it in fruit ice creams and sherbets for its flavor; it also discourages formation of ice crystals.

EMMENTHALER CHEESE
Probably the most common Swiss cheese, made from part-skim raw or pasteurized milk. Identified by its large holes, some almost an inch (2.5cm) in diameter. Norwegian Jarlsberg or supermarket Swiss cheese are excellent substitutes.

FERMENTED BLACK BEANS
Available in small plastic bags at Chinese grocery stores or well stocked supermarkets. A small amount of the 1/4-inch (6mm) beans adds rich, pungent flavor to food. Keep indefinitely in screw-cap jar in refrigerator.

FETA CHEESE
White, crumbly cheese, sold in rectangular pieces, originally used in Greek cooking. Salty and tangy, can be made from goats', cows' or sheeps' milk. Each has slightly different flavor; sample several to find what suits you best. Available at supermarkets, cheese

shops and specialty food stores. Wrap securely in plastic wrap and store in refrigerator, where it will keep for several weeks.

FLOUR
How To Measure Flour
Most recipes in this book specify weight for flour. When 1 cup of flour is given as 5 ounces (140g), measure flour by the "stir, scoop and sweep method." *Stir* flour in its container to aerate it; *scoop* it up with dry-measure cup, heaping flour in cup; and *sweep* off excess with straight-edged utensil or chopstick. Don't shake cup to settle flour and don't pack flour into cup.

Some recipes call for sifted flour. To measure it, sift it onto large sheet of waxed paper to aerate it. (Use any kind of sifter.) Spoon flour lightly into dry-measure cups to overflow-ing and sweep off excess, using swift stroke with straight-edged utensil or chopstick. Don't shake cup or bang it on counter; that would settle flour and give incorrect measurement. One cup of sifted flour weighs 4 ounces (115g).

All-Purpose Flour.
White flour made from bulk of wheat kernel, the endosperm, which is rich in starch and special proteins called gluten. Outer coating of wheat kernel (bran) and embryo (germ) are removed during milling. Only some of nutrients removed during processing are returned when flour is enriched. Called all-purpose because it is a mixture of hard (high-gluten) and soft (low-gluten) wheats. Balanced formula makes it usable in large variety of cakes, pastries, cookies and breads. Available bleached (pure white) or unbleached (pale cream). I always use unbleached flour because it has been subjected to less chemical processing. Unbleached flour also has a slightly higher gluten content, making it better for breads.

Bread Flour.
A combination of high-gluten, high-protein enriched flours, produced especially for bread making. Protein content is 14 grams per cup compared with 11 grams per cup for unbleached all-purpose flour. Bread flour should be used only when specified; not every bread recipe requires it. Two brands currently marketed nationally are widely available in supermarkets. Look for bags labelled "Bread Flour" or "Better for Bread."

Buckwheat Flour.
Strongly flavored low-gluten flour used for Russian pancakes called blini. It also makes tasty pasta. Not made from grain but from a member of the rhubarb family.

Cake Flour.
Made from enriched, bleached, white, soft-wheat flour (8 grams of protein per cup compared with 11 grams per cup for all-purpose flour). Its very fine consistency produces an especially tender and light texture. Cake flour mixed with all-purpose flour results in light and tender pastries.

Rye Flour.
In medium rye flour, the type most commonly available, the bran is usually

removed from the rye kernels during milling. Gives subtle yet rich flavor to breads. Less commonly available are dark rye and pumpernickel flours. In these, the whole kernel, including the bran, is milled, giving breads made with these flours a full, rich flavor with a pleasantly sour taste. Pumpernickel flour usually contains more bran than dark rye flour. If you cannot find either of these, use medium rye flour instead. Because rye flour is low in gluten, it must be combined with gluten-rich wheat flour to produce high-rising loaves.

Semolina.
Golden, granular, coarsely-ground flour, milled from polished kernels of durum wheat. Popular for pasta because it imparts good flavor and firm texture. Available in Italian markets or specialty food shops.

Soy Flour.
Pale yellow flour manufactured from ground raw soybeans. Very high in protein but contains no gluten. Must be combined with wheat flour to make bread that is light in texture. Breads made with soy flour brown nicely and keep well, but only a little

is needed. Store, covered, in refrigerator, where it keeps up to 3 months.

Stone-Ground Flour.
Refers to process, not type of flour. Grain crushed and pulverized between stone grinding wheels (millstones) is labelled "stone-ground". (Ordinary flour is ground between steel rollers.) Many people consider stone-ground flours to be more "natural" than steel-ground varieties because heat generated during stone grinding is relatively low compared to that of steel grinding. Stone-grinding produces very fine flour suitable for all-purpose baking. Some brands are finer than others; experiment to see what suits you best.

Whole-Wheat Flour.
More nutritious than white flour because the entire wheat kernel is ground. Some brands are more finely milled than others. Approximate composition by weight of whole-wheat kernel is: bran, 15%; wheat germ, 3%; endosperm, 82%. Because gluten is found only in endosperm, 1 cup of whole-wheat flour contains about 18% less gluten than 1 cup of all-purpose flour, which is 100% endosperm.

White flour is added to most whole-wheat breads to provide gluten needed for elasticity or tenderness. Since it contains the oily wheat germ, whole-wheat flour must be refrigerated to prevent it from becoming rancid. Buy small quantities and use it up quickly for best results.

FONTINA CHEESE
Semi-soft cheese with a nutty, sweet flavor, made from cows' or sheeps' milk and sold in wedges from large wheel. Two widely available types come from Denmark and Italy. The Danish variety is sweeter and milder. Available in supermarkets, delicatessens and cheese shops.

Delicious plain and in recipes like Gougère and Fontina Quiche with Roasted Red Peppers.

GINGER
Fresh ginger is now widely available in markets everywhere. Knobby, with tan

peel, should feel firm and have shiny skin. Don't buy if it is shriveled or has

spots of mold. Wrap securely in plastic wrap and store in refrigerator, where it will keep for 2 or 3 weeks. Cut and peel only what you need.

GRUYERE CHEESE
Swiss cheese with firm texture and tiny holes. Has decidedly nutty flavor and richer taste than Emmenthaler. If you can't get it, substitute Emmenthaler.

HERBS
Dried herbs, like fresh ones, lose fragrance and flavor over time. Buy them in small quantities and store airtight, in cool, dry place. To substitute fresh herbs for dried, triple amounts specified.

HOISIN SAUCE
Thick, mahogany-colored sauce made from soy beans, sugar, water, salt, fermented rice, vinegar and seasonings. Widely used in Chinese cooking, it contrib-

utes flavor reminiscent of good barbecue sauce. (In fact, I recommend adding some to your favorite barbecue sauce.) Sold in cans or jars in Oriental food sections of many supermarkets. After opening it, store covered in refrigerator, where it will keep indefinitely.

JALAPENO CHILES

About 2½ inches (6cm) long and 1-inch (2.5cm) wide, somewhat triangular in shape, hot and extremely flavorful, they add delightful zip to many foods. Now widely available nationwide. Oil from seeds and

veins can be highly irritating. Handle them, like all chiles, carefully; wear rubber or plastic gloves and wash your hands thoroughly afterwards in soapy water. Store fresh chiles, unwrapped, on paper towels in refrigerator for up to 1 week. Don't wrap them in plastic, which hastens spoilage.

JERUSALEM ARTICHOKES

A neglected root vegetable belonging to the sunflower family and also known as sunchokes. Unrelated to

more familiar globe artichoke, it has crunchy texture and mild, pleasant taste. Knobby, ranging in size from 1 to 3 inches (2.5 to 7cm), they have thin peel and white flesh. Select those that feel very firm. Usually it is not necessary to peel them; simply brush away any dirt under cold running water. Low in calories and rich in carbohydrate called inulin (a long chain of linked fructose molecules), which can be tolerated by diabetics. In addition, they are delicious! Try them raw in salad, or cooked.

JICAMA

A tuber that looks somewhat like an overgrown

turnip with thick, light brown skin, and roots protruding from one end. Available from September through June in most parts of the country. Ranges in weight from about 1 to 6 pounds (455g to 3kg). Smaller ones are more tender and less pithy than larger ones. Select jicama that feels firm, with no soft or moldy spots. Jicama does not discolor after it's cut. Remove fibrous peel completely from crunchy, pure white flesh by cutting into flesh about ⅛-inch (3mm) with sharp paring knife. Serve slices sprinkled with lime juice as low-calorie appetizer, or use in stir-fry dishes for sweet-tasting crunch. I routinely substitute it for water chestnuts. After cutting it, wrap in plastic wrap and refrigerate. Leftovers will keep from 1 to 2 weeks.

NUOC MAM

Often spelled Nuok Mam, also known as Vietnamese fish sauce. A staple in the cooking of Southeast Asia, made from fish extract, water and salt. It is a brown liquid that comes in clear plastic or glass bottles. Available in Oriental grocery stores or well stocked supermarkets. Substitute it for soy sauce in Oriental

dishes for a different taste. Also useful in salad dressing. Like soy sauce, it keeps indefinitely in cupboard or refrigerator.

ORIENTAL SESAME OIL

Dark-brown oil extracted from roasted sesame seeds, it is aromatic and has a wonderful, strong, nutty flavor. Not to be confused with the light yellow oil called sesame oil; they are not the same. Oriental sesame oil is specified in several recipes in this book. Refrigerate to prevent it from becoming rancid.

OYSTER SAUCE

Thick sauce sold in bottles and found in Oriental markets, specialty food shops, and well stocked supermarkets. Made from extract of oysters, it is very salty. Mix a little into hamburger patties for a delicious flavor. Also excellent in marinades and in sauces for stir-fry dishes. Store in refrigerator, where it keeps indefinitely.

PHYLLO DOUGH

Paper-thin pastry that comes in rectangular sheets; generally available in supermarkets and delicatessens. Almost always frozen, in 1-pound (455g) boxes containing 25 to 30 sheets measuring 12 by 17 inches (30 by 45cm). Always follow package directions for storing and thawing. Sometimes called "filo" or "fillo", or even strudel dough. Easy to work with if kept covered, otherwise it dries and is hard to fold or roll. Cover unwrapped phyllo first with dry towel, then damp one, to keep it pliable. Work with 1 sheet at a time, keeping remainder under wraps

until needed. Roll unused sheets in plastic wrap, return to original container, and seal airtight. Refrigerate leftovers for up to 1 week; do not refreeze or sheets may stick together. Always bring to room temperature before opening package.

RICE-STICK NOODLES
Whitish, opaque, thin noodles made from rice flour. Several stacks are packaged together. They are deep-fried, and become crisp and puffy seconds after being placed in oil.

May also be soaked for 30 minutes in hot water to soften, then drained and stir-fried or added to soups. Those allergic to wheat may find them a pleasant alternative to pasta.

SHALLOTS
Brownish-skinned bulbs with pale purple flesh, members of Lily family (which also includes garlic and onions). Commonly used in French cooking, they add wonderful flavor to any dish that needs mild onion or garlic taste. Easy

to grow in quantity in small patch of garden.

TAHINI
Made from lightly roasted and ground sesame seeds and commonly sold in 1-pound (455g) cans. Also known as sesame seed

paste, it is used in Middle Eastern dishes and Oriental cooking. Has oil layer above paste, much like old-fashioned peanut butter. Stir oil into paste thoroughly. If paste is very stiff, empty into food processor and process a few seconds with metal blade to make mixture smooth. Thoroughly mixed, it has consistency of very thick, pourable cream. Available in health or ethnic food sections of supermarkets, specialty food shops, and Middle Eastern or Oriental markets.

TOFU
Prepared from pulverized soy beans and formed into square cakes or rectangular blocks. Popular because it is high in good-quality protein and low in calories and fat. Contains no cholesterol. Very bland when eaten plain, but a favorite staple of Oriental cooking because it absorbs flavor of soups and sauces. Tofu-Mushroom Stir-Fry uses it to good advantage. Also known as bean curd, it is white and usually sealed in plastic containers. Look for it with refrigerated produce in supermarkets or health-food stores. To store, immerse in water in covered container and refriger-

ate. If you change water every 3 days, it will keep well for about 1 week.

WHEAT GERM
The "germ" or embryo of the wheat kernel, removed during milling of white flour. Golden in color and rich in oils and Vitamins B and E. Adds nutty taste and pleasant texture to breads, pastries and other food. Comes in 2 forms: toasted and untoasted (raw). Some recipes specify one kind, but in many recipes they're interchangeable. Untoasted wheat germ is usually so designated or labelled "raw". Read labels carefully; some containers marked "regular" contain the toasted kind. Sold in supermarkets and health-food stores. Store, tightly covered, in refrigerator, where it will keep for a few months. Before using, taste a little to be sure it is not rancid.

INDEX

Low-fat recipes appear in blue.